WEALTH

—— OVER ——

HEALTH

THE COST YOU CAN'T AFFORD TO PAY

DR. JASON WEST & JORDAN DORSEY

ISBN:
978-1-967451-03-6 (Paperback)
978-1-967451-04-3 (Ebook)

PERFORMANCE
PUBLISHING

CONTENTS

PART FOUR:
THE HIGH-PERFORMANCE LIFESTYLE FOR LONGEVITY & SUCCESS

PART FIVE:
THE HEALTH-WEALTH LEGACY PLAN

Introduction

In today's fast-paced world, success is often measured by financial accumulation. People work tirelessly, sacrifice sleep, skip meals, ignore their bodies, and push their limits—all in the name of building wealth. The logic seems sound: Work harder now, achieve financial success, and enjoy the rewards later. But what happens when "later" comes, and the body is broken, the mind is exhausted, and the wealth that took years to accumulate is funneled into medical treatments, prescription medications, and attempts to regain lost health?

It's a painful paradox. People spend their youth and vitality chasing financial success, only to spend their financial success trying to restore the youth and vitality they lost along the way. The price of wealth, if pursued without balance, often includes stress-induced illnesses, chronic disease, and premature aging. Many high-achievers only realize too late that their relentless pursuit of money has left them bankrupt in the one currency that truly matters: health. Imagine an executive who spent decades climbing the corporate ladder.

He skipped workouts, lived off caffeine and convenience foods, and justified the endless stress as "part of the game." His bank account grew, but so did his blood pressure, his cholesterol, and his reliance on prescription drugs. One day, he faces a wake-up call—a heart attack, a diabetes diagnosis, or severe burnout. Suddenly, he finds himself in the frustrating position of trying to use his financial resources to buy back what he lost. But money cannot reverse years of neglect.

The best doctors, the most advanced medical treatments, and even the most luxurious wellness retreats cannot undo the damage of chronic stress, inflammation, and poor lifestyle choices. This is the shocking truth that most people ignore until it's too late. Many wealthy individuals have been conditioned to believe that money is the ultimate goal. Their schedules revolve around meetings, deals, investments, and expansion strategies, while their health becomes an afterthought. They operate under the illusion that success will allow them to relax later—that they can always "get healthy" when they have more time. But time is not a renewable resource.

Neither is healthy. The wealthy often underestimate the impact of chronic stress, poor nutrition, and lack of movement on their long-term performance and longevity. They assume that a high income will provide solutions to any health problem they encounter. But true health is not something that can simply be purchased when it becomes necessary. It must be cultivated, maintained, and prioritized—just like financial investments.

Even more concerning, the delayed gratification model that works so well in wealth-building often backfires when it comes to health. In the world of finance, it makes sense to sacrifice short-term pleasures for long-term gains. Save now, invest wisely, and enjoy compounded wealth later. But when applied to health, this mindset leads to irreversible damage. The body does not wait patiently for attention. It accumulates stress, inflammation, and deficiencies, often without obvious symptoms—until the breaking point.

The truly successful individuals—those who build and sustain wealth over a lifetime—understand that their most valuable asset is not their business, portfolio, or net worth. It is their health. Without a strong, vibrant body and a sharp, clear mind, even the greatest fortunes are useless. For many, the concept of legacy wealth is about leaving behind financial security for future generations. Parents and grandparents work hard to create generational wealth, ensuring that their children and grandchildren have financial stability. But what if we expanded the definition of legacy wealth beyond money? True legacy wealth starts with health. It is not just about the assets you leave behind, but the quality of life you model and pass down. What good is a multimillion-dollar inheritance if the next generation inherits chronic disease, stress, and the same unhealthy habits that led to poor health in the first place? A real legacy includes vitality, longevity, and functional health. It means living in a way that allows you to be fully present—not just financially, but physically, mentally, and emotionally—for your family, your business, and your personal aspirations. It means creating a culture of health within your family and professional circles, demonstrating that wealth and well-being are not mutually exclusive. Imagine a legacy where children grow up seeing their parents prioritize exercise, nutrition, and stress management. Imagine a generational shift where chronic disease is not an inheritance, but optimal health is. Imagine being able to enjoy the wealth you worked so hard for—not just from a financial perspective, but from a state of abundant energy, mental clarity, and physical strength. This is the real meaning of wealth.

It is not just the size of your bank account but the quality of your years. It is the ability to live fully, contribute meaningfully, and inspire future generations to do the same. Most health books focus solely on diet, exercise, or specific medical treatments. Most financial books focus on investing, saving, and wealth accumulation. But very few books bridge the gap between health and wealth, offering a blueprint for maximizing both. This book is different because it does not just preach the importance of health. It provides a practical, actionable strategy that integrates cutting-edge medical science with proven financial wisdom. It is designed for high performers, business owners, executives, and entrepreneurs—people who want to build wealth without sacrificing their well-being. How to structure your lifestyle like a high-performance asset—ensuring that your body and mind function at peak levels so you can continue creating and leading. The hidden costs of neglecting your health—and how small, strategic shifts can prevent the need for expensive medical interventions later in life. The science behind longevity and peak performance—how proper nutrition, movement, sleep, and stress management directly enhance your financial success.

How to create a health investment strategy—treating your body with the same level of foresight and discipline as your financial portfolio. How to implement a long-term wellness plan—so that you can enjoy your wealth without being limited by disease, fatigue, or aging. This is not just another book on health. It is a blueprint for sustainable success—one that ensures that you do not fall into the trap of spending your best years working only to spend your later years trying to fix what could have been prevented. It is a book that redefines success—one that proves that true wealth is not measured in dollars alone, but in the ability to wake up every day feeling strong, focused, and ready to take on life's challenges. Because in the end, money means nothing if you do not have the health to enjoy it. If you are ready to break free from the cycle of sacrificing health for wealth—and then wealth for health—this book will show you the way forward. It is time to build a legacy that includes both prosperity and longevity. The best time to start was ten years ago. The second-best time is today.

PART ONE

THE HEALTH-WEALTH FORMULA

The Biggest Financial Mistake: Neglecting Your Health

Health and wealth are not separate pursuits; they are inextricably linked. While financial success can provide access to better healthcare, it cannot replace the foundation of well-being that is built over years of conscious choices. Likewise, good health alone does not guarantee financial prosperity, but it does create the conditions necessary for sustained success. The truly successful understand that these two pillars must be developed simultaneously, not sequentially.

Far too many people operate under the belief that they can focus on wealth now and worry about their health later. This mindset is not only flawed but also dangerous. Every financial plan should include a health plan, just as every wealth-building strategy should include measures to safeguard and enhance physical and mental vitality. The people who thrive in both areas are those who recognize that maintaining their well-being is just as important as making wise financial investments.

Imagine an entrepreneur who views their body as an asset rather than an afterthought. They understand that without energy and mental clarity, they cannot make sound decisions, innovate, or lead effectively. They make time for exercise because they know it enhances their productivity. They prioritize sleep because they understand its role in memory consolidation, creativity, and stress management. They fuel their bodies with nutrient-rich foods because they recognize that proper nutrition is not just about longevity but about optimizing daily performance.

On the flip side, consider the executive who disregards their health while climbing the corporate ladder. They push through exhaustion, rely on caffeine and sugar to stay alert, and assume that a future vacation or a luxury wellness retreat will undo the damage. Eventually, their body rebels. Chronic fatigue, metabolic disorders, and cardiovascular issues take hold. They start missing work due to illness. Their once-sharp mind becomes sluggish, and their ability to handle stress diminishes. They begin losing what they worked so hard to build—not because of financial missteps but because their body could no longer keep up with their ambitions.

This is why the concept of health as an investment is so crucial. People often think of investing in financial terms—putting money into stocks, real estate, or businesses to yield future returns. But health follows the same principles. The small, daily deposits you make into your well-being—through nutrition, exercise, stress management, and sleep—accumulate over time, providing the resilience and longevity necessary to sustain success.

Those who ignore this truth often find themselves spending more money on medical bills than they ever anticipated. They become trapped in a cycle of prescription medications, invasive procedures, and declining energy levels. Their hard-earned wealth is funneled into managing preventable diseases rather than being used to enjoy life. This is not just a personal tragedy; it is an economic reality that affects families, businesses, and entire industries.

Many people fail to recognize the ripple effects that poor health has on every aspect of life. It is not just about medical expenses—it is about lost time, lost opportunities, and a diminished ability to contribute to the world. Chronic illness does not only deplete financial resources; it robs individuals of their most precious commodity: time.

Chronic illness does not only deplete financial resources; it robs individuals of their most precious commodity: time. Think about the number of people who dream of traveling the world in retirement but find themselves unable to do so because their bodies are no longer capable. Consider the parents who worked tirelessly to provide for their families but are too fatigued to play with their children. Reflect on the business owners who had incredible ideas but lacked the stamina to execute them.

These are not hypothetical situations; they are the stories of countless individuals who believed they could postpone health until a later date—only to realize that later never arrived the way they had hoped. What makes this situation even more tragic is that most health issues are preventable. The vast majority of chronic diseases—heart disease, diabetes, hypertension, obesity—are lifestyle-related. They do not develop overnight; they are the cumulative result of years of neglect. The good news is that just as poor habits create disease, good habits create health. The body has an incredible ability to heal when given the right conditions. Imagine a different scenario—one where people approach their health with the same level of strategy and discipline that they apply to their finances.

What if, instead of waiting for illness to force a change, they proactively invested in their well-being? What if they viewed nutrition, movement, and recovery not as optional luxuries but as non-negotiable components of success? This shift in mindset is what separates those who thrive from those who struggle. The most successful individuals do not wait until they are sick to start caring about their health. They understand that the best time to start was ten years ago, but the second-best time is today.

True abundance is not measured solely in financial terms. It is about having the energy, mobility, and mental clarity to experience life to the fullest. It is about waking up every day feeling strong, focused, and capable. It is about knowing that your body will support your ambitions, not hinder them. For this to happen, health must become a core value—not something that is pursued only when convenient, but something that is prioritized regardless of external circumstances. Just as a financially disciplined person does not abandon their investment strategy during market fluctuations, a health-conscious individual does not abandon their well-being during busy seasons of life. Building sustainable habits is key. This does not mean adopting extreme diets or spending hours in the gym. It means making consistent, intelligent choices that support long-term vitality. It means recognizing that the small decisions—what you eat, how you move, how you manage stress—all compound over time.

It also means redefining what success looks like. A thriving career or business is meaningless if it comes at the expense of your health. True success is being present for your family, having the stamina to pursue passions, and maintaining the freedom to live life on your terms. It is about creating a future where you are not just financially secure but physically and mentally capable of enjoying that security. The wealthiest people in the world do not simply think about how much money they can accumulate; they think about how long they can maintain their ability to create, contribute, and enjoy life. They know that health is the ultimate wealth—one that allows them to continue building, innovating, and leading for decades.

At the end of the day, success is not just about how much money you have in the bank. It is about how well you live, how deeply you love, and how fully you experience the world. It is about being able to wake up each morning with energy, confidence, and excitement for the day ahead. If you are healthy, you can always earn more money. But if you lose your health, no amount of money can buy it back. This book is not just a guide to improving your well-being—it is a blueprint for sustainable success. It is about bridging the gap between health and wealth, proving that the two are not opposing forces but complementary ones. The time to start is now. Your future self will thank you. productivity due to illness and fatigue disrupt workflow, leading to lost income and stalled career progression.

The average American spends over $12,000 per year on medical care, and proactive health measures can drastically reduce this burden. Many individuals are forced to retire earlier than planned due to deteriorating health. Studies show that medical expenses are the number one cause of bankruptcy in the United States. Yet, much of this financial and physical suffering is preventable. Investing in one's health is not an expense—it's a wealth-building strategy. When people proactively care for their bodies, they are not just preventing illness; they are increasing their ability to generate wealth, maintain independence, and enjoy the rewards of their labor. Preventive care is the key to longevity and financial stability. Simple lifestyle habits— such as staying hydrated, consuming nutrient-dense foods, engaging in daily movement, and managing stress—compound over time, just like financial investments. The earlier one prioritizes health, the greater the long-term return.

The body, much like a business, requires constant attention, regular maintenance, and strategic upgrades. A person who exercises regularly, maintains a balanced diet, and invests in high-quality supplements will experience far fewer medical complications than someone who disregards their health until it becomes a crisis. In the entrepreneurial world, burnout is a silent killer of success. Many business owners and executives push themselves to extreme limits, operating under the false assumption that sleep deprivation and excessive stress are necessary sacrifices for wealth accumulation. However, research consistently proves the opposite: chronic stress weakens the immune system, impairs memory, accelerates aging, and increases the risk of serious conditions such as hypertension and cardiovascular disease.

Those who prioritize their health build resilience against stress, enabling them to sustain peak performance for decades rather than burning out prematurely. The key to long-term wealth and success lies in harmonizing health and productivity. True prosperity is not just about financial gain—it's about having the energy, mental clarity, and physical well-being to fully enjoy and sustain that wealth. Without health, vacations become burdensome, time with loved ones is overshadowed by medical concerns, and the joy of financial success is diminished by physical limitations. For those who aspire to achieve both wealth and well-being, the solution is clear: prioritize health as diligently as financial planning. Schedule workouts as seriously as business meetings. Invest in high-quality nutrition just as one would invest in an expanding portfolio. Protect sleep as fiercely as a retirement fund. Build habits that support longevity, mental sharpness, and resilience.

The most successful individuals understand that their body is their most valuable asset. By taking care of it, they don't just extend their lifespan—they enhance their ability to create, innovate, and generate wealth for years to come. After all, if you're healthy, you can always earn more money. But if you're sick, no amount of money can restore the time, opportunities, and vitality lost. prematurely, cutting short their earning potential. By investing in health, one safeguards financial security, ensuring wealth is built without being siphoned away by preventable medical issues. A longer, healthier life extends one's ability to generate wealth and enjoy financial security.

A strong, resilient body ensures decades of peak performance and continued financial growth. Take billionaire investor Warren Buffett, who remains actively involved in managing Berkshire Hathaway well into his 90s. His longevity is a connection between health and financial success cannot be overstated. While money can buy comfort and access to resources, it cannot replace lost years, rebuild a broken body, or restore vitality once it has deteriorated. Those who understand this truth take proactive steps to maintain their health as a core strategy for long-term success. Health is not simply a factor in wealth accumulation—it is the very foundation upon which sustainable success is built. Conversely, many who neglect their well-being experience a sharp decline, forcing them into early retirement or financially draining medical care. They enter a vicious cycle of declining energy, poor decision-making, and increasing dependence on medications that manage symptoms rather than address root causes.

Instead of thriving, they spend their later years battling preventable diseases, watching their hard-earned wealth disappear into hospital bills, prescription costs, and long-term care facilities. Critical longevity-promoting habits include regular exercise, which reduces the risk of chronic disease, preserves cognitive function, and enhances metabolic health. Movement is not just about aesthetics or fitness—it is about ensuring that the body remains functional, resilient, and capable of sustaining high performance in both business and life. Cardiovascular exercise supports heart health and circulation, while strength training preserves muscle mass, which is directly linked to longevity and quality of life.

An anti-inflammatory diet plays a crucial role in longevity as well. Whole foods, lean proteins, and healthy fats combat oxidative stress and inflammation, which are at the root of most chronic diseases. Processed foods, excessive sugars, and inflammatory oils contribute to degenerative conditions that sap energy and impair cognitive function. Those who fuel their bodies with the right nutrients enjoy better focus, higher energy levels, and stronger immunity, allowing them to work and invest in their futures without frequent illness or fatigue slowing them down. Stress management is another pillar of long-term success. Chronic stress is a silent killer, contributing to high blood pressure, weakened immunity, and accelerated aging. Business leaders and investors operate in high-stakes environments, often facing unpredictable market fluctuations and intense pressure. Without effective stress management techniques such as meditation, breathwork, and nature exposure, the body remains in a constant state of fight-or-flight, leading to burnout and poor decision-making.

Lowering cortisol levels through mindfulness practices enhances emotional resilience, allowing individuals to navigate challenges with clarity and composure. By prioritizing health early in life, one extends the ability to create, invest, and enjoy wealth for decades. Instead of spending their later years managing disease, those who take care of their bodies are able to expand their influence, contribute meaningfully to their industries, and continue accumulating wealth while enjoying a high quality of life. The road to wealth is rarely smooth. Economic downturns, market fluctuations, and personal setbacks test even the most seasoned investors and entrepreneurs. A body burdened by chronic illness, inflammation, or hormonal imbalances is ill-equipped to handle these stressors. Fatigue, brain fog, and mood instability weaken resilience, making it difficult to think strategically or seize new opportunities.

A well-nourished, optimally functioning body provides a stronger stress response by balancing cortisol levels to facilitate rational decision-making under pressure. It ensures faster recovery by strengthening the immune system and minimizes downtime from illness. Additionally, balanced neurotransmitters support calm, focused thinking in high-stakes situations, preventing emotional reactivity from derailing success. Successful individuals recognize that emotional and physical resilience go hand in hand. Strengthening the body through nutrition, movement, and recovery fosters the endurance necessary to navigate financial and personal challenges. Just as one would diversify investments to protect against market volatility, maintaining physical and mental well-being creates a buffer against unexpected hardships. The most intelligent investors strategize decades ahead, making incremental investments that compound over time. Health should be approached with the same mindset. Preventative measures include annual health screenings to detect deficiencies before they escalate, nutrient optimization through strategic supplementation, and detoxification to reduce exposure to heavy metals, pesticides, and toxins. These measures protect long-term health, ensuring that the body remains strong and capable of sustaining high performance.

Those who invest in prevention enjoy uninterrupted careers, reduced medical expenses, and sustained vitality. Instead of being forced to slow down due to chronic illness, they remain at the top of their game well into their later years. They avoid the common pitfalls of aging—loss of mobility, cognitive decline, and dependence on pharmaceuticals—and instead experience extended years of productivity, influence, and financial growth. A healthy body fosters confidence, presence, and influence—three non-negotiable traits in wealth-building. People are naturally drawn to leaders who exude vitality and discipline. First impressions matter, whether negotiating a deal, delivering a keynote, or networking, and physical presence and mental acuity make a lasting impact. Beyond appearances, health promotes self-discipline. The habits required for peak health— exercise, clean eating, and consistent sleep—translate into discipline in business and investing. Those who commit to daily physical and mental well-being cultivate the same focus and consistency in their financial decisions.

A person who can control their diet, maintain a fitness routine, and manage stress is also more likely to exercise discipline in their investment strategies and career choices. Higher energy levels also allow individuals to pursue more opportunities, connect with influential people, and take calculated risks. Fatigue leads to avoidance, procrastination, and hesitation. In contrast, those with optimal health have the endurance to seize opportunities that others may shy away from. They can outwork, outthink, and outperform the competition simply because they have the stamina to do so. The wealthiest individuals understand that health is their ultimate competitive edge. Money holds little value without the health to enjoy it.

What good is a fortune if one is too exhausted, sick, or mentally foggy to reap its benefits? True wealth encompasses more than financial success—it is the ability to wake up with energy, clarity, and the freedom to pursue one's ambitions without limitation. By prioritizing health, one increases earning potential through heightened productivity, protects financial assets by avoiding preventable medical expenses, and extends career longevity, maximizing wealth accumulation. Additionally, a strong and resilient body strengthens the ability to navigate economic uncertainties, ensuring that challenges are met with clarity and perseverance rather than fatigue and overwhelm. The most successful individuals don't wait until illness strikes—they invest in their health long before it's needed. They understand that success is a marathon, not a sprint. Those who take care of their bodies early on will be the ones standing strong, thriving, and leading decades down the road.

Because, in the end, the greatest investment one can make is in their own vitality. The best time to prioritize health was ten years ago. The second-best time is today. Throughout history, many brilliant minds and industry leaders have neglected their health in pursuit of success, only to realize too late that wealth means little without well-being. These cautionary tales serve as powerful reminders that health should never be sacrificed for ambition.

One of the most well-documented examples is Steve Jobs, co-founder of Apple Inc. A visionary who revolutionized the technology industry, Jobs was known for his obsessive work ethic, perfectionism, and relentless drive. Yet, he ignored his health for years, pushing himself to extremes while disregarding critical warning signs. When he was diagnosed with pancreatic cancer, he initially pursued alternative treatments instead of immediate medical intervention. His decision, coupled with years of immense stress and an irregular diet, may have contributed to his declining condition. Despite his immense wealth and access to the best healthcare, he ultimately lost his battle with cancer in 2011.

His story serves as a stark reminder that no amount of financial success can compensate for neglected health, and delaying essential care can have dire consequences. Howard Hughes, once one of the wealthiest and most powerful men in the world, offers another sobering example. A brilliant businessman, aviator, and filmmaker, Hughes was known for his extraordinary ambition and genius. However, his neglect of both physical and mental health led to a tragic decline. Plagued by severe obsessive-compulsive disorder (OCD) and chronic pain, Hughes turned to prescription drugs to cope, leading to a deepening addiction. Over the years, his health deteriorated to such an extent that he became a reclusive figure, avoiding social interaction and shutting himself away from the world.

His body suffered from malnutrition, his mind spiraled into paranoia, and he was barely recognizable by the time of his death. Despite his massive fortune, Hughes spent his final years in agony, a prisoner of his own declining health. His story underscores the devastating impact of ignoring mental health and how even the richest individuals can be undone by neglecting self-care. The entertainment world has also seen its share of cautionary tales. Anthony Bourdain, the celebrated chef, writer, and television host, seemed to have it all—global fame, creative freedom, and the ability to explore the world doing what he loved.

Yet, beneath the surface, he struggled with personal demons, including depression, substance abuse, and the physical toll of a grueling career. Bourdain was constantly on the move, often neglecting rest and recovery. The stress, combined with emotional and mental exhaustion, weighed heavily on him. His tragic passing in 2018 sent shockwaves through the world, serving as a painful reminder that outward success does not always equate to inner peace. Burnout, chronic fatigue, and untreated mental health struggles can erode even the strongest individuals, cutting lives short despite their achievements. A similar pattern can be seen in the life of Elvis Presley. The King of Rock and Roll captivated the world with his talent, charisma, and larger-than-life performances. However, his lifestyle was far from healthy. Over time, the relentless pressures of fame, combined with poor dietary habits and an overreliance on prescription drugs, took a toll on his body. Struggling with addiction and chronic health issues, Presley's once vibrant energy waned.

By the time of his passing at just 42 years old, he had suffered from multiple health complications, including heart disease and digestive disorders, conditions that could have been managed with better self-care and lifestyle choices. His story serves as a poignant example of how fame and fortune offer little protection against the consequences of long-term health neglect. Another modern example is Bernie Madoff, the infamous financier behind one of the largest Ponzi schemes in history. While Madoff's downfall is often examined from a financial and ethical perspective, his health also deteriorated significantly due to chronic stress and the pressures of maintaining his fraudulent empire.

Stress-related illnesses, anxiety, and long-term sleep deprivation likely contributed to his declining well-being. By the time he was incarcerated, his body had begun breaking down under the weight of years of unrelenting tension and anxiety. His case highlights how high levels of stress and unethical business practices can not only ruin financial legacies but also destroy personal health. Each of these stories, while unique in their circumstances, shares a common theme: the failure to prioritize health leads to tragic outcomes, regardless of status or wealth. Whether it is chronic stress, lack of sleep, poor nutrition, or ignoring mental well-being, the repercussions are often irreversible.

These individuals, despite their remarkable achievements, ultimately paid the price for neglecting the one thing money cannot buy—good health. The lesson here is clear. Health should never be treated as an afterthought or something to be addressed only when problems arise. It must be nurtured, protected, and prioritized as a fundamental part of success. After all, what good is wealth if one is too sick to enjoy it? By making conscious choices to care for the body and mind, individuals can ensure that their success is not just temporary but sustainable, allowing them to truly enjoy the fruits of their labor for years to come. One thing I know for sure after treating thousands of patients is this: If you're healthy, you can always earn more money. It's a simple principle, yet it's one that people overlook every day.

Too many people chase money, promotions, and business success while sacrificing their health. They work long hours, neglect their bodies, and tell themselves they'll focus on their health once they've "made it." But what happens when they finally achieve their financial goals? More often than not, their health is in shambles. They have money, but they are exhausted, in pain, or struggling with chronic illnesses. Suddenly, all the success they worked so hard for feels meaningless because they don't have the energy to enjoy it. I have seen it time and time again. Patients come to me after years of grinding in their careers, only to realize they've spent so much time focused on money that they've lost their most valuable asset—their health. Many of them tell me they would trade all their money just to feel good again. But what if we didn't have to choose between health and wealth? What if we could have both? The truth is, when you prioritize your health, your ability to create wealth increases exponentially.

Money is a renewable resource. You can always earn more. You can start a new business, land a new job, or create new income streams. But your body? You only get one. When it breaks down, it doesn't matter how much money you have in the bank. If you don't have your health, you have nothing. This is something many people don't fully understand until it's too late. I've worked with patients who spent decades building their wealth, believing they could always "fix" their health later. But when later came, it wasn't so simple. Their energy was gone, their minds were foggy, and they were facing serious medical conditions that could have been prevented.

On the other hand, I've seen people who invest in their health early on, and as a result, they continue thriving well into their later years. They have the energy, stamina, and clarity to keep creating, innovating, and earning. That's the difference. Healthy people are capable of growth. They can keep building. They can enjoy the fruits of their labor. Ignoring your health doesn't just affect your body—it affects your productivity, your relationships, and ultimately, your success. When you don't take care of yourself, the price you pay is far greater than most people realize. Poor health leads to low energy, chronic fatigue, mental fog, and reduced performance in every area of life. Many of my patients have struggled for years with joint pain, brain fog, and exhaustion.

They assumed these issues were just part of getting older. But once we addressed their health, they couldn't believe how much better they felt. Suddenly, they had more energy, more focus, and more drive. Their businesses took off. Their relationships improved. Their entire outlook on life changed. I've also seen entrepreneurs go from barely keeping up with their workload to launching new ventures with ease. Their secret? They invested in their health. They made sleep a priority. They improved their diet. They took the right supplements. They exercised regularly. And in return, their minds and bodies operated at peak performance.

They didn't wait for a health crisis to force them to take action. They made their well-being a priority before they ever had a reason to worry about it. Too many people view health as an expense. They hesitate to spend money on high-quality supplements, organic food, or integrative healthcare. Yet, they have no problem spending thousands on cars, vacations, or luxury goods. The irony is that when their health collapses, they'll pay whatever it takes to get it back. But why wait until there's a problem? The smartest financial decision you can make is to invest in your health now. Every dollar you spend on prevention today saves you thousands in medical bills, lost productivity, and missed opportunities in the future.

More importantly, it gives you the ability to enjoy your life. Because when you're healthy, everything becomes easier. You think better, work better, and feel better. You wake up with energy. You show up to your job or business with confidence. You make smarter decisions. You handle stress more effectively. You have the stamina to keep going when others burn out. That is what creates long-term success. If you run a business, manage a team, or work in a high-performance career, your health is the engine that drives your success. If you're constantly sick, exhausted, or in pain, you are operating at a fraction of your potential. Think of it this way: Imagine a high-performance sports car running on cheap fuel and never getting maintenance. It might still move, but eventually, it will break down. Your body is no different. You can push it hard for a while, but if you neglect it, it will fail. The most successful people in the world don't leave their health to chance.

They treat their bodies like high-performance machines. They fuel themselves with the right nutrients. They optimize their sleep. They manage their stress. They stay active. They don't see health as optional. They see it as essential. It's no coincidence that many of the world's most successful people prioritize their health. There is a direct connection between how you feel physically and how you perform financially. When you feel good, you're more confident. You take bigger risks. You have the mental clarity to solve problems. You have the endurance to keep going when others give up. But when you're exhausted, inflamed, and stressed, everything feels harder. You procrastinate. You doubt yourself. You struggle to stay focused. You make impulsive decisions because you don't have the mental bandwidth to think strategically. When you're at your best physically, you're at your best mentally.

Your decisions are sharper. Your emotions are more stable. Your stress levels are lower. Your ability to handle challenges increases. I've worked with people who thought they were "too old" to compete in their industries, but once they made a commitment to their health, they outperformed colleagues half their age. They had better focus, greater endurance, and a renewed sense of purpose. Your body is an investment. You wouldn't expect a house to stand strong without a solid foundation, and you shouldn't expect to sustain long-term success without a healthy body.

When you invest in your well-being, you're ensuring that you can continue to perform at a high level for decades to come. Health isn't about vanity. It's about longevity. It's about ensuring that you have the physical and mental capacity to live the life you've worked so hard to build. Many people wait until they're forced to take their health seriously. They wait until they're diagnosed with a disease, experience burnout, or feel the effects of chronic stress before they make changes. But by then, they've already lost valuable time, energy, and opportunities. The key is to be proactive. Start prioritizing your health before you "need" to. That way, you never find yourself in a situation where your body limits your ability to achieve your goals.

The truth is, wealth without health is meaningless. What's the point of financial success if you're too exhausted to enjoy it? What's the point of building a business if you don't have the energy to sustain it? What's the point of accumulating wealth if you have to spend it all on medical treatments, prescription drugs, and hospital bills? The people who thrive—those who build empires, create legacies, and enjoy the fruits of their labor—are the ones who understand this. They don't wait until it's too late. They make their health a priority from the start. They understand that their body is their most valuable asset. They recognize that success isn't just about financial gain—it's about having the freedom to live fully, without limitations. When you make health a non-negotiable part of your life, everything else improves. Your work becomes more enjoyable.

Your creativity flourishes. Your relationships deepen. Your ability to contribute to the world expands. You have the energy to chase your dreams, explore new opportunities, and take on challenges with confidence. You become unstoppable. So don't wait for a wake-up call. Don't wait for illness to remind you of the importance of your body. The time to invest in your health is now. Eat foods that nourish you.

Move your body daily. Get enough sleep. Manage your stress. Take the supplements your body needs. Surround yourself with people who support your well-being. Make your health a priority, and you'll be amazed at what you're capable of achieving. Because at the end of the day, if you're healthy, you can always earn more money. But if you're sick, no amount of money can buy back your time, your energy, or your vitality. Success isn't just about what you build—it's about having the health to enjoy it. And that starts with the choices you make today.

2

The 4 Biggest Threats to Your Health & Wealth

S tress is an invisible force that quietly dictates the course of our health, often without us realizing its full impact until it's too late. It creeps into our daily lives, masquerading as a normal part of existence, until its effects manifest in ways we can no longer ignore—fatigue, anxiety, weight gain, digestive distress, and even chronic disease. But what if I told you that stress is not just an emotional response but a biochemical reaction capable of wreaking havoc on every system in the body?

Chronic stress is one of the most pervasive and insidious threats to modern health. Often dismissed as an unavoidable part of daily life, stress silently undermines well-being, contributing to a host of chronic conditions. While not a disease in itself, stress amplifies nearly every health problem, making it a significant risk factor for long-term illness.

The body's response to stress is deeply ingrained in our evolutionary biology. Imagine stepping outside and encountering a wild animal—a bear, a snake, or a tarantula. Instantly, your body would trigger a cascade of physiological changes: blood flow would be redirected away from the digestive system, breathing would become rapid and shallow, pupils would dilate, and blood pressure would surge. These reactions, governed by the fight-or-flight response, are designed to optimize survival. However, in the modern world, the sources of stress are rarely as tangible as a wild predator. Instead, they come in the form of financial concerns, work-related pressures, relationship struggles, and environmental factors. Unfortunately, the body does not distinguish between an immediate physical threat and chronic psychological stress—it reacts in the same way, perpetuating a state of heightened alert that depletes energy reserves and disrupts normal physiological function.

The statistics are alarming. Research suggests that 43% of Americans experience health problems related to stress. It accounts for an estimated 70 to 90% of doctor visits and costs the U.S. economy up to $300 billion annually. Given these staggering figures, stress management should be considered a cornerstone of preventative healthcare.

One of the most critical steps in mitigating the effects of chronic stress is establishing a structured routine. The human body thrives on consistency, and disruptions to natural rhythms exacerbate stress responses. When daily routines are neglected, symptoms such as digestive distress, hormonal imbalances, and chronic fatigue often emerge. A simple yet powerful test to assess the impact of stress on the body is Raglan's test, which evaluates adrenal function. This test measures blood pressure while lying down and again immediately after standing. Ideally, blood pressure should rise slightly upon standing, but individuals suffering from adrenal fatigue often experience a drop, sometimes leading to dizziness or faintness. This condition, known medically as postural orthostatic tachycardia syndrome (POTS), indicates dysfunction in the body's ability to regulate stress.

Chronic stress affects multiple systems in the body, with particularly severe consequences for the gastrointestinal and endocrine systems. Stress-induced digestive issues arise because the body frequently diverts resources away from the gut to prioritize survival mechanisms. Over time, this can lead to conditions such as irritable bowel syndrome (IBS), acid reflux, and nutrient malabsorption. Similarly, chronic stress taxes the adrenal glands, which play a crucial role in managing hormonal balance. As the adrenal glands become overburdened, the thyroid often compensates, eventually leading to hypothyroidism. This condition is characterized by fatigue, weight gain, depression, and a slowed metabolism, creating a cycle of deteriorating health.

Beyond these immediate effects, stress has a profound impact on cardiovascular health. Chronic stress contributes to high blood pressure, increased heart rate, and elevated cholesterol levels. Over time, these factors significantly raise the risk of heart disease and stroke. The inflammatory response triggered by chronic stress also accelerates the progression of atherosclerosis, leading to arterial plaque buildup and restricted blood flow. Research has shown that individuals who experience high levels of chronic stress have a significantly greater likelihood of developing cardiovascular conditions compared to those who manage stress effectively.

Additionally, stress can suppress immune function, making the body more susceptible to infections, autoimmune diseases, and even cancer. The immune system is highly responsive to stress hormones, particularly cortisol. When stress levels remain elevated for extended periods, the immune system weakens, impairing the body's ability to fight off infections and repair damaged tissues. This explains why individuals under chronic stress are more prone to colds, flu, and slow wound healing.

Addressing chronic stress requires a multifaceted approach. First, establishing a structured routine is essential. Consistent sleep patterns, nourishing whole foods, and regular exercise all contribute to improved stress resilience. A healthy sleep environment, free from electronic distractions, significantly enhances sleep quality and allows the body to repair and recover from daily stressors.

Exercise is one of the most effective natural stress relievers. Physical activity helps regulate cortisol levels, increase endorphin production, and improve overall mood. Engaging in regular movement, whether through cardio workouts, strength training, or activities like yoga and tai chi, can have profound effects on stress reduction. Even simple activities such as walking in nature or stretching can help lower cortisol levels and promote relaxation.

Diet plays a foundational role in stress management. Consuming fresh, natural foods optimizes bodily function, while processed foods and artificial stimulants exacerbate stress-related imbalances. It is vital to minimize foods that come in boxes, wrappers, or cans, as well as to limit the intake of sugar, caffeine, and alcohol. These substances may offer temporary relief, but they ultimately compound stress by destabilizing energy levels and hormone regulation. By prioritizing whole, nutrient-dense foods, the body receives the fuel it needs to function optimally.

In addition to lifestyle modifications, specific vitamins and supplements can support the body's stress response. Adaptogenic herbs, B vitamins, magnesium, and vitamin C play crucial roles in adrenal function and overall stress resilience. Testing for thyroid function, metabolic efficiency, and liver health can also reveal underlying imbalances that contribute to stress-related disorders.

Mental and emotional well-being are equally critical in managing stress. Practices such as meditation, deep breathing, and time spent in nature can significantly reduce stress levels. Journaling is another powerful tool, facilitating communication between the brain's analytical and creative centers and promoting emotional clarity. Writing down concerns often illuminates the fact that many worries are unfounded, leading to a more balanced perspective.

A particularly effective technique for stress management is the "I Am Enough" affirmation exercise. Standing in front of a mirror and affirming self-worth may feel awkward at first, but over time, it fosters a profound sense of self-acceptance. The mind-body connection is undeniable, and positive self-talk plays a crucial role in breaking the cycle of chronic stress.

While pharmaceutical interventions exist for stress-related disorders, they should be considered a secondary approach rather than a first-line treatment. Medications can provide relief, but they often mask symptoms rather than addressing the underlying cause. Instead, a holistic approach that integrates functional medicine, lifestyle modifications, and emotional wellness strategies yields the most sustainable results.

Effectively managing stress significantly reduces the risk of chronic diseases, from cardiovascular conditions to autoimmune disorders. By embracing structured habits, nourishing the body with wholesome foods, incorporating targeted supplementation, and fostering emotional well-being, individuals can regain control over their health and well-being. Stress may be an inevitable part of life, but our response to it determines the course of our long-term vitality.

The pursuit of health is an ongoing journey—one that requires conscious effort and commitment. By addressing stress proactively, we can cultivate resilience, prevent disease, and ultimately lead more fulfilling, vibrant lives. Stress significantly impacts sleep patterns, leading to insomnia, restless sleep, and daytime fatigue. When the body is in a heightened state of alert due to stress, falling asleep and staying asleep become challenging. Racing thoughts, anxiety, and physical tension disrupt the natural sleep cycle, preventing the body from entering deep restorative sleep stages. Over time, sleep deprivation exacerbates stress levels, creating a vicious cycle of insomnia and heightened anxiety.

Additionally, stress can trigger unhealthy coping mechanisms, such as excessive caffeine or alcohol consumption, which further disrupt sleep patterns. By prioritizing stress management techniques, such as relaxation exercises, meditation, and establishing consistent sleep routines, individuals can improve sleep quality and break the cycle of stress-induced insomnia. Stress also contributes to weight gain and metabolic dysfunction. Cortisol, the primary stress hormone, influences appetite and fat storage. When cortisol levels remain elevated due to chronic stress, the body tends to crave high-calorie, sugary foods, leading to overeating and weight gain. Additionally, cortisol promotes fat storage, particularly around the abdomen, which is associated with an increased risk of metabolic diseases such as type 2 diabetes and heart disease. Stress can also disrupt blood sugar regulation, leading to insulin resistance and further metabolic imbalances. By managing stress effectively and adopting healthy eating habits, individuals can mitigate the impact of stress on weight and metabolic health. The relationship between stress and mental health is complex and bidirectional.

Chronic stress can contribute to the development of mental health disorders such as anxiety, depression, and post-traumatic stress disorder (PTSD). When stress levels remain elevated for extended periods, the brain's chemistry and structure can be altered, leading to changes in mood, cognition, and behavior. Additionally, stress can trigger unhealthy coping mechanisms, such as substance abuse, social isolation, and self-harm, which further exacerbate mental health problems. Conversely, pre-existing mental health conditions can increase vulnerability to stress, making it more challenging to cope with daily stressors. By addressing both stress and mental health concerns through therapy, medication, and lifestyle changes, individuals can improve their overall well-being and resilience. Stress can strain relationships, leading to conflict, communication breakdowns, and emotional distance. When individuals are stressed, they may be more irritable, impatient, and less emotionally available to their loved ones. This can lead to misunderstandings, arguments, and a breakdown of trust. Additionally, stress can lead to unhealthy coping mechanisms, such as withdrawing from social interaction or engaging in substance abuse, which further strain relationships. By prioritizing stress management techniques and open communication, individuals can navigate the challenges of stress and maintain healthy relationships.

Work-related stress is a common and significant source of chronic stress. Demanding workloads, tight deadlines, interpersonal conflicts, and job insecurity can all contribute to high levels of stress. When work-related stress becomes chronic, it can lead to burnout, decreased productivity, and a host of health problems. Additionally, work-related stress can spill over into personal life, affecting relationships and overall well-being. By setting boundaries, prioritizing self-care, and seeking support when needed, individuals can manage work-related stress and maintain a healthy work-life balance. Chronic stress accelerates the aging process, both physically and mentally. Telomeres, the protective caps at the ends of chromosomes, shorten with age, and stress can accelerate this process.

Shortened telomeres are associated with an increased risk of age-related diseases such as heart disease, cancer, and Alzheimer's disease. Additionally, stress can contribute to premature aging of the skin, hair loss, and cognitive decline. By managing stress effectively and adopting healthy lifestyle habits, individuals can slow down the aging process and maintain their vitality as they age. Environmental factors, such as noise pollution, air pollution, and exposure to toxins, can also contribute to stress levels. These environmental stressors can trigger the body's stress response, leading to physiological and psychological changes. Additionally, environmental stressors can interact with other sources of stress, such as work or relationship stress, exacerbating their effects.

By minimizing exposure to environmental stressors and adopting stress management techniques, individuals can mitigate the impact of these factors on their health and well-being. While stress is an inevitable part of life, individuals can build resilience and develop effective coping mechanisms. By adopting healthy lifestyle habits, such as regular exercise, a balanced diet, and sufficient sleep, individuals can improve their ability to manage stress. Additionally, mindfulness practices, such as meditation and deep breathing, can help individuals cultivate a sense of calm and inner peace. Building strong social connections and seeking support from loved ones can also provide a buffer against stress. By prioritizing self-care and developing healthy coping mechanisms, individuals can navigate the challenges of life with greater ease and resilience.

Poor Diet

Everybody knows they should eat healthier. But let's be real—knowing isn't enough. You need a reason to take action. You need a WHY. That's where this book comes in. I'm Dr. Jason West, and I'm about to give you 20 compelling, undeniable reasons to change your diet today. You don't have to overhaul everything at once—just start somewhere. The goal is progress, not perfection.

Let's start with one of the biggest myths about healthy eating— it's expensive. People assume eating well will drain their wallets, but that's not true. There's a toll road on the journey of life: one leads to the doctor's office, the other to the grocery store. You choose where to invest. Studies show that for every dollar you spend on nutritious food, you save about three dollars in future medical costs. So, would you rather pay a little more now or a whole lot later?

An apple a day isn't just a saying. A study from New Zealand found that people who eat whole, natural foods experience greater emotional stability. Less moodiness, less anxiety—just calm, collected energy. Eating well isn't just about physical health. It's about mental health, too. Your immune system is your body's defense force, and it can't fight off invaders without the right fuel. Garlic, cayenne, green leafy vegetables, and vitamin C-rich foods are natural immune boosters. Eat well, and you'll find yourself dodging the flu and common colds like a pro.

One of the saddest things I see in my office? Advanced osteoporosis. The spine compresses, bones become fragile, and suddenly, life changes forever. But guess what? You can prevent it. Healthy eating builds strong bones, reduces your risk of fractures, and helps you maintain mobility. Trust me—you want to skip osteoporosis. And ladies, if you suffer from brutal PMS, diet plays a huge role. Nutrient-rich foods balance estrogen and progesterone, reducing cramps, bloating, and mood swings. Plus, eating a colorful diet (no, Skittles don't count) can significantly improve reproductive health.

Sex hormones aren't just about reproduction. They play a massive role in energy, stamina, and overall well-being. If you want your thyroid, adrenals, and reproductive organs functioning optimally, you need to eat right. A healthy diet provides the raw materials your body needs to balance hormones naturally. And speaking of hormones, if you're struggling with insomnia, poor diet is often the culprit. Nutrient-rich foods help regulate sleep hormones like melatonin and serotonin, improving sleep quality and duration.

Your gut health determines how well you absorb nutrients, how strong your immune system is, and even how clear your skin looks. Leaky gut, IBS, and digestive distress are rampant today, and they're largely diet-related. If you want to improve digestion, reduce bloating, and enhance nutrient absorption, cut out junk food. Your gut microbiome thrives on whole, nutritious foods—not processed garbage. What you eat also affects your future generations. Studies show that pregnant women who consume omega-3s and essential fatty acids have children with higher IQs. Translation: What you eat today can impact the health and intelligence of future generations. That's powerful.

Think of your brain as a high-performance engine. If you feed it junk, it sputters. If you give it premium fuel—like omega-3s, healthy fats, and whole foods—you get sharper memory, better focus, and improved problem-solving skills. Eating right makes you smarter. Period. And while you're at it, proper nutrition also reduces cravings. When your body gets what it needs, you stop reaching for junk food.

Want to maximize your workouts? It's not just about reps and sets. Nutrition fuels muscle recovery, endurance, and strength gains. The right food amplifies every single benefit of exercise. And if you want natural stress relief, look no further than your plate. Sugar spikes, caffeine crashes, and processed foods send your stress levels through the roof. Eating whole foods helps regulate blood sugar and keeps you calm, collected, and in control. Feeling sluggish? That's because most people arc. Your body needs real food to generate sustainable energy. If you're constantly tired, check your diet first.

Your skin reflects what's happening inside your body. Acne, eczema, and dull skin often stem from inflammation and poor diet. Load up on antioxidants and watch your complexion transform. The same goes for muscle recovery—eating right speeds up muscle repair and reduces soreness after workouts. Load up on anti-inflammatory foods, and your body will thank you.

When you nourish your body properly, you don't just feel better—you become stronger, faster, and more efficient in everything you do. Your body is a high-performance machine, and the fuel you provide determines how well it runs. If you want to improve your endurance, strengthen your muscles, and increase your lifespan, the answer is simple: eat better. Healthy eating isn't a punishment—it's a privilege. It's not about deprivation, but empowerment. Every bite is an opportunity to invest in your future. Whether you start small or go all-in, remember: Progress is better than perfection.

This is your chance to take control of your health and your future. The power is in your hands, and the food you choose to eat will shape your energy levels, your mood, your longevity, and your ability to thrive. Make the choice today to eat better, live better, and be better. We've already explored a handful of compelling reasons to prioritize healthy eating, but we're just scratching the surface. The human body is a marvel of intricate systems, each influenced by the fuel we provide. Let's delve deeper into the profound connection between your diet and your overall well-being.

Your brain is your most valuable asset, and it demands premium fuel to function optimally. A diet rich in omega-3 fatty acids, found in fatty fish, walnuts, and flaxseeds, has been shown to enhance cognitive function, memory, and focus. Antioxidants, abundant in colorful fruits and vegetables, protect brain cells from damage and may reduce the risk of cognitive decline.

Ever heard of the "gut-brain" connection? It's real. Your gut and brain communicate constantly, and the health of your gut microbiome directly impacts your mood and emotional well-being. A diet rich in fiber and fermented foods nourishes beneficial gut bacteria, leading to improved mood, reduced anxiety, and a greater sense of calm. Chronic diseases like heart disease, type 2 diabetes, and certain cancers are often preventable through dietary choices. A diet low in saturated and trans fats, refined sugars, and processed foods, and high in fruits, vegetables, whole grains, and lean protein can significantly reduce your risk of these debilitating conditions. Maintaining a healthy weight is crucial for overall health and longevity. A balanced diet, combined with regular physical activity, is the most sustainable way to achieve and maintain a healthy weight.

By focusing on whole, nutrient-dense foods, you'll feel satisfied and energized, making it easier to manage your weight and avoid the pitfalls of fad diets. Tired of feeling sluggish and drained? Your diet could be the culprit. Processed foods and sugary drinks provide a quick burst of energy, followed by a crash, leaving you feeling worse than before. Whole foods, on the other hand, provide sustained energy, keeping you feeling vibrant and alert throughout the day. Calcium, vitamin D, and other essential nutrients are vital for maintaining strong bones and joints. Dairy products, leafy green vegetables, and fatty fish are excellent sources of these nutrients, helping to prevent osteoporosis, arthritis, and other musculoskeletal problems.

Aging is inevitable, but the quality of your aging is largely within your control. A nutritious diet, rich in antioxidants and anti-inflammatory compounds, can slow the aging process, protect against age-related diseases, and keep you feeling young and vibrant for years to come.

Your outer appearance reflects your inner health. A diet rich in vitamins, minerals, and antioxidants nourishes your skin, hair, and nails from the inside out, promoting a healthy glow, strong hair, and resilient nails. Whether you're a weekend warrior or a professional athlete, your diet plays a crucial role in your performance.

Proper nutrition fuels your workouts, enhances recovery, and helps you reach your full athletic potential. Your food choices impact not only your health but also the health of the planet. By choosing sustainably sourced, plant-based foods, you can reduce your environmental footprint and contribute to a healthier planet for future generations.Healthy eating doesn't have to break the bank. By planning your meals, cooking at home, and choosing seasonal produce, you can eat well on a budget. Plus, as we discussed earlier, investing in healthy food now can save you a fortune on healthcare costs down the road.

Food is often at the center of social gatherings and celebrations. By sharing healthy meals with loved ones, you can strengthen relationships, create lasting memories, and promote healthy habits within your community. Taking control of your diet is an act of self-care and empowerment. By making conscious choices about what you eat, you're prioritizing your health and well-being, setting a positive example for others, and taking an active role in shaping your future.

Your health is not just about you. It affects your family, your friends, your community, and even future generations. By prioritizing your health through nutritious food choices, you're creating a ripple effect of positive change that extends far beyond yourself. Remember, the goal is progress, not perfection. Start by making small, sustainable changes to your diet. Add more fruits and vegetables to your plate, swap sugary drinks for water, and choose whole grains over refined carbohydrates.

Every healthy choice you make is a step in the right direction. Your health is not simply the absence of disease; it's a state of complete physical, mental, and social well-being. And your diet is the cornerstone of your health. By nourishing your body with wholesome, nutrient-dense foods, you're investing in your greatest asset – your health. And that's a wealth that no amount of money can buy.

Lack of Movement

Every day, there's a new diet trend, a new superfood, or a new "miracle" weight loss secret being hyped up in the media. Some of them sound fantastic; some are outright ridiculous. But here's the reality: dieting isn't just about losing weight. It's about fueling your body with the right nutrients to live a long, healthy, and vibrant life. If you feel sluggish, struggle with focus, or battle chronic pain, the problem isn't just your age or genetics—it's often your diet. Just like you wouldn't put bad fuel in a high-performance car, you can't expect your body to run efficiently on poor-quality food. Your diet impacts every part of your life—your energy, your hormones, your mental clarity, and even your happiness. This book isn't about fad diets, starvation, or counting every single calorie. It's about eating in a way that makes sense for your body, supports your health, and keeps you thriving. Let's dive into the 25 reasons why you should start dieting the right way today.

Your diet is a natural antidepressant. Did you know your gut is often called your second brain? That's because your digestive system produces about 90% of your serotonin—the neurotransmitter responsible for happiness and emotional stability. When you eat processed junk, excess sugar, and bad fats, you disrupt your gut, and in turn, you mess with your mood. A whole-food, nutrient-dense diet can naturally boost your mental well-being. Your diet can help balance hormones. Hormones are the body's chemical messengers, responsible for everything from energy levels to metabolism to mood. When your diet is high in processed foods, artificial additives, and bad fats, it throws off your hormone balance, leading to weight gain, fatigue, and brain fog. Eating whole foods rich in healthy fats, fiber, and quality protein can keep your hormones in check.

Good nutrition reduces anxiety and stress. Have you ever noticed that you crave sugar or junk food when you're stressed? That's because your adrenal glands—responsible for handling stress—burn through nutrients like magnesium and B vitamins at lightning speed. A nutrient-rich diet replenishes these reserves, helping your body handle stress more effectively. A good diet boosts creativity and mental clarity. If you've ever had a big meal and felt sluggish afterward, you know what food fog feels like. The wrong foods slow you down mentally, making it harder to focus and be creative. A diet rich in antioxidants, omega-3s, and essential vitamins keeps your brain sharp and your ideas flowing.

Healthy eating strengthens your immune system. Your immune system is like a shield, constantly working to protect you from viruses, bacteria, and chronic diseases. But if your diet is filled with sugar, preservatives, and inflammatory foods, that shield gets weaker. Whole foods, especially fruits, vegetables, and lean proteins, give your immune system the support it needs to keep you healthy year-round. Your heart loves a clean diet. Heart disease is the leading cause of death worldwide, and diet plays a major role in preventing it. Too much sugar, bad fats, and processed foods can clog arteries and lead to high blood pressure. On the flip side, heart-healthy foods like leafy greens, avocados, nuts, and fatty fish help protect your heart and keep it strong.

Good nutrition helps curb cravings. Junk food cravings aren't just about willpower; they're about nutrient deficiencies. If you're constantly craving sugar or carbs, your body might be missing essential nutrients like magnesium or chromium. A balanced diet helps stabilize blood sugar and reduce the urge to reach for unhealthy snacks. A proper diet fights metabolic syndrome. Metabolic syndrome is a cluster of conditions—including obesity, high blood sugar, and high cholesterol—that increase your risk for diabetes and heart disease. The best way to combat it? A clean, whole-food diet rich in fiber, lean protein, and healthy fats.

A healthy diet can prevent chronic disease. Diabetes, cancer, arthritis, Alzheimer's—the list goes on. Many chronic diseases stem from inflammation and poor nutrition. A whole-food diet packed with anti-inflammatory foods like turmeric, ginger, and green tea can help reduce your risk of developing these conditions. Eating right protects your eyesight. Your eyes need specific nutrients—like vitamin A, lutein, and omega-3s—to function properly. A diet high in colorful vegetables, fish, and nuts can help protect against macular degeneration and other vision issues.

A good diet adds years to your life. Want to live longer and feel younger? Your diet plays a critical role in longevity. The longest-living populations in the world eat whole, nutrient-dense foods with minimal processed junk. Eating well enhances your quality of life. Longevity isn't just about the number of years you live—it's about the quality of those years. Proper nutrition keeps you mobile, strong, and independent as you age.

Healthy eating respects your body. You only get one body, and food is either fuel or poison. Choosing nutrient-dense foods is the ultimate act of self-respect. A clean diet supports strong bones. Calcium, vitamin D, and magnesium are crucial for bone health. Skip the processed junk and get your nutrients from whole foods to prevent osteoporosis. Proper nutrition saves you money on medical bills. For every dollar you spend on healthy food, you could be saving nearly three dollars on future medical expenses. Think of it as an investment in your health.

A healthy diet supports fertility and hormonal balance. If you're trying to conceive, nutrition plays a huge role. Whole foods can improve reproductive health in both men and women. Proper nutrition supports a healthy sex life. Feeling sluggish? Low libido? The right nutrients can enhance energy, circulation, and hormone balance, all of which are essential for a vibrant sex life. Good nutrition helps you sleep better. Poor diet equals poor sleep. If you're struggling with insomnia, improving your nutrition can make a huge difference.

Eating right keeps your skin looking younger. Collagen, healthy fats, and antioxidants from food are your best anti-aging tools. Skip the expensive creams—eat for your skin. A healthy diet supports your body's natural detox process. Your liver, kidneys, and gut detoxify your body, but they need the right nutrients to function optimally. Whole foods help your body clear toxins efficiently.

Your diet is one of the most powerful tools you have for improving your health. Whether you're looking to lose weight, boost energy, or just feel amazing, it all starts with food. If you're ready to take charge of your health, start making better choices today. The Role of Hydration While we've focused heavily on the importance of whole foods and nutrient-dense meals, we can't overlook the critical role that hydration plays in our overall health and well-being. Our bodies are largely composed of water, and every cell, tissue, and organ relies on it to function properly. Dehydration can lead to a host of problems, including fatigue, headaches, constipation, and even cognitive impairment.

Drinking enough water throughout the day helps flush out toxins, regulate body temperature, and transport nutrients to where they're needed. It also plays a role in maintaining healthy skin, lubricating joints, and supporting digestive health. Aim to drink at least eight glasses of water per day, and more if you're active or live in a hot climate. You can also get fluids from other sources, such as herbal tea, fruits, and vegetables.

It's not just about *what* you eat, but also *how* you eat. Mindful eating is a practice that involves paying close attention to your food and the experience of eating it. This means slowing down, savoring each bite, and tuning into your body's hunger and fullness cues. When you eat mindfully, you're more likely to make healthier choices and avoid overeating. You're also more likely to appreciate your food and feel satisfied with your meals. Mindful eating can also help reduce stress and improve your relationship with food.

Sleep is often overlooked when it comes to health and wellness, but it's just as important as diet and exercise. When you sleep, your body repairs itself, consolidates memories, and regulates hormones. Lack of sleep can lead to a host of problems, including weight gain, fatigue, and impaired cognitive function. Aim to get seven to eight hours of sleep per night, and create a relaxing bedtime routine that helps you wind down. Avoid caffeine and electronics before bed, and create a dark, quiet, and cool environment in your bedroom. Chronic stress can take a toll on your physical and mental health.

It can weaken your immune system, disrupt your sleep, and contribute to a host of chronic diseases. Finding healthy ways to manage stress is essential for your overall well-being. Some effective stress management techniques include exercise, meditation, yoga, spending time in nature, and connecting with loved ones. Find what works for you and make it a regular part of your routine. Exercise isn't just about losing weight or building muscle. It's about feeling good, boosting your energy, and improving your overall health. Regular physical activity can reduce your risk of chronic diseases, improve your mood, and enhance your cognitive function.

Find an activity you enjoy and make it a part of your daily routine. Aim for at least 30 minutes of moderate-intensity exercise most days of the week.

You can also break it up into shorter sessions throughout the day. Social connection is essential for our well-being. Strong relationships with family, friends, and community members can provide support, reduce stress, and enhance our overall quality of life. Make time for the people you care about, and find ways to connect with others who share your interests. Taking care of yourself is not selfish—it's essential. Self-care involves making time for activities that nourish your mind, body, and soul.

This might include reading, taking a bath, getting a massage, or simply spending time in nature. When you prioritize self-care, you're better able to cope with stress, maintain healthy relationships, and show up as your best self. Make self-care a non-negotiable part of your routine. Remember, optimal health is not a destination—it's a journey. There will be ups and downs along the way, but the key is to keep moving forward. Focus on progress, not perfection, and celebrate your successes along the way.

By making small, sustainable changes to your diet, lifestyle, and mindset, you can create a life of vibrant health and well-being. It's never too late to start, and every step you take is a step in the right direction. In a world that often prioritizes material possessions and external achievements, it's easy to forget that our health is our most valuable asset. Without good health, everything else suffers. By investing in your health today, you're creating a foundation for a fulfilling and abundant life. Remember, you are worth it.

Wrong Doctor

"I did everything my doctor told me to do—and I'm still sick."

I hear this every single day from driven professionals, entrepreneurs, and go-getters—the very people who refuse to settle for mediocrity in their careers but are unknowingly settling for mediocre healthcare. Conventional medicine excels in acute care. If you break a bone, have a heart attack, or need emergency surgery, we have the best system in the world. But when it comes to chronic conditions—fatigue, hormone imbalances, autoimmune disorders, or neurological decline—it's a different story. The truth is, high-achievers are not getting the medical care they need because they don't fit into the standard, symptom-suppressing model of medicine.

Patients who come to my clinic are often exhausted by a cycle of prescriptions, band-aid treatments, and dismissive specialists who don't listen to them. They don't have time to be sick, yet they find themselves trapped in a revolving door of medical appointments that go nowhere. They're told their labs are normal, their symptoms are stress-related, and their concerns are overblown. They're offered antidepressants, sleep aids, and painkillers instead of answers. Take

James, a 42-year-old executive who came into my office after seeing a dozen specialists. He told me, *"Doc, I was running two companies, but I couldn't get out of bed. My doctors ran tests, said everything looked fine, and handed me an antidepressant. I didn't need a pill—I needed someone to figure out why I felt like a shadow of myself."*

What James really needed was a doctor willing to look beyond the standard labs and protocols. His testosterone was technically normal, but only if you compared him to the average 70-year-old. His inflammatory markers were high, but his primary care doctor dismissed them as 'not significant enough.' When we dug deeper, we found underlying adrenal dysfunction, micronutrient deficiencies, and chronic inflammation. Within three months of targeted therapy—IV nutrition, bioidentical hormone support, and mitochondrial repair— James was back in his element, leading his companies and feeling better than he had in a decade.

Then there's Sarah, a 38-year-old entrepreneur, who came in with debilitating brain fog, extreme fatigue, and unexplained weight gain. Her doctors told her it was just stress—a convenient excuse when they don't know the real answer. They suggested more exercise and offered her an anti-anxiety medication. But Sarah wasn't just stressed—she was in biochemical burnout. Her cortisol was flatlined, her gut microbiome was wrecked, and she was severely deficient in magnesium, B vitamins, and omega-3 fatty acids. After a deep-dive evaluation, we customized a recovery protocol for her. Three months later, she was back to running her business at full capacity, telling me, *"I finally feel like myself again. Why didn't anyone tell me this was possible?"*

The problem isn't that conventional doctors don't care. It's that they've been trained to treat disease, not to optimize health. Medical school teaches doctors to diagnose pathology and prescribe pharmaceuticals—but what if your labs are normal and you still feel terrible? What if you're not technically sick, but you're far from thriving? Most doctors don't know what to do with that. They were never taught to look for functional imbalances, only for outright disease. If you don't fit into a tidy diagnostic box, you're sent home with a prescription or told, *"Everything looks fine, maybe you're just getting older."*

This approach may work for the average person, but high-performers operate differently. They push harder, take on more stress, and demand more from their bodies than the average person. But conventional medicine doesn't account for that. It treats everyone the same—regardless of whether you're a desk worker or a CEO running on six hours of sleep and sheer willpower. When high-achievers crash, they crash hard. The warning signs—fatigue, irritability, gut issues, hormonal swings—are ignored or brushed off until suddenly, their system can't compensate anymore. They burn out. They get hit with autoimmune conditions, neurological decline, or chronic pain that no one can explain. This is why the standard medical model doesn't work for them. They need a system designed for optimization, not just disease management.

So, what do high-performers actually need? They need a doctor who listens deeply—not just to symptoms, but to patterns, lifestyle, and stressors. They need a doctor who runs the right tests—beyond the standard bloodwork, looking at hormones, inflammation, micronutrients, and mitochondrial function. They need a doctor who treats the root cause—not just the symptoms, but the underlying imbalances that are creating dysfunction. And most importantly, they need a doctor who focuses on recovery and performance—not just getting rid of symptoms, but unlocking energy, resilience, and longevity.

I've seen countless patients transform simply because they finally got the right kind of medical support. Mark, a 50-year-old attorney, came in feeling like his brain was 'short-circuiting.' His memory was slipping, his focus was gone, and he was terrified he was developing early dementia. His neurologist told him it was normal aging. We ran deeper tests and found sky-high inflammation, a leaky blood-brain barrier, and severe B12 and omega-3 deficiencies. With targeted therapies, diet optimization, and IV nutrients, Mark's cognitive function came back. Within six months, he was sharper than ever, telling me, *"I don't just feel normal—I feel unstoppable."*

Jessica, a 44-year-old CEO, was an elite-level entrepreneur but was struggling with debilitating joint pain and extreme fatigue. Rheumatologists ruled out major diseases and simply told her it was 'probably fibromyalgia.' When we tested her thoroughly, we found hidden infections, chronic mold exposure, and an autoimmune trigger in her thyroid. After detoxifying her system and using regenerative medicine strategies, she was back to training for triathlons within a year.

These are just a few of the many patients who have walked into my clinic feeling dismissed, misdiagnosed, and exhausted by the traditional healthcare system. They were stuck in a medical hamster wheel, going from doctor to doctor with no real solutions. They weren't looking for a quick fix or another prescription. They were looking for answers, for someone to see the bigger picture, and for a medical approach that aligned with their level of performance and ambition.

If this resonates with you—if you've been dismissed, misdiagnosed, or told "everything is fine" while feeling the worst you've ever felt—you're not alone. The standard medical system is designed to keep people from dying, not to make them truly well. But here's the truth: you don't have to settle. You can work with a doctor who actually understands how to optimize your body, your mind, and your performance.

If you're a high-achiever stuck in the medical hamster wheel, it's time to ask yourself: are you seeing the wrong doctor? And more importantly, are you ready to find the right one? The gap between the needs of high-achieving individuals and the conventional healthcare system is both vast and deeply problematic. These individuals, accustomed to pushing boundaries and demanding excellence in their professional lives, often find themselves underserved by a medical model that prioritizes disease management over health optimization.

For high performers, simply avoiding illness is not enough—they strive for peak physical and cognitive function, seeking to unlock their full potential in every aspect of life. Yet, conventional medicine, with its symptom-based approach and reactive strategies, often fails to address their unique challenges.

Traditional healthcare is designed to intervene once symptoms appear or diseases are diagnosed, whereas high performers require a proactive approach that anticipates and mitigates potential health risks before they escalate. The one-size-fits-all nature of standard medical care does not account for the physiological, genetic, and lifestyle variations that define high achievers. Instead of merely suppressing symptoms, these individuals need solutions that address the root causes of dysfunction, ensuring long-term health and sustained peak performance.

A fundamental flaw in conventional medicine is its reliance on standardized testing, which primarily detects disease markers rather than assessing overall function and vitality. High performers need more advanced evaluations that go beyond the basics—comprehensive hormonal panels, micronutrient assessments, and in-depth metabolic testing that can uncover subtle imbalances before they become full-blown health issues. When standard treatment protocols fail to consider the specific demands placed on a high achiever's body and mind, they risk being left with generic recommendations that do not align with their performance-driven lifestyle.

The consequences of inadequate healthcare for high-achievers can be profound, affecting both their personal well-being and professional success. Chronic fatigue, cognitive decline, hormonal imbalances, and undiagnosed inflammation can silently erode their ability to perform at their best. Without targeted interventions and personalized care, these individuals may find themselves in a relentless cycle of underperformance, frustration, and deteriorating health.

High performers refuse to accept mediocrity in their careers, and they should demand the same high standards in their healthcare. They require a medical approach that goes beyond disease prevention, one that actively enhances resilience, maximizes energy, and sustains peak cognitive and physical function. The future of healthcare for high achievers must shift from reactive disease management to a proactive, precision-based wellness model, ensuring that those who push the limits in every other area of life receive the medical support they need to thrive.

When health issues go unaddressed or are poorly managed, they can significantly impact professional success. Decreased productivity, missed deadlines, and impaired decision-making are common consequences, leading to frustration and underperformance. The relentless pursuit of excellence, often accompanied by inadequate self-care and suboptimal health, can eventually result in burnout—characterized by exhaustion, cynicism, and a diminished sense of efficacy. Left unchecked, these issues can escalate into chronic conditions that further erode performance and quality of life. Beyond professional setbacks, health struggles can strain relationships with family, friends, and colleagues, leading to isolation and withdrawal from social and professional circles. Additionally, financial losses due to decreased income, rising medical expenses, and lost opportunities only compound the problem.

The shortcomings of conventional medicine in addressing the needs of high-achievers underscore the urgent need for a new model of healthcare—one that is specifically tailored to their physiology, lifestyle, and performance goals. This model must prioritize prevention and early intervention, identifying and mitigating potential health risks before they escalate. It should offer treatment plans customized to the individual's unique biology, genetics, and lifestyle demands. Rather than merely suppressing symptoms, it must focus on addressing the root causes of health issues to create long-lasting solutions. Advanced testing and assessment tools should be integral, providing a comprehensive understanding of an individual's health status and identifying imbalances before they manifest as disease. Most importantly, this approach must optimize both physical and cognitive function, enhancing overall performance and well-being.

Functional medicine provides a promising solution to the healthcare needs of high achievers. Unlike conventional medicine, which often isolates symptoms and treats them in silos, functional medicine takes a holistic view, recognizing the intricate connections between different systems in the body. Practitioners consider the interplay of lifestyle, nutrition, genetics, and environmental factors to uncover and address underlying imbalances that contribute to disease and diminished performance. By focusing on the root causes of health concerns rather than masking symptoms, functional medicine empowers individuals to reclaim their energy, mental clarity, and vitality.

The future of high-performance healthcare lies in a personalized, proactive, and root-cause-driven approach that equips individuals to take control of their health and optimize their performance. By partnering with healthcare providers who understand their unique needs, high achievers can break free from the limitations of conventional medicine and achieve a level of well-being that supports their pursuit of excellence. True health is not just the absence of disease—it is the foundation upon which peak performance, resilience, and a life of sustained success are built.

High-achievers operate at a level of intensity that places unique demands on both their bodies and minds, yet conventional healthcare often fails to address their specific needs. A standardized approach to medicine overlooks the fact that individuals have different genetic predispositions, lifestyles, and health goals. True optimization requires a healthcare model that tailors treatment plans to the individual, recognizing that peak performance is not a one-size-fits-all pursuit. By implementing personalized care strategies, healthcare providers can support high-achievers in sustaining energy, mental clarity, and resilience while preventing the chronic health issues that often arise from relentless stress and overexertion. Achieving this level of personalization requires advanced diagnostic tools and a deep understanding of the interconnected systems that influence overall health.

Traditional healthcare often relies on reactive testing—waiting for symptoms to emerge before investigating potential health concerns. However, high-achievers require a proactive approach that anticipates imbalances before they escalate into serious conditions. Advanced diagnostic tools provide a wealth of information about an individual's health status, uncovering hidden deficiencies and potential risks that could compromise performance. Genetic testing can reveal predispositions to certain diseases or identify variations that influence how an individual responds to specific treatments. Comprehensive blood panels provide insights into key biomarkers, including nutrient levels, hormone balances, and inflammation markers, allowing for precise interventions tailored to the individual's unique biochemistry. Microbiome analysis offers an in-depth look at gut health, which plays a crucial role in immunity, mental well-being, and metabolic function. Toxicology testing helps identify exposure to environmental toxins, heavy metals, and other harmful substances that may be silently affecting health and performance.

By leveraging these advanced tools, healthcare providers can develop targeted interventions that not only treat symptoms but address the root causes of dysfunction. For high-performers who demand precision in every aspect of their lives, this kind of healthcare approach ensures they are operating at their absolute best.

Preventive healthcare is a critical component of high-performance living. Instead of waiting for illness to strike, a proactive approach emphasizes early intervention, helping individuals maintain long-term health and peak performance. By identifying potential risks before they become debilitating conditions, individuals can take charge of their well-being and make strategic lifestyle modifications to safeguard their health. Nutritional interventions, stress management techniques, and bio-individual supplementation can help prevent chronic conditions such as adrenal fatigue, metabolic disorders, and inflammatory diseases—common issues among high-achievers who push themselves beyond their biological limits.

Additionally, maintaining peak performance requires continuous monitoring and adjustments. Regular check-ups that go beyond standard medical exams can help track progress, identify shifts in biomarkers, and fine-tune personalized treatment plans. By staying ahead of potential health risks, individuals can sustain high levels of productivity and performance without the setbacks of preventable health issues.

Success-driven individuals often face intense mental and emotional stress, which can have significant repercussions on physical health. Chronic stress impacts hormonal balance, weakens the immune system, and disrupts cognitive function, ultimately diminishing performance in both personal and professional life. A holistic healthcare approach acknowledges the deep interconnection between the mind and body, recognizing that true health extends beyond physical wellness.

Integrating stress-reduction techniques such as mindfulness, meditation, and cognitive-behavioral therapy into a healthcare regimen can have profound effects on mental resilience and physical well-being. Mindfulness practices help regulate cortisol levels, reducing the wear and tear of chronic stress on the body. Cognitive-behavioral strategies empower individuals to reframe negative thought patterns, improving focus, emotional regulation, and decision-making. By prioritizing mental well-being alongside physical health, high-achievers can cultivate the emotional resilience necessary to sustain long-term success without succumbing to burnout.

The future of healthcare for high-achievers lies in a collaborative model—one that fosters a partnership between individuals and healthcare providers to create personalized, strategic health plans. This approach moves beyond the conventional "treat and release" method and instead provides ongoing support, empowering individuals to maintain optimal health throughout their demanding careers and lifestyles. Regular health assessments utilizing advanced diagnostics will play a vital role in continuously monitoring health markers and identifying emerging risks before they manifest into serious conditions. Personalized treatment plans will address the root causes of health concerns rather than simply suppressing symptoms, ensuring long-term vitality and resilience.

Beyond medical interventions, lifestyle coaching will become an integral component of high-performance healthcare. Educating individuals on nutrition, movement, sleep optimization, and recovery strategies will allow them to implement daily habits that support sustained energy and peak mental function. Additionally, prioritizing stress management and mental health support will create a more comprehensive wellness framework, helping individuals navigate high-pressure environments without sacrificing their well-being.

High-achievers are accustomed to taking charge in their professional lives, and their healthcare should be no different. By providing them with the knowledge, tools, and resources to optimize their health, healthcare providers can empower them to make informed decisions and implement strategies that support long-term performance. Education plays a crucial role in this process—individuals need to understand the key factors that influence their health, from metabolic function to hormonal balance and gut health. Self-monitoring tools, such as wearable technology and at-home biomarker testing, can help track progress and provide real-time feedback, allowing individuals to make data-driven adjustments to their health routines.

In addition to knowledge and self-tracking, access to a supportive community can be a game-changer. Surrounding oneself with like-minded individuals who prioritize health and performance fosters accountability and provides a network for shared learning and motivation. Whether through professional networks, mastermind groups, or specialized healthcare communities, having a support system in place can make the pursuit of optimal health more effective and sustainable.

High-achievers demand excellence in every area of their lives, and their healthcare should be no exception. Conventional medicine, with its reactive and generalized approach, often falls short in meeting the needs of those who strive for more than just the absence of disease. By embracing a personalized, proactive, and holistic healthcare model, individuals can optimize their physical and cognitive function, sustain high levels of energy, and prevent the long-term consequences of untreated health imbalances. True health is not merely the absence of illness—it is the foundation upon which peak performance, resilience, and long-term success are built. By partnering with forward-thinking healthcare providers who understand the demands of high-achievers, individuals can unlock their full potential and ensure that their greatest asset—their health—remains strong and uncompromised.

The four biggest threats to your health—chronic stress, poor diet, lack of movement, and inadequate healthcare—are not just obstacles;

they are silent saboteurs of your well-being, performance, and financial future. These factors do not operate in isolation but rather intertwine, creating a vicious cycle that can erode your health, productivity, and overall quality of life. The high-achieving individual, driven to excel in every aspect of life, must recognize that success is unsustainable without a foundation of robust health. Without energy, mental clarity, and physical resilience, even the most brilliant minds and ambitious spirits will eventually falter.

Chronic stress, often disguised as a necessary byproduct of ambition, is a biochemical storm that disrupts every major system in the body. Left unchecked, it accelerates aging, weakens immunity, and fuels chronic disease. Poor diet compounds this stress, starving the body of the essential nutrients needed for optimal function while flooding it with inflammatory and hormone-disrupting substances. Lack of movement further exacerbates these issues, leading to metabolic dysfunction, decreased circulation, and cognitive decline. Meanwhile, conventional medicine, designed to manage disease rather than optimize performance, often fails to provide high-achievers with the level of care they truly need.

The good news? You have the power to take control. True health is not a matter of luck or genetics—it is a choice, a series of daily decisions that determine whether you will thrive or merely survive. By adopting a proactive approach to health, prioritizing prevention, and investing in personalized strategies that align with your unique physiology and goals, you can break free from the limitations of traditional healthcare and reclaim your vitality.

This chapter has laid bare the real threats standing between you and your highest potential. The question now is—what are you going to do about it? Will you continue to tolerate stress, neglect your nutrition, and settle for a healthcare system that does not serve you? Or will you take charge, seek out the right knowledge, and partner with practitioners who understand the science of peak performance?

The choice is yours, and it starts today. Your health is your most valuable asset—protect it, optimize it, and watch every other area of your life transform as a result.

3

The Investment Professional's Perspective: Money and Longevity

Imagine this: You've spent decades working hard, building your portfolio, making smart investments, and planning for a future of financial security. You picture yourself finally stepping away from the daily grind, enjoying the fruits of your labor, traveling, spending time with family, and living without financial stress. But then reality hits—you're physically exhausted, dealing with chronic illnesses, and unable to enjoy the wealth you worked so hard to build. This is the harsh reality for millions of high-performing professionals who meticulously plan their finances but neglect their most valuable asset: their health.

We often hear financial advisors stress the importance of preparing for retirement, ensuring there's enough money to sustain us well into our 80s and 90s. However, what most fail to consider is the distinction between lifespan and healthspan. Lifespan is the number of years you live, but healthspan is the number of years you live in good health—free from chronic disease, mental decline, and physical limitations. The problem is that most financial plans assume that these two are the same, but the truth is they rarely are. If your health deteriorates long before your money runs out, what's the point of all that financial success?

The irony is that the very habits that drive financial success—long hours, high stress, and constant productivity—are the same habits that lead to poor health. Business owners, executives, and high achievers often sacrifice sleep, proper nutrition, and physical activity in the pursuit of career milestones. Stress becomes a badge of honor, and burnout is seen as a necessary evil for professional growth. Financial success without health is like having a high-performance sports car but never maintaining it. It looks great on the outside, but internally, the engine is breaking down. Most people don't think about their health until they experience a wake-up call—a heart attack, a diabetes diagnosis, or debilitating chronic pain. By that point, years of neglect have taken their toll, and reversing the damage becomes a complex, costly, and sometimes impossible endeavor.

There are a few reasons why people meticulously plan for wealth but neglect health. Society glorifies financial success. We are taught from a young age to chase wealth, secure high-paying jobs, invest wisely, and build assets. However, health education is often secondary. While personal finance is a common topic in adulthood, proactive health education remains inadequate. Financial planning inherently involves delayed gratification—saving now for rewards later. On the other hand, health often involves immediate choices that may not have visible consequences until years later. Poor diet, lack of exercise, and chronic stress don't immediately manifest as disease, making it easy to ignore their impact. Many people believe that financial success is a result of discipline and strategy, whereas health issues are often seen as genetic or luck-based. In reality, lifestyle choices play a massive role in long-term health outcomes, but because the effects are gradual, they are often underestimated. Many assume that modern medicine can fix whatever goes wrong. While advancements in healthcare have certainly increased lifespan, they have not necessarily improved healthspan. Treating chronic conditions with medication rather than addressing root causes often leads to dependency on medical interventions instead of true wellness.

Most financial planners talk about retirement in terms of money: How much do you need to retire comfortably? But what about the real cost of poor health? Chronic diseases such as diabetes, heart disease, and neurodegenerative conditions can rack up enormous medical bills. Even with insurance, the cost of medications, treatments, and hospital stays can erode savings faster than anticipated. Poor health can force early retirement or reduced work capacity. Many high-income earners find themselves unable to work at peak performance due to chronic fatigue, stress-related illnesses, or mobility issues. Beyond finances, the emotional and psychological toll of poor health is immense. Chronic pain, limited mobility, and dependency on others for basic needs can strip away the joy of retirement and personal freedom.

So, how can we shift the focus from just financial wealth to a balance between wealth and health? Just like financial investments compound over time, so do health investments. Small, consistent actions—regular exercise, healthy eating, stress management—pay dividends in the form of vitality, longevity, and reduced medical costs. Financial experts recommend diversifying investments; the same principle applies to health. A well-rounded approach includes physical fitness, nutrition, mental well-being, and preventative care. Work with a health professional the same way you would with a financial advisor. Set milestones, track progress, and make necessary adjustments over time. Allocate time and resources for self-care. Consider budget allocations for high-quality supplements, organic foods, health coaching, gym memberships, or alternative therapies like ozone therapy, IV vitamin therapy, and neural therapy to enhance vitality. Shift the definition of success from just financial milestones to a holistic view that includes energy levels, physical capabilities, emotional resilience, and relationships. After all, true wealth is the ability to enjoy life without limitations.

If you've spent decades focused on financial wealth, making the shift to prioritizing health can seem daunting. But the key is to start small and integrate healthy habits into your routine, just as you would with a long-term investment strategy. Just 15-20 minutes of stretching, walking, or light exercise can set a positive tone for the day. Begin with simple swaps: replace processed foods with whole foods, increase water intake, and focus on balanced meals rich in vitamins and minerals. Sleep is the foundation of health. Poor sleep leads to cognitive decline, weight gain, and weakened immunity. Aim for seven to nine hours of quality sleep per night. Incorporate meditation, deep breathing, or time in nature to balance stress hormones. Prevention is always better than treatment. Regular functional health assessments can catch issues early, giving you a roadmap to optimize your well-being.

In the grand scheme of life, wealth without health is a hollow victory. The most successful individuals are those who not only secure their financial future but also invest in their longevity, vitality, and well-being. By shifting the focus from mere lifespan to healthspan, we can redefine retirement—not as a time of decline, but as a time of abundance, energy, and fulfillment. The question is: Will you wait for a wake-up call, or will you take proactive steps today to ensure that you can fully enjoy the wealth you've worked so hard to build? The choice is yours.

In today's world, chronic disease is one of the biggest financial liabilities you can have. The cost of healthcare in the U.S. is staggering, with an estimated 90% of the $4.3 trillion spent annually going toward chronic disease management. Heart disease, diabetes, neurodegenerative disorders, and autoimmune conditions are all largely preventable, yet they drain savings, decrease productivity, and lower quality of life.

Many people assume that healthcare expenses will be covered by insurance or Medicare in retirement, but they fail to account for out-of-pocket costs, long-term care, and lost earning potential due to declining health. Medical bills, prescription medications, specialized treatments, and home care services can easily drain retirement accounts, turning what should be a period of enjoyment into one of financial and physical suffering.

The financial impact doesn't stop there. Chronic disease leads to lost productivity and missed opportunities. Fatigue, brain fog, and physical limitations reduce an individual's ability to perform at their peak, leading to fewer promotions, lost business deals, and diminished investment decision-making. For entrepreneurs and business leaders, declining health can mean an inability to lead effectively, which can have a direct financial impact on their businesses and investments.

From an investment perspective, waiting until illness strikes is a high-risk strategy. The alternative? Investing in prevention. Just as a savvy investor diversifies their portfolio to mitigate risk, a wise individual prioritizes proactive health measures to avoid the financial burden of disease. Regular health check-ups, personalized nutrition, exercise, stress management, and functional medicine approaches may seem like expenses today, but they are among the highest-yield investments anyone can make.

The financial devastation of chronic illness extends beyond direct medical costs. Indirect costs, such as lost wages and reduced productivity, accumulate over time. Employees suffering from chronic conditions often require more sick days, experience reduced work performance, and may even be forced into early retirement due to declining health. Employers, in turn, face increased costs related to absenteeism, higher insurance premiums, and diminished workforce efficiency. For self-employed individuals or business owners, the impact can be even more severe, as their livelihood depends on their ability to function optimally.

Another overlooked cost is the burden placed on family members. Chronic illness often necessitates unpaid caregiving from spouses, children, or other relatives, who may need to reduce their work hours or leave their jobs entirely to provide care. This not only affects the caregiver's financial stability but also compounds the economic strain on the entire household. The emotional toll of caregiving can be immense, leading to burnout, depression, and a reduced quality of life for everyone involved.

Long-term care costs represent another major financial challenge. Many chronic illnesses require extended care, which can be exorbitantly expensive. Assisted living facilities, nursing homes, and in-home healthcare services can deplete savings rapidly, with costs ranging from thousands to tens of thousands of dollars per month. While some individuals have long-term care insurance, many do not, leaving them vulnerable to financial ruin. The misconception that

Medicare or Medicaid will cover all costs often leads to inadequate financial planning, resulting in difficult decisions and compromised quality of care in later years.

Prescription medications constitute another significant expense. The cost of managing chronic diseases through pharmaceuticals is steadily rising, with many patients requiring multiple medications to control symptoms and prevent complications. Even with insurance, copays and deductibles can add up quickly, not to mention the expenses for those who fall into the Medicare Part D "donut hole," where coverage gaps lead to increased out-of-pocket costs. Many patients are forced to choose between paying for their medications and covering basic living expenses, creating a dire situation that impacts overall well-being.

One of the most frustrating aspects of chronic disease management is the reactive nature of conventional healthcare. Traditional medical systems are designed to treat illness rather than prevent it, leading to a cycle where patients are prescribed medications to manage symptoms rather than addressing the root cause. This approach results in long-term dependency on pharmaceuticals and treatments, increasing financial strain without necessarily improving quality of life. Functional and preventive medicine, which emphasizes lifestyle modifications, nutritional interventions, and holistic therapies, offers a more sustainable alternative but is often not covered by insurance, making it an out-of-pocket expense for most individuals.

Insurance limitations further exacerbate the problem. Many policies do not fully cover alternative or integrative treatments that could significantly reduce the risk of chronic disease. Preventive measures such as nutritional counseling, stress management programs, and functional medicine consultations often fall outside the scope of coverage, discouraging people from seeking proactive healthcare solutions. Consequently, individuals may avoid preventive care due to cost concerns, only to face significantly higher expenses when a chronic condition develops.

The psychological and emotional burden of chronic illness also contributes to financial distress. Depression and anxiety are common among individuals with chronic diseases, impacting their ability to work, maintain relationships, and engage in activities that bring joy and fulfillment. Mental health challenges often require therapy, counseling, or medication, further adding to medical costs. The cycle of financial and emotional strain becomes self-perpetuating, making it difficult for individuals to break free from the grip of chronic disease.

Given these realities, the importance of investing in health cannot be overstated. Proactive health measures, including regular physical activity, a balanced diet rich in nutrients, adequate sleep, stress reduction techniques, and personalized supplementation, can dramatically reduce the risk of developing chronic illnesses. Functional medicine approaches that focus on optimizing gut health, reducing inflammation, and balancing hormones offer promising results for disease prevention and reversal.

Exercise is one of the most cost-effective ways to protect against chronic disease. Regular physical activity has been shown to reduce the risk of heart disease, diabetes, obesity, and even certain cancers. Strength training, cardiovascular exercise, and flexibility training improve overall function, increase energy levels, and enhance mental clarity. Despite the well-documented benefits, many individuals fail to prioritize movement in their daily lives, leading to preventable health complications.

Nutrition is another critical factor. The modern diet, laden with processed foods, artificial additives, and excessive sugar, contributes to inflammation and metabolic dysfunction, increasing the likelihood of chronic disease. Prioritizing whole, nutrient-dense foods supports cellular function, enhances immune resilience, and promotes longevity. While some argue that healthy eating is expensive, the long-term savings from reduced medical expenses far outweigh the short-term costs of quality food.

Stress management plays a crucial role in disease prevention. Chronic stress triggers inflammation, hormonal imbalances, and immune system dysfunction, all of which contribute to chronic illness. Practices such as meditation, deep breathing exercises, yoga, and spending time in nature have been shown to reduce stress hormones and improve overall well-being. Investing time in these practices can lead to improved health outcomes and a reduced financial burden over time.

Sleep is another often overlooked yet essential component of health. Poor sleep quality has been linked to obesity, diabetes, cardiovascular disease, and cognitive decline. Creating a sleep-friendly environment, maintaining a consistent sleep schedule, and addressing underlying issues such as sleep apnea can significantly enhance overall health and longevity. Prioritizing rest is a simple yet powerful investment in long-term well-being.

The financial implications of chronic disease extend far beyond individual households. As the prevalence of chronic conditions rises, healthcare systems become overburdened, leading to increased insurance premiums and higher taxes to support government-funded healthcare programs. A society with a healthier population experiences lower healthcare costs, improved workforce productivity, and greater economic stability.

Ultimately, the choice between proactive health investment and reactive disease management is one of financial foresight. Just as individuals plan for retirement by saving and investing, they must also plan for health by making daily choices that support long-term well-being. The cost of prevention is a fraction of the cost of treatment, making it a wise financial decision for anyone seeking to maintain financial independence and quality of life.

In conclusion, chronic disease is not just a health crisis—it is a financial crisis. The staggering costs associated with medical care, lost productivity, caregiving, and long-term care make chronic illness one of the greatest financial threats of our time. However, by shifting the focus toward prevention and investing in proactive health measures, individuals can safeguard their financial future while enhancing their quality of life. The best investment anyone can make is in their health, ensuring not only longevity but also the ability to fully enjoy the wealth and experiences they have worked so hard to achieve.

The world's top investors, entrepreneurs, and business leaders understand a simple but profound truth: health is the foundation of performance. A sharp mind, boundless energy, and resilience under pressure are essential traits for success in competitive industries. However, many professionals fall into the trap of believing that working harder and sacrificing sleep, exercise, and proper nutrition is the price of success. In reality, this approach is financially and professionally unsustainable.

A high-performance investor treats their health just as they would their portfolio—by making calculated, strategic decisions that yield long-term gains. They understand that peak cognitive function, stamina, and resilience aren't just nice-to-haves; they are the competitive edge that allows them to make better decisions, sustain productivity, and stay ahead of the curve. This is why elite performers invest in advanced health diagnostics, bio-individualized nutrition, recovery protocols, and cutting-edge therapies to optimize their energy, mental clarity, and longevity.

There is a direct correlation between physical well-being and financial success. A fatigued, stressed, and inflamed body leads to poor decision-making, reduced creativity, and decreased problem-solving ability—traits that directly affect financial outcomes. On the other hand, an optimized body and brain lead to better business performance, greater wealth-building potential, and the ability to sustain success over a longer period.

The science behind this connection is compelling. The brain consumes a significant portion of the body's energy. When the body is under stress or deprived of essential nutrients, cognitive function declines. Decision fatigue sets in, impulse control diminishes, and risk assessment suffers. A well-nourished, well-rested brain, however, operates with clarity, precision, and foresight, enabling high-performance individuals to navigate complex financial landscapes with confidence and efficiency.

One of the most undervalued components of high performance is sleep. Many high achievers wear sleep deprivation as a badge of honor, believing that cutting back on rest allows them to be more productive. However, the evidence suggests otherwise. Studies show that inadequate sleep impairs cognitive function, increases stress hormones, and weakens immune response—all of which can lead to burnout and poor financial decisions.

Quality sleep enhances memory consolidation, emotional regulation, and decision-making abilities. A well-rested investor or entrepreneur is more likely to analyze data accurately, remain calm under pressure, and execute long-term strategies with greater clarity. Optimizing sleep through proper sleep hygiene, maintaining a consistent sleep schedule, and minimizing exposure to blue light before bedtime can significantly enhance both mental and physical resilience.

Elite investors and business leaders recognize that food is more than just sustenance—it is fuel for peak performance. Nutrient-dense foods rich in antioxidants, healthy fats, and essential vitamins play a crucial role in maintaining energy levels and cognitive sharpness. A diet high in processed foods, sugar, and artificial additives leads to inflammation, energy crashes, and brain fog, all of which diminish productivity and decision-making ability.

Strategic eating habits, such as incorporating high-quality proteins, omega-3 fatty acids, and phytonutrients, can enhance mental acuity and endurance. Bio-individualized nutrition, based on personal health assessments, can further optimize digestion, hormone balance, and metabolic efficiency. Intermittent fasting, ketogenic diets, and anti-inflammatory meal plans have gained popularity among high-performance individuals for their ability to boost mitochondrial function and sustain energy throughout the day.

Physical movement is another cornerstone of the high-performance lifestyle. Exercise not only improves cardiovascular health and muscular endurance but also plays a critical role in brain function. Regular physical activity increases the production of brain-derived neurotrophic factor (BDNF), a protein essential for learning, memory, and cognitive resilience.

Many successful entrepreneurs and investors incorporate exercise into their daily routines, whether through high-intensity interval training (HIIT), strength training, or mindfulness-based practices like yoga and meditation. These activities reduce stress, enhance focus, and contribute to a strong, resilient mindset—all of which are necessary for sustained financial success.

The ability to handle stress effectively separates the best from the rest. Chronic stress leads to elevated cortisol levels, which impair cognitive function, weaken the immune system, and contribute to burnout. High-performance individuals employ proactive stress management techniques, including breathwork, meditation, and mindfulness practices, to maintain emotional balance and clarity.

Cold exposure therapies, such as ice baths and cryotherapy, have gained traction among elite performers for their ability to enhance resilience, boost immune function, and accelerate recovery. Similarly, biofeedback, neurofeedback, and heart rate variability (HRV) tracking provide real-time insights into stress levels, allowing individuals to optimize their performance state.

True high performance isn't just about pushing harder; it's about recovering smarter. Recovery protocols such as infrared sauna therapy, hyperbaric oxygen therapy, and IV nutrient therapy are becoming mainstream among investors and entrepreneurs looking to sustain peak performance. These modalities accelerate cellular repair, reduce oxidative stress, and replenish essential nutrients that are often depleted by high-stakes decision-making and travel-intensive lifestyles.

Another emerging trend in recovery is the use of adaptogens and nootropic supplements. Adaptogens like ashwagandha, rhodiola, and ginseng help the body adapt to stress and maintain hormonal balance. Nootropic compounds, such as L-theanine, phosphatidylserine, and citicoline, support cognitive function and mental endurance.

High-performance investors think in decades, not just quarters. Just as they seek to build sustainable wealth, they also prioritize longevity and healthspan—the number of years spent in optimal health. Cutting-edge therapies such as NAD+ supplementation, peptide therapy, and stem cell treatments are being adopted by forward-thinking individuals who want to extend their health and productivity well into their later years.

The science of longevity is advancing rapidly, with research pointing to epigenetic modifications, autophagy-inducing diets, and regenerative medicine as potential keys to extending lifespan. By investing in these innovations, high performers ensure that they can continue to lead, innovate, and create wealth for as long as possible.

The modern era has glorified hustle culture, encouraging professionals to work longer hours and sacrifice their health for short-term gains. However, the most successful individuals understand that true wealth isn't just about financial abundance—it's about having the energy, vitality, and mental clarity to enjoy the journey. Sustainable high performance isn't about working harder; it's about working smarter by optimizing the body and mind.

By shifting the focus from short-term hustle to long-term health investment, investors and entrepreneurs can unlock unprecedented levels of success. They can make better decisions, execute with greater precision, and sustain their impact over decades. Health is the ultimate investment, yielding the highest returns in both business and life.

The secret to high performance isn't a mystery—it's a science-backed approach to optimizing health for better business outcomes. By prioritizing sleep, nutrition, exercise, stress management, and recovery, elite performers create an environment where cognitive function, energy, and resilience thrive. The high-performance investor doesn't leave their success to chance; they take calculated steps to ensure their body and mind operate at peak efficiency.

Just as a wise investor diversifies their portfolio to mitigate risk and maximize returns, a high-performance individual invests in their health to sustain long-term success. The return on this investment is unparalleled: greater wealth, sharper decision-making, and an extended career filled with purpose and fulfillment. In the end, optimizing your body is the ultimate strategy for optimizing your business.

Health is often viewed as a personal issue, something that primarily affects an individual's well-being and quality of life. However, the repercussions of neglecting health extend far beyond the individual, impacting families, legacy planning, and generational wealth in profound and often overlooked ways. A well-structured financial plan typically incorporates legacy planning, with the goal of building and preserving wealth that benefits not only the individual but also their children and grandchildren. Yet, poor health can systematically dismantle these efforts, causing financial devastation, emotional distress, and the perpetuation of unhealthy lifestyle habits across generations.

Medical debt, long-term care costs, and disability expenses can swiftly drain assets intended for inheritance. When individuals fail to prioritize their health, they often find themselves facing chronic illnesses and medical conditions that require extensive and expensive treatment. In the United States, where healthcare costs are notoriously high, medical debt is a leading cause of financial hardship, even for those with insurance. Unplanned hospital visits, prescription medications, and specialized care can deplete savings, forcing families to dip into resources meant for future generations. Moreover, the need for long-term care—whether in the form of in-home care or assisted living—adds another financial burden that can easily erode accumulated wealth.

Beyond the direct costs of medical treatment, the financial strain of health neglect also manifests through lost income and reduced earning potential. Chronic illness and disability can limit an individual's ability to work, resulting in decreased productivity, missed career opportunities, and early retirement. In cases where a primary breadwinner is affected, the entire family's financial stability is jeopardized. The spouse or children may have to step in as caregivers, sacrificing their own careers and financial aspirations to support the ailing family member. This not only affects immediate income but also diminishes long-term financial growth through missed promotions, reduced retirement savings, and an overall decline in economic mobility.

The burden of caregiving further exacerbates the financial and emotional toll on families. Many families find themselves unprepared for the responsibilities that come with caring for a loved one suffering from a preventable or manageable condition. The role of a caregiver is demanding, often requiring significant time, effort, and emotional resilience. As a result, caregivers may experience burnout, stress-related health issues, and financial strain from cutting back on work hours or leaving their jobs altogether. The ripple effects of this burden extend to younger generations as well, as children of caregivers may receive less financial and emotional support for their education, career development, and personal growth.

Another significant yet often overlooked consequence of health neglect is the generational transmission of poor lifestyle habits. Children of unhealthy parents frequently adopt the same dietary patterns, exercise habits, and stress management techniques they observe in their household. If a parent struggles with obesity, diabetes, or heart disease due to poor lifestyle choices, their children are more likely to develop similar conditions. This creates a vicious cycle where poor health is not just an individual problem but a family legacy. Moreover, financial instability stemming from medical expenses and lost income can limit access to education, extracurricular activities, and opportunities that would otherwise empower the next generation to break free from the cycle of poverty and poor health.

Conversely, prioritizing health serves as an investment in both personal well-being and long-term financial security. When individuals take proactive steps to maintain their health through proper nutrition, regular exercise, and preventive care, they significantly reduce the risk of chronic diseases that lead to financial strain. Health-conscious individuals are more likely to sustain higher energy levels, maintain productivity, and extend their earning potential well into their later years. This, in turn, strengthens their ability to contribute to generational wealth by continuing to work, save, and invest for longer periods.

Beyond the financial benefits, maintaining good health establishes a powerful legacy of strength, resilience, and vitality. A leader who optimizes their well-being serves as a role model for their family, demonstrating that success is not merely about accumulating wealth but about sustaining the energy and vitality to enjoy it and pass it forward. Healthy parents are better equipped to engage with their children, participate in meaningful experiences, and instill values that promote well-being and prosperity. They create an environment where self-care is normalized, and prioritizing health is seen as a fundamental aspect of a successful life.

Additionally, a well-rounded approach to health can enhance longevity, allowing individuals to actively contribute to their family's financial and emotional well-being for an extended period. The ability to witness and support children and grandchildren throughout their milestones—whether it be graduations, weddings, or entrepreneurial pursuits—adds immeasurable value to the family unit. The wisdom, experience, and guidance of elders who maintain their health can significantly shape the direction of younger generations, providing them with the tools and mindset necessary for long-term success.

The intersection of health and wealth extends beyond the individual and into broader societal implications. When families prioritize health, they contribute to a healthier workforce and economy. Reduced medical expenses mean less dependency on government healthcare programs, fewer medical bankruptcies, and increased financial contributions to local businesses and investments. On a macroeconomic level, a population that values preventive health measures fosters greater economic stability and growth.

Addressing health neglect requires a cultural shift in how we perceive both personal well-being and financial planning. Healthcare should not be viewed as a reactive measure but as a proactive investment that safeguards both individual and generational wealth. Employers, policymakers, and financial advisors must recognize the intrinsic link between health and wealth and advocate for holistic strategies that integrate wellness into financial planning. Encouraging workplace wellness programs, promoting health education, and incentivizing preventive care can all contribute to a more sustainable approach to wealth preservation.

For individuals and families, making health a priority requires conscious effort and commitment. It involves making informed decisions about diet, exercise, stress management, and regular medical check-ups. It means setting an example for children by demonstrating that self-care is not selfish but a crucial element of long-term success. Financial planning should include considerations for health-related expenses, long-term care insurance, and emergency funds to mitigate the risks associated with unexpected medical issues.

Ultimately, the true cost of health neglect extends far beyond medical bills and lost wages. It permeates every aspect of life, from the quality of relationships to the opportunities available to future generations. By recognizing the profound impact that health has on family, legacy, and generational wealth, individuals can take meaningful steps to protect not only their own well-being but also the financial security and prosperity of their loved ones. Health is not just a personal responsibility—it is a cornerstone of lasting wealth and a legacy worth preserving.

Investors don't wait until a stock crashes to take action. They analyze trends, anticipate risks, and make strategic decisions to ensure long-term success. Your health should be treated the same way. The notion that one should only seek medical attention when illness strikes is akin to waiting for a financial portfolio to plummet before making any adjustments. By then, much of the damage has already been done. Instead, the intelligent approach involves proactive measures designed to sustain optimal performance and prevent irreversible setbacks.

A truly strategic health plan starts with regular, comprehensive testing that extends far beyond standard medical checkups. Traditional medical exams typically focus on detecting disease once it has already manifested, but the best investors in health know that prevention is the key to longevity and sustained well-being. Advanced functional medicine testing can assess micronutrient levels, inflammation markers, heavy metal toxicity, gut microbiome balance, and genetic predispositions. These tests provide a deeper insight into the body's internal environment, offering a roadmap for personalized intervention. By understanding what is happening at a cellular level, individuals can take corrective actions before minor imbalances evolve into serious conditions.

For example, many people suffer from undiagnosed deficiencies in essential vitamins and minerals, which can lead to chronic fatigue, impaired cognitive function, and increased susceptibility to illness. Standard blood panels often fail to detect these subtle yet significant issues. However, functional testing can reveal early warning signs, allowing for targeted nutritional interventions. Investing in regular testing is not an expense but a strategic allocation of resources to safeguard long-term health.

Another critical aspect of a proactive health strategy is the implementation of a personalized nutrition and supplementation plan. Just as a financial portfolio is tailored to an individual's risk tolerance, investment goals, and market conditions, a nutrition plan should be customized based on genetics, lifestyle, and performance objectives. There is no one-size-fits-all diet that guarantees optimal health. Instead, an individualized approach considers factors such as metabolic rate, food sensitivities, and genetic markers related to nutrient absorption and detoxification pathways.

A strategic nutrition plan begins with foundational principles: consuming whole, unprocessed foods rich in essential nutrients while eliminating inflammatory substances such as processed sugars, industrial seed oils, and artificial additives. But beyond these basics, fine-tuning macronutrient ratios and incorporating targeted supplementation can significantly enhance performance and resilience. For example, an individual with a genetic predisposition for poor methylation may require additional B vitamins to support detoxification and neurological function. Someone with a family history of cardiovascular disease may benefit from omega-3 supplementation and endothelial support nutrients such as nitric oxide precursors. This level of precision enables individuals to optimize their health much like a well-diversified investment portfolio minimizes risk while maximizing returns.

Equally important to nutrition is the prioritization of sleep, stress management, and movement. Many people view these elements as secondary to diet and supplementation, yet they form the bedrock of true health optimization. Chronic sleep deprivation is the equivalent of making high-risk, uninformed investment decisions—it depletes energy reserves, impairs cognitive function, and accelerates biological aging. High-performing individuals recognize that quality sleep is non-negotiable. Deep, restorative sleep is necessary for cellular repair, immune function, and hormonal balance. Without it, even the best nutrition plan cannot compensate for the systemic damage caused by poor sleep habits.

Managing stress is another essential component of a proactive health strategy. Chronic stress leads to sustained elevations in cortisol, which can contribute to insulin resistance, cardiovascular disease, and cognitive decline. Effective stress management techniques— whether through meditation, breathwork, adaptive stress response supplementation, or intentional downtime—are crucial for maintaining physiological equilibrium. The ability to regulate stress effectively is a hallmark of longevity and peak performance. Likewise, consistent movement and exercise help maintain metabolic health, cardiovascular function, and musculoskeletal integrity. Whether through resistance training, cardiovascular conditioning, or mobility work, movement ensures that the body remains resilient and adaptable to stressors.

For those truly committed to staying ahead of aging and disease, cutting-edge therapies provide a strategic advantage. Just as sophisticated investors use advanced market analysis and algorithmic trading to maintain an edge, health-focused individuals can leverage therapies such as IV nutrition, peptide therapy, and regenerative medicine to maintain peak performance.

IV nutrition therapy delivers essential vitamins, minerals, and amino acids directly into the bloodstream, bypassing the limitations of oral absorption. This method allows for higher bioavailability and more immediate cellular uptake, making it particularly effective for individuals with digestive issues, high levels of oxidative stress, or increased nutrient demands due to athletic performance or chronic illness recovery. For example, high-dose intravenous vitamin C has been shown to support immune function, collagen synthesis, and even act as a pro-oxidant against certain cancer cells when administered at therapeutic levels.

Peptide therapy represents another frontier in health optimization. Peptides are short chains of amino acids that act as signaling molecules within the body, regulating various physiological processes. Certain peptides, such as BPC-157, have been shown to accelerate tissue healing and reduce inflammation, making them valuable for injury recovery and musculoskeletal health. Others, like thymosin alpha-1, enhance immune function and resilience against infections. By incorporating peptide therapy into a health strategy, individuals can harness the body's innate regenerative potential and mitigate the effects of aging.

Regenerative medicine, including stem cell therapy and platelet-rich plasma (PRP) treatments, further extends the possibilities for longevity and disease prevention. These therapies leverage the body's natural repair mechanisms to regenerate damaged tissues, reduce inflammation, and support cellular health. While once considered experimental, regenerative therapies are now at the forefront of medical innovation, offering viable solutions for conditions ranging from joint degeneration to neurodegenerative diseases.

Ultimately, the principles that guide successful investing—foresight, discipline, diversification, and long-term thinking—should also apply to health. Just as a financial portfolio is continuously monitored and adjusted based on shifting market conditions, health requires ongoing evaluation and refinement. Those who proactively invest in their well-being through comprehensive testing, personalized nutrition, strategic supplementation, lifestyle optimization, and advanced therapies are positioning themselves for long-term success.

The greatest wealth is health, and the savviest investors understand that without physical and mental vitality, financial success loses much of its value. A future of longevity, resilience, and peak performance is not left to chance but designed through intentional actions taken today. By treating health as the most valuable asset, individuals can ensure that they not only live longer but thrive at the highest levels throughout their lifespan.

The question is not whether to invest in health, but rather how soon one will realize that waiting until symptoms appear is the most expensive mistake of all. The smart investor's plan is clear: take control now, optimize proactively, and build a foundation for a future where health and wealth are seamlessly aligned.

Throughout history, humanity has pursued wealth as a means of achieving security, status, and comfort. Financial success has long been the metric by which many measure their accomplishments. Yet, a significant flaw in this mindset emerges when financial wealth is pursued at the expense of personal health. True financial security is not just about accumulating assets or achieving career milestones—it is about whether one has the physical and mental well-being to fully enjoy the fruits of their labor. The best investment strategy is one that accounts for both wealth and longevity, ensuring that financial success is matched by a strong, resilient body and mind.

In modern society, people often chase financial success with singular focus. They work long hours, sacrifice sleep, consume convenience foods, and neglect exercise—all in the name of building wealth. The irony is that many individuals reach their financial goals only to find themselves physically depleted, dealing with chronic illness, stress-related conditions, or lifestyle-induced diseases. What good is a hefty bank account if one's body is too frail to travel, too fatigued to enjoy leisure, or too sick to spend time with loved ones? Wealth without health leads to a diminished quality of life, often accompanied by exorbitant medical bills that erode financial gains. Conversely, prioritizing health does not mean neglecting wealth-building. It means recognizing that financial success and physical well-being are interconnected. The healthier you are, the more energy, focus, and resilience you bring to your career or business endeavors. This synergy enables a life of sustained productivity and fulfillment rather than one marked by burnout and regret.

Ignoring one's health today invariably results in costly consequences in the future. Chronic diseases such as diabetes, heart disease, and obesity often stem from years of poor lifestyle choices. These conditions not only shorten lifespan but also diminish the quality of life, making every task more challenging and painful. They also introduce significant financial burdens, including medical expenses, long-term care, and loss of income due to disability or reduced work capacity. According to studies, healthcare costs for chronic conditions account for the majority of medical expenses in the United States. Preventative healthcare, which includes proper nutrition, exercise, stress management, and regular medical check-ups, is a fraction of the cost of treating advanced illnesses. The choice is clear: invest in health now or pay exponentially more later.

Beyond direct medical costs, there is the issue of lost potential. A lack of physical vitality can hinder career progression, reduce cognitive performance, and lead to mental health struggles such as anxiety and depression. Studies consistently show that healthier individuals tend to have higher earning potential, stronger leadership capabilities, and better problem-solving skills. Smart investors understand that compounding returns apply to health just as much as they do to wealth. Just as an early and disciplined approach to financial investments can lead to exponential growth over time, prioritizing health decisions early yields long-term benefits that extend into every area of life.

Consider the concept of metabolic health. People who maintain healthy habits from a young age—eating nutrient-dense foods, engaging in regular exercise, and managing stress effectively—build a metabolic advantage that protects them from chronic diseases. Over time, their health investments accumulate, leading to extended longevity, reduced healthcare costs, and sustained energy levels that allow them to pursue both professional and personal goals with vigor. Additionally, investing in high-quality nutrition, functional medicine, and preventative healthcare strategies leads to fewer sick days, increased mental clarity, and greater physical endurance. When compounded over decades, these small daily choices create a future where health is not an obstacle but an asset.

We often discuss wealth in terms of financial resilience—having enough resources to withstand economic downturns and unforeseen financial hardships. However, physical resilience is equally important. A strong, well-nourished body is more capable of handling stress, recovering from illness, and adapting to life's inevitable challenges. The same principles that apply to financial success apply to health. Just as diversifying investments reduces financial risk, maintaining a balanced lifestyle that includes proper nutrition, movement, mental well-being, and regular health check-ups reduces the risk of disease. Just as building passive income streams creates financial stability, developing habits like proper hydration, sleep optimization, and mindfulness creates long-term health stability.

Moreover, the healthier an individual is, the more they can take calculated risks in business, seize opportunities, and maintain the stamina required to build and sustain wealth. Many of the world's top entrepreneurs and executives recognize this connection and prioritize their health as a key component of their professional success. They view exercise, nutrition, and wellness practices not as optional luxuries but as essential tools for peak performance. Attaining a high-performance life requires strategic planning in both financial and health domains. It is not enough to work hard; one must also work smart by incorporating habits that support long-term well-being.

Prioritizing preventative healthcare is essential. Just as financial planning involves forecasting future needs, proactive health measures can prevent chronic diseases and improve overall longevity. Regular check-ups, functional medicine assessments, and diagnostic testing help identify health risks before they become serious problems. Optimizing nutrition is a critical component. Quality nutrition is the foundation of health. Investing in organic, nutrient-dense foods and avoiding processed, inflammatory ingredients ensures that the body receives the essential building blocks for optimal function. Supplementation with vitamins, minerals, and adaptogenic herbs can further enhance resilience and vitality.

Incorporating movement and recovery is non-negotiable. Consistent physical activity strengthens the cardiovascular system, maintains musculoskeletal integrity, and boosts cognitive function. Whether through strength training, yoga, high-intensity interval training, or outdoor activities, movement is essential. Equally important is recovery—adequate sleep, active rest, and relaxation techniques such as sauna therapy, ice baths, and meditation. Managing stress effectively is another critical element. Chronic stress accelerates aging, disrupts hormonal balance, and contributes to various diseases. Financially successful individuals often experience high levels of stress, but those who master stress management techniques—such as breathwork, meditation, journaling, or therapy—maintain better long-term health outcomes.

Partnering with experts is also vital. Just as financial advisors provide expertise in wealth management, working with healthcare providers who specialize in high-performance medicine ensures that you receive personalized strategies to optimize your health. Functional medicine doctors, nutritionists, and wellness coaches can help tailor a plan suited to your specific needs. If you're serious about achieving peak performance in both your business and your life, you need a health strategy as strong as your financial strategy. The most successful individuals understand that their greatest asset is not just their investment portfolio—it is their physical and mental capacity to generate, sustain, and enjoy wealth.

No amount of money can buy back lost time, and no financial windfall can reverse years of neglecting personal health. However, making the decision today to prioritize health will pay dividends for years to come. This is not a matter of choosing between wealth and health—it is about recognizing that they are two sides of the same coin. When optimized together, they create a life of abundance, fulfillment, and longevity. Because in the end, the real measure of wealth is not just money—it's the ability to live a life full of strength, purpose, and vitality. The question remains: Are you willing to invest in your health with the same diligence as your wealth? The choice is yours, and the best time to start is now.

PART TWO

THE ANNUAL HEALTH INVESTMENT STRATEGY

4

The Core Labs – What Every High Achiever Must Test Annually

Success is never accidental. It is the result of careful planning, continuous evaluation, and strategic adjustments. High achievers in every field—whether business, athletics, or personal development—rely on measurable data to track progress and optimize outcomes. A business leader does not make decisions based on gut instinct alone; they analyze financial statements, revenue streams, and performance metrics to determine whether they are on track to achieve their goals. An elite athlete does not simply train harder and hope for the best; they monitor heart rate variability, muscle recovery times, and nutritional intake to ensure they are fine-tuning their body for peak performance. Yet, when it comes to health—the very foundation upon which all other achievements are built—most people fail to apply this same level of precision. They wait until symptoms appear, only seeking medical attention when something feels off, rather than proactively monitoring their body's internal data.

The truth is, your body requires an annual health audit just like any other high-performing system. Without regular health assessments, even the most disciplined individual may unknowingly be on the path to burnout, chronic illness, or diminished vitality. Ignoring core lab testing is like running a business without ever checking the financials. You might think you are doing well, but beneath the surface, inefficiencies, imbalances, and silent risks could be accumulating. The body, much like a business, thrives when properly managed. And just as a company can go bankrupt if financial problems go unnoticed for too long, the body can experience serious health consequences if issues are not detected and addressed early.

The core lab tests discussed in this chapter are non-negotiable. They are not optional add-ons for those with existing medical conditions, nor are they just for individuals who feel unwell. These tests serve as the profit and loss statements of your health, providing the necessary data to detect deficiencies, imbalances, and potential risks before they escalate into serious problems. When monitored consistently, they offer a roadmap for optimizing energy levels, longevity, and peak physical and mental performance.

Despite the vast amounts of health information available today, most people are still in the dark about what is happening inside their own bodies. They may assume they are in good health simply because they feel fine. But symptoms are often the last stage of disease, not the first. High blood sugar, insulin resistance, and metabolic dysfunction do not cause pain until they have progressed significantly. Elevated cholesterol and inflammation levels may remain unnoticed for years before contributing to heart disease. Declining red blood cell counts, indicating poor oxygenation and energy production, may not trigger fatigue until the body is struggling to compensate. These hidden imbalances do not announce themselves with flashing warning signs; they reveal themselves in bloodwork—if you take the time to look.

The world's most successful individuals do not leave their health to chance. They understand that testing is not just about diagnosing disease—it is about optimizing performance. When an entrepreneur tracks their financials, they are not just checking for signs of bankruptcy; they are looking for ways to increase profitability and efficiency. When an athlete monitors their VO2 max or lactic acid threshold, they are not just avoiding injury; they are actively improving endurance, strength, and recovery. The same mindset must be applied to health.

Routine lab testing is not a luxury—it is a necessity. Without it, there is no way to truly understand how well the body is functioning or what adjustments need to be made for sustained peak performance. These tests provide the biological data required to make informed decisions about nutrition, supplementation, lifestyle, and training. They highlight where the body is thriving and where it may need additional support. More importantly, they allow for early intervention, preventing small imbalances from turning into major health challenges.

Some people hesitate to engage in proactive testing because they assume that if they feel fine, everything must be fine. But this is the equivalent of saying that if a business has not yet gone bankrupt, there is no need to check its financial records. By the time a problem becomes obvious, the opportunity for early correction has passed. The body is incredibly adaptive and can compensate for deficiencies for long periods before they manifest as noticeable symptoms. This means that waiting for warning signs is a dangerous strategy. The better approach—the high-achiever's approach—is to stay ahead of problems by tracking trends, identifying risks, and making adjustments before performance declines.

The core lab tests covered in this chapter have been carefully selected based on their ability to provide a comprehensive overview of metabolic health, immune function, cardiovascular status, and systemic inflammation. These tests are fundamental for everyone, regardless of age or current health status. They serve as a baseline for evaluating progress over time, allowing individuals to measure the impact of dietary choices, exercise routines, stress management strategies, and supplementation programs.

The real advantage of testing lies in its ability to create a personalized approach to health. Many people waste time and money on generic health advice, following diets or supplement plans that may not be right for their unique physiology. Without lab data, they are essentially guessing about what their body needs. Core lab tests eliminate this uncertainty, providing clear, actionable insights that allow for precise health optimization.

Understanding and implementing data-driven health strategies is what separates those who merely exist from those who thrive. The human body is capable of extraordinary feats when given the right support. With the right balance of nutrients, hormones, and metabolic function, energy levels soar, cognitive performance sharpens, and physical recovery accelerates. The immune system strengthens, resilience to stress increases, and longevity is maximized. These are not abstract concepts; they are measurable outcomes that can be tracked, tested, and optimized.

The concept of health as an asset is one that many overlook until it is too late. Just as financial investments require careful monitoring and strategic decision-making, health must be actively managed. Those who ignore their health data until a crisis arises are taking an unnecessary risk. But those who prioritize routine lab testing and use the insights gained to refine their approach to diet, exercise, and supplementation gain an unmatched advantage. They are the ones who maintain boundless energy, clarity of thought, and the ability to perform at their highest level—year after year.

This chapter will break down the essential lab tests that every high achiever must run annually. These tests will empower you with the knowledge needed to take full control of your health, ensuring that you are not just surviving, but thriving. If you are serious about achieving long-term success in any area of life, health must be at the forefront of your strategy. You would not run a business without tracking performance metrics. You would not train for an athletic event without measuring progress. And you should not expect to maintain peak health without regularly testing and analyzing your biological data.

Your body is your most valuable asset. How you take care of it determines how well you perform, how long you live, and how much vitality you experience along the way. The elite do not leave their health to chance. They measure, they track, and they optimize. It is time to apply this principle to your own life—starting with the essential lab tests that will give you the insight and advantage you need to reach your highest potential.

In the pursuit of excellence, high achievers track their progress meticulously. Athletes monitor their performance metrics, business leaders analyze financial reports, and students measure their academic progress. Yet, when it comes to personal health, many individuals neglect the most critical data set of all—their own biological markers. The reality is that your body is the most important system you will ever manage. Without optimal health, no amount of success in other areas can be fully enjoyed.

For most people, lab testing is an afterthought, something done only when symptoms become impossible to ignore. But this reactive approach to health is akin to waiting for a car engine to fail before checking the oil. By the time a major issue emerges, irreversible damage may have already occurred. The elite—the top one percent—take a different path. They do not leave their health to chance. They test proactively, track their physiological trends, and make data-driven decisions to optimize performance, longevity, and vitality.

Baseline testing is the profit and loss statement of your health. Just as a business owner reviews financial records to detect inefficiencies and prevent losses, individuals must assess their internal biomarkers to ensure their body is functioning at peak efficiency. These tests measure critical aspects of health, including red blood cell counts, immune function, metabolic efficiency, and inflammation levels. By analyzing these markers regularly, it is possible to detect imbalances before they lead to disease, ensuring that the body remains in an optimal state for productivity, energy, and long-term wellness.

Ignoring baseline testing is like flying a plane without instruments. The outside conditions may seem fine, but turbulence could be approaching, and without the right data, there is no way to adjust course. Health, like aviation or finance, requires precision. Those who monitor their biomarkers gain an unparalleled advantage, allowing them to maximize performance, prevent illness, and extend both lifespan and healthspan.

Health is not just about avoiding sickness—it is about thriving. Just as businesses assess revenue, expenses, and profitability, the body operates on a system of inputs and outputs. Energy levels, immune function, metabolism, and inflammation all play a role in determining how well a person feels and performs each day. The problem is that, unlike financial statements, these indicators are not always visible unless tested.

Red blood cells, for example, are responsible for delivering oxygen to tissues. When levels are low, fatigue, brain fog, and poor athletic performance can result. White blood cells indicate how well the immune system is functioning. If levels are too high or too low, it may suggest chronic stress, an underlying infection, or immune dysfunction. Inflammatory markers provide insight into the body's overall state of stress. Elevated levels indicate that the body is in a constant state of repair, which can lead to accelerated aging and chronic disease if left unchecked.

Blood sugar and lipid levels serve as critical indicators of metabolic efficiency. While many assume that conditions like diabetes or cardiovascular disease emerge suddenly, the truth is that these disorders develop gradually over years, sometimes decades. A person may feel perfectly fine even as their fasting glucose levels steadily rise. By the time they are diagnosed with insulin resistance or diabetes, significant damage may already be present. However, by testing regularly and tracking trends, these conditions can be prevented entirely with the right lifestyle interventions.

A single lab test provides valuable information, but real power comes from analyzing trends over time. Just as a business owner does not make financial decisions based on one month of revenue, health-conscious individuals should not rely on a single blood test to assess their well-being. By tracking biomarkers annually, it becomes possible to see patterns and make adjustments before minor issues become major health concerns.

Dr West's Core Lab Recommendation:

1. Complete blood cell count with auto differentiation
2. Complete metabolic panel
3. 12 hour fasting cholesterol
4. Thyroid panel - T3, T4, TSH
5. Vitamin D3
6. Total iron, ferritin
7. Highly selecdtive C Reactive Protein

5

The Secret Health Markers of the Ultra-Wealthy

O ne of the most damaging myths about health is the idea that disease happens suddenly. In reality, most chronic conditions develop silently over years. By the time a person receives a diagnosis, dysfunction has often been present for a long time. This is true for high cholesterol, diabetes, heart disease, liver dysfunction, and even neurodegenerative conditions.

Many people mistakenly believe that if they feel fine, their health must be in good shape. But the body is highly adaptive, capable of compensating for imbalances until it can no longer keep up. By the time symptoms appear, the problem is often well advanced. This is why relying on how you feel is a poor strategy for managing health. Data, not perception, is what drives success.

For example, a person with developing insulin resistance may experience subtle shifts in energy, cravings, and focus. These changes might be dismissed as stress or poor sleep, but in reality, their fasting blood sugar and A1C levels may be creeping higher each year. Without regular testing, they would remain unaware until a full-blown metabolic disorder emerges.

Similarly, elevated cholesterol or inflammatory markers do not cause immediate pain or discomfort. But over time, they contribute to arterial plaque buildup, increasing the risk of heart attack and stroke. Had these markers been monitored and addressed early, a simple change in diet, exercise, or supplementation could have prevented years of cumulative damage.

This is why high performers prioritize early detection over crisis management. They recognize that waiting for symptoms to appear is a losing game. Instead of reacting to health problems after they arise, they track their numbers proactively and make adjustments to keep their body in a state of high performance.

Health is not static—it is a dynamic, ever-changing system influenced by lifestyle, diet, stress, environment, and genetics. Just as businesses monitor market trends and adjust their strategies accordingly, individuals must track their health markers and make course corrections over time.

A single lab test provides a snapshot, but real power comes from analyzing trends. If fasting blood sugar is increasing year over year, it signals the need for better metabolic control. If white blood cell counts fluctuate significantly, it may indicate underlying immune challenges or chronic stress. If inflammatory markers steadily rise, adjustments to diet, exercise, or stress management may be necessary.

This is the difference between precision health and guesswork. Most people take a haphazard approach to wellness, assuming that if they eat well and exercise, they must be healthy. While lifestyle choices play a crucial role, testing removes uncertainty and provides clarity. It allows individuals to move beyond vague assumptions and take targeted action based on concrete data.

When trends are monitored consistently, small imbalances can be corrected before they spiral into major health issues. This is the ultimate advantage of preventive medicine—it allows people to stay ahead of problems rather than chasing solutions after damage has already occurred.

The ultimate goal of regular baseline testing is not just to avoid disease but to optimize health for maximum performance, energy, and longevity. Health is not simply the absence of illness; it is the foundation for everything else in life.

When lab markers are in optimal ranges, the body functions at its highest potential. Mental clarity is sharp, energy remains consistent, and productivity soars. Recovery from exercise and stress is faster, immune function is stronger, and aging is slowed at a cellular level.

A well-balanced body is resilient. It can handle stress more effectively, repair damage efficiently, and sustain high levels of activity without burnout. This is why professional athletes, executives, and top performers in every field take their health seriously. They know that how they feel and function directly impacts their ability to succeed.

Those who take control of their health through regular testing and strategic interventions do not just live longer—they live better. They have more energy, sharper focus, and greater resilience than those who neglect their physiological markers. They move through life with confidence, knowing that they are not just surviving but thriving.

Health is an asset, one that must be managed with the same diligence as finances, career, and relationships. Baseline testing is the foundation of this process. It provides the roadmap for longevity, performance, and overall well-being. Those who prioritize it will always have an edge over those who ignore it. By making health data a non-negotiable part of life, individuals can ensure that they are not just reacting to problems, but actively creating the conditions for sustained success, vitality, and longevity. The choice is clear: track it, optimize it, and thrive.

Health is the foundation upon which all success is built. Whether you are an athlete, entrepreneur, executive, or anyone striving for peak performance, your ability to function at your best depends on the internal workings of your body. Every decision, from the food you eat to the supplements you take, should be informed by data rather than guesswork. Just as a mechanic would never attempt to fix an engine without first diagnosing the problem, you should never attempt to optimize your health without first understanding what is happening beneath the surface.

The difference between those who sustain long-term success and those who burn out often comes down to how well they manage their health metrics. Many individuals invest thousands of dollars into coaching, education, and performance-enhancing strategies yet fail to assess the very foundation of their capabilities—their physiological health. While it is easy to track external metrics like weight, strength, and endurance, the true indicators of longevity and sustained performance lie within the bloodstream. The body provides clues long before issues become symptomatic, and those who take the time to interpret these signals have a significant advantage over those who wait for problems to surface.

To stay at the top of your game, there are three core lab tests that should be run annually at a minimum. These tests provide crucial insights into oxygen transport, immune function, metabolic efficiency, detoxification pathways, hydration, and cardiovascular health. They are not optional. They are non-negotiable for anyone serious about maintaining long-term vitality, cognitive sharpness, and physical endurance. Each of these tests serves as a fundamental checkpoint, ensuring that your body is functioning at its highest level and providing early warning signs of imbalances that could hinder performance or lead to disease.

The power of these tests lies not only in their ability to diagnose existing health concerns but in their capacity to prevent potential issues before they arise. Most people operate under the illusion that if they "feel fine," they must be in good health. This is a flawed assumption. Many of the most devastating chronic illnesses—such as cardiovascular disease, diabetes, and neurodegenerative conditions—develop silently over years or even decades before symptoms become apparent. By the time noticeable warning signs appear, the opportunity for easy intervention has often passed. The human body is an adaptive machine, capable of compensating for deficiencies and dysfunctions for long periods before reaching a breaking point. The key to avoiding this downward spiral is early detection and proactive management, and these core lab tests provide exactly that.

Testing is not just for those who are experiencing health concerns. In fact, the individuals who stand to benefit the most from routine lab work are those who already feel strong, energetic, and high-performing. A person may think they are in peak condition, but unless they are tracking key biomarkers over time, they are merely operating on assumption rather than factual evidence. Regular lab work allows high achievers to fine-tune their approach, whether that means optimizing nutritional intake, improving recovery protocols, adjusting exercise regimens, or implementing targeted supplementation strategies.

Every successful professional understands the importance of continuous feedback loops. In business, financial statements provide insight into profitability and efficiency. In sports, performance metrics help refine training strategies. In personal development, assessments and reflection drive growth. Why should health be any different? Without objective data, even the most well-intentioned efforts to optimize performance become a game of trial and error. Routine testing eliminates guesswork, allowing for precision-based interventions that maximize longevity, resilience, and overall well-being.

The most significant advantage of incorporating lab testing into a health optimization strategy is the ability to track progress over time. A single test provides a valuable snapshot, but the real power lies in establishing a trendline of key biomarkers. By analyzing these markers year after year, individuals can detect subtle shifts and make small, strategic adjustments before minor imbalances escalate into major concerns.

Long-term success is not about quick fixes or reactive measures; it is about sustainable, proactive decision-making. Those who prioritize their health data gain an unfair advantage—one that allows them to maintain higher energy levels, sharper cognitive function, and superior physical endurance compared to those who neglect these crucial insights.

For anyone striving for high performance, longevity, and sustained success, routine lab testing is not just advisable—it is essential. The three core tests outlined in this chapter serve as the cornerstone of any effective health strategy, providing the information necessary to make data-driven choices that enhance vitality and ensure continued peak performance. Whether you are an elite athlete, a driven entrepreneur, or simply someone committed to maintaining optimal health, integrating these tests into your annual routine will transform the way you approach your well-being—allowing you to operate at your absolute best for years to come.

The Complete Blood Count (CBC) is one of the most fundamental yet powerful lab tests available. It provides a comprehensive overview of your blood cells, which are responsible for oxygen transport, immune defense, and clotting. Since blood is the medium that delivers oxygen and nutrients throughout the body, even small changes in blood cell levels can have significant consequences on energy levels, endurance, recovery, and resilience.

This test measures red blood cells (RBC), hemoglobin, and hematocrit, which are direct indicators of how efficiently oxygen is being transported throughout the body. Red blood cells carry oxygen from the lungs to tissues, fueling muscles, organs, and the brain. If these levels are too low, oxygen delivery is compromised, leading to chronic fatigue, sluggishness, and a reduced ability to recover from exertion. Hemoglobin, the protein in red blood cells that binds oxygen, is equally crucial. A low hemoglobin count is often associated with anemia, a condition that significantly impairs endurance, strength, and overall cognitive function.

White blood cells (WBC) are another critical component of the CBC. These immune cells act as the body's first line of defense against infection, inflammation, and chronic stressors. An elevated white blood cell count can indicate that the immune system is fighting an infection, even if symptoms are not yet present. Chronic low-grade infections, which many people unknowingly carry, can drain energy levels and interfere with focus and productivity. On the other hand, a suppressed white blood cell count may signal immune dysfunction, making you more susceptible to illness.

Platelets, the third major component of a CBC, are responsible for blood clotting and wound healing. Their levels can indicate whether your body is prone to excessive bleeding or, conversely, whether you are at increased risk for dangerous clot formation. Abnormal platelet levels may also suggest underlying inflammation or other systemic imbalances.

Tracking CBC levels annually is essential for anyone pushing their limits, whether in the gym, at work, or in daily life. Suboptimal oxygen transport can impair endurance, weak immune function can lead to frequent illness, and abnormal clotting markers can increase the risk of cardiovascular complications. By monitoring these values consistently, adjustments can be made through diet, supplementation, and lifestyle interventions to ensure that the body remains in a state of peak performance.

While the CBC provides a snapshot of blood cell function, the Complete Metabolic Panel (CMP) evaluates the biochemical processes that keep the body running smoothly. This test assesses kidney function, liver function, electrolyte balance, and blood sugar regulation, all of which play a critical role in energy levels, detoxification, and metabolic health.

The kidneys are responsible for filtering toxins from the blood, regulating hydration, and maintaining electrolyte balance. The CMP measures markers such as creatinine and blood urea nitrogen (BUN), which indicate how efficiently the kidneys are removing waste products from the body. If these values are elevated, it may suggest impaired kidney function, dehydration, or excessive protein breakdown. Since the kidneys also play a role in blood pressure regulation, tracking these markers is essential for preventing cardiovascular complications.

Liver function is another key area assessed by the CMP. The liver is the body's primary detoxification organ, responsible for metabolizing toxins, drugs, and hormones. When liver enzymes such as AST and ALT are elevated, it often indicates stress on the liver due to poor diet, environmental toxins, or excessive alcohol consumption. Since the liver also plays a crucial role in processing fats and producing energy, impaired liver function can lead to fatigue, sluggish metabolism, and hormonal imbalances.

Electrolytes such as sodium, potassium, and calcium are vital for nerve conduction, muscle function, and hydration. An imbalance in these minerals can lead to muscle cramps, dehydration, poor endurance, and even cognitive dysfunction. Many people, particularly athletes, overlook the importance of maintaining optimal electrolyte levels, yet even slight deviations can have profound effects on performance.

Blood sugar regulation, another key component of the CMP, provides insight into metabolic efficiency and insulin function. Elevated fasting glucose levels suggest insulin resistance, a precursor to type 2 diabetes and metabolic syndrome. Even if blood sugar levels are within the normal range, tracking trends over time is critical. Many high achievers unknowingly operate with suboptimal blood sugar control, leading to energy crashes, brain fog, and poor recovery. By identifying early signs of insulin resistance, dietary and lifestyle interventions can be implemented to maintain stable energy levels and prevent long-term metabolic dysfunction.

The CMP provides a real-time snapshot of how the body processes energy, detoxifies waste, and regulates hydration. Without this data, it is impossible to optimize diet, supplementation, and hydration strategies. Running this test annually allows for early intervention and ensures that all metabolic processes are functioning at their highest capacity.

Cardiovascular health is often overlooked by individuals who feel physically fit, but internal markers of heart health can be silently deteriorating long before symptoms appear. The lipid panel is an essential test for assessing cardiovascular risk, measuring cholesterol levels and lipid ratios that influence blood flow, inflammation, and heart disease risk.

The lipid panel measures LDL, or low-density lipoprotein, often referred to as "bad" cholesterol. While LDL is necessary for cellular function, excessively high levels can lead to arterial plaque buildup, increasing the risk of heart attack and stroke. More important than total LDL levels, however, is the size and type of LDL particles. Small, dense LDL particles are more likely to contribute to atherosclerosis, whereas large, buoyant LDL particles are less harmful. Many standard lipid panels do not differentiate between these types, but advanced lipid testing can provide a deeper understanding of cardiovascular risk.

HDL, or high-density lipoprotein, is considered "good" cholesterol because it helps remove excess LDL from the bloodstream. Higher HDL levels are associated with reduced heart disease risk, but it is the ratio of HDL to LDL that truly matters. A favorable lipid ratio indicates efficient cholesterol metabolism, while an unfavorable ratio may suggest increased inflammation and metabolic dysfunction.

Triglycerides, another key marker in the lipid panel, measure the amount of stored fat in the blood. Elevated triglycerides are strongly correlated with insulin resistance, metabolic syndrome, and an increased risk of cardiovascular disease. High triglyceride levels often result from excessive carbohydrate intake, poor fat metabolism, or hormonal imbalances.

Contrary to popular belief, cholesterol alone is not the problem—it is cholesterol in combination with inflammation that drives heart disease. High LDL levels in the absence of inflammation may not pose a significant risk, but when coupled with elevated inflammatory markers, the risk of cardiovascular events increases dramatically.

Running a lipid panel annually provides a crucial checkpoint for cardiovascular health. It allows for adjustments to diet, exercise, and supplementation to maintain optimal cholesterol balance, reduce inflammation, and ensure proper blood flow. By proactively monitoring these markers, high achievers can prevent cardiovascular disease before it ever becomes a concern.

The world's top performers do not leave their success to chance, and they do not gamble with their health. They use data-driven strategies to optimize every aspect of their performance, including nutrition, recovery, and disease prevention. These three core lab tests—CBC, CMP, and lipid panel—are the foundation of this approach, offering a direct look into the body's internal workings. Those who embrace routine testing gain an immense advantage over those who rely solely on how they feel, because feelings are subjective while biological data tells the truth.

Health is not just about avoiding illness; it is about maximizing energy, mental clarity, and physical resilience. The best in any field know that performance is only as strong as the body's ability to sustain output. Fatigue, brain fog, and sluggish recovery are not just inconveniences—they are barriers to peak performance. Without tracking critical markers, it is impossible to know whether these barriers are caused by nutritional deficiencies, metabolic imbalances, inflammation, or early-stage disease processes.

By integrating these lab tests into an annual routine, individuals gain unparalleled insight into their body's internal state, allowing for precision-based interventions that keep them operating at peak levels. Routine testing ensures that small issues are corrected before they snowball into larger health concerns. Instead of waiting for energy crashes, muscle weakness, or unexplained weight gain to force change, high performers take a proactive approach by using data to fine-tune their health strategy year-round.

Testing is not a reactive measure—it is a proactive strategy that ensures longevity, vitality, and sustained high performance. It is the difference between reacting to a crisis and engineering a long-term plan for success. Those who make data-driven health decisions are always ahead of the curve, continuously adjusting their lifestyle, diet, and supplementation to meet their body's changing demands.

Every professional understands the importance of long-term strategy. A high-level CEO does not make business decisions without reviewing financial data. An elite athlete does not train blindly without tracking performance metrics. In the same way, no high performer should attempt to optimize health without objective data.

The mindset shift from reactive healthcare to proactive health optimization is the key to long-term vitality. Many people assume they are in good health simply because they are not experiencing symptoms. This assumption is a costly mistake. The body is incredibly adaptive, and it can compensate for underlying deficiencies or dysfunctions for long periods before reaching a breaking point. By the time symptoms appear, what could have been an easy fix may now require a more aggressive intervention.

Testing allows individuals to track trends over time, making incremental adjustments rather than facing a sudden health crisis. By monitoring red blood cell counts, immune function, metabolic markers, and cardiovascular health annually, individuals can avoid performance declines, chronic fatigue, and metabolic dysfunction before they take root.

This is the mindset of the elite performer—they treat health as a priority, not an afterthought. They see lab testing not as an inconvenience but as an investment in their greatest asset—their body and mind. The sooner this mindset is embraced, the longer and stronger one can sustain excellence, resilience, and vitality in all areas of life.

Understanding your lab results is more than just reviewing numbers on a page. It is about identifying patterns, trends, and opportunities for optimization so you can function at the highest level. Many people view lab work as a one-time assessment, but this is a flawed approach. A single test provides valuable information, but real insight comes from tracking changes over time. When used correctly, lab testing is not just a diagnostic tool; it is a roadmap to peak health, longevity, and sustained performance.

The body is constantly adapting, responding to stress, diet, exercise, and environmental factors. What may be a normal lab result today could shift dramatically in a year if left unmonitored. Many early signs of dysfunction—such as rising blood sugar, creeping inflammation, or subtle shifts in immune function—are only detectable when you compare test results over time. By taking a proactive approach and using lab data to fine-tune your health strategy, you can avoid common pitfalls that lead to disease, fatigue, and performance decline.

Lab tests provide snapshots of your health at a given moment, but a single test does not reveal the full picture. The real value comes from tracking results year after year to recognize patterns. A one-time high blood sugar reading might not seem concerning, but if that number has been creeping up for the last three years, it indicates a trend toward insulin resistance. Inflammation markers that fluctuate slightly within the normal range may not seem urgent, but a steady increase over time suggests chronic stress, poor diet, or underlying immune dysfunction.

By evaluating lab trends, it becomes possible to identify hidden stressors that may not yet be causing noticeable symptoms. An elevated white blood cell count, for example, could indicate low-grade infection or chronic stress on the immune system, even if you feel fine. A slow but consistent drop in hemoglobin might signal nutrient deficiencies or reduced oxygen transport, impacting endurance and mental clarity. These trends provide an early warning system, allowing for preventative interventions before problems escalate into full-blown disease.

Another important aspect of tracking lab trends is measuring the effectiveness of lifestyle changes. If you have improved your diet, increased exercise, or optimized your supplement regimen, your lab results should reflect those changes. A well-designed health strategy will lead to lower inflammation markers, improved metabolic function, and enhanced immune resilience. If your lab results are not improving despite healthy habits, it signals the need for further adjustments. Perhaps your diet is not as nutrient-dense as you think, or your exercise routine is placing excess stress on your body. Without data, making these refinements is guesswork. With data, you can make precise changes that deliver real results.

Most doctors rely on standard lab reference ranges to determine whether results are normal. However, these ranges are based on the average population, which includes a large percentage of people who are overweight, sedentary, inflamed, or pre-disease. Being within a "normal" range does not necessarily mean you are in optimal health. In fact, many people with suboptimal lab values feel exhausted, inflamed, or mentally foggy, even though their doctors assure them everything looks fine.

Functional medicine takes a different approach by focusing on optimal ranges, which represent the levels associated with high energy, longevity, and peak performance. For example, standard glucose ranges consider anything up to 99 mg/dL to be normal, but functional medicine practitioners know that high performers typically function best in the 75-85 mg/dL range. Even if your doctor tells you that a fasting glucose of 95 mg/dL is fine, it may indicate that your body is trending toward insulin resistance and poor metabolic efficiency. By optimizing rather than just accepting "normal," you take control of long-term health and performance.

Another example is inflammation markers like C-reactive protein (CRP). Many physicians will only flag CRP levels if they are significantly elevated, but even low levels of chronic inflammation can impair recovery, cognitive function, and immune resilience. Functional medicine aims to keep CRP as low as possible, ideally under 0.5 mg/L, rather than merely under the conventional threshold of 3 mg/L. The same principle applies to cholesterol, thyroid markers, and liver function tests—functional ranges prioritize performance and longevity, not just disease prevention.

Optimizing health requires a higher standard than simply not being sick. True vitality comes from fine-tuning the body for optimal function, energy production, and resilience. This is why using functional lab ranges instead of conventional ones is essential for anyone looking to stay in the top 1%. Once you have your lab results, the next question is: What do you do with this information? Identifying imbalances is only the first step. The real value comes from taking action—making strategic lifestyle modifications, adjusting nutrition, and implementing advanced therapies to optimize health and performance.

For those with deficiencies or imbalances, targeted nutrition plays a crucial role. Magnesium is one of the most important supplements for recovery, muscle function, and nervous system regulation. Many people are unknowingly deficient, leading to poor sleep, muscle cramps, and increased stress response. Omega-3 fatty acids, found in fish oil, are another critical nutrient for brain function, reducing inflammation, and supporting cardiovascular health. If lipid panel results show high triglycerides or a poor LDL-to-HDL ratio, increasing omega-3 intake can be a powerful corrective measure.

Lifestyle adjustments are equally important. If fasting blood sugar trends upward, refining carbohydrate intake, increasing fiber, and implementing intermittent fasting can improve insulin sensitivity. If inflammation markers are elevated, optimizing hydration, sleep quality, and stress management techniques such as meditation and breathwork can dramatically reduce systemic inflammation. Sleep is one of the most overlooked pillars of recovery. Even mild sleep deprivation raises cortisol levels, disrupts metabolic function, and impairs immune resilience. By analyzing lab trends, individuals can identify whether chronic stress and poor sleep are contributing to underlying health concerns.

For those looking to take optimization further, advanced therapies such as IV nutrition, hormone balancing, and detoxification strategies can be game-changers. Intravenous (IV) nutrient therapy delivers high doses of vitamins and minerals directly into the bloodstream, bypassing digestive limitations. This is especially beneficial for individuals with gut issues, nutrient absorption problems, or high performance demands. Hormone optimization, including balancing testosterone, estrogen, and thyroid hormones, can dramatically improve energy levels, muscle recovery, and cognitive performance. Detoxification strategies, including infrared sauna therapy and liver-supportive protocols, help reduce toxic burden and inflammation.

Knowing your numbers puts you in control, giving you the roadmap to optimize health, longevity, and peak performance. The most successful individuals in any field do not wait for problems to arise—they anticipate, adapt, and optimize. By taking a data-driven approach to health, you can make intelligent, informed decisions that support your highest level of performance.

The key to long-term success is not guesswork; it is precision-based interventions that build resilience and longevity. Health is not something you react to—it is something you engineer. The information provided by routine lab testing is the foundation for a strategy that allows you to perform at your best, feel energized, and avoid the common health traps that slow others down. Those who use this approach will always have an advantage, because true success is built on a foundation of vibrant, optimized health.

Elite performers understand that leaving health to chance is a losing strategy. Just as financial success requires tracking income, expenses, and investments, sustained peak performance demands rigorous health monitoring and optimization. Those who thrive in business, athletics, and personal development recognize that their greatest asset is not money, status, or power—it is their physical and mental vitality. Without a strong foundation of health, even the most ambitious goals become unattainable.

Tracking and testing are the cornerstones of data-driven health. The difference between those who maintain lifelong energy, resilience, and cognitive sharpness and those who experience premature decline lies in the ability to see problems before they arise, take early action, and consistently refine their approach. Health is not static; it is an evolving system influenced by diet, stress, sleep, movement, and environmental exposures. The only way to stay ahead of the curve is through continuous self-monitoring, using lab data as a roadmap for precision-based health decisions.

Many people still operate under the assumption that health is something to be addressed only when symptoms appear. This outdated mindset leads to a reactionary, crisis-based approach to wellness, where individuals wait until they are fatigued, overweight, inflamed, or experiencing cognitive decline before making changes. By the time warning signs are evident, damage has already accumulated. The elite take a different approach. They invest in preventative health measures, track their biomarkers regularly, and make strategic adjustments long before issues become irreversible.

The key to outpacing disease and aging is the ability to identify trends and patterns rather than waiting for an emergency. When lab work is reviewed over months and years, it reveals subtle shifts in metabolism, inflammation, immune function, and nutrient status that would otherwise go unnoticed. A single test might suggest that all is well, but repeated testing tells the true story. The best performers use this knowledge to optimize their energy, brain function, and physical performance, ensuring they remain at the top of their game regardless of age.

Taking control of health starts with scheduling annual labs and tracking personal health trends. This single action step separates those who live with vitality and endurance from those who unknowingly drift toward decline. The most successful individuals treat their health with the same level of diligence as they do their businesses and investments. They do not wait for external circumstances to dictate their well-being. They leverage data, take decisive action, and continuously refine their approach.

For those looking to elevate their health beyond standard recommendations, specialty testing provides an even greater advantage. The ultra-wealthy and elite performers are not just testing basic biomarkers—they are diving deep into hidden variables that influence longevity, resilience, and cognitive dominance.

One of the most overlooked factors in health optimization is nutrient sufficiency at the cellular level. Standard blood tests may indicate that vitamin and mineral levels are within range, but these do not account for how effectively nutrients are being absorbed and utilized at the cellular level. Many high performers struggle with hidden deficiencies, leading to chronic fatigue, poor recovery, and suboptimal cognitive function—even when eating a nutrient-dense diet. Cellular-level vitamin and mineral testing reveals whether the body is truly nourished at a functional level. Those who optimize their nutrient status experience greater energy, better immune resilience, and improved mental clarity.

Another silent disruptor of long-term health is heavy metal toxicity. Industrial pollutants, contaminated water, and certain foods expose individuals to heavy metals such as lead, mercury, cadmium, and arsenic. These toxic elements accumulate in tissues over time, interfering with hormone function, brain health, and immune regulation. Heavy metal burden testing is one of the secret weapons of high performers, as it allows for early detoxification before metals impair cellular function. Many of the unexplained symptoms experienced by individuals—such as brain fog, chronic fatigue, and persistent inflammation—can often be linked to hidden heavy metal exposure. By testing and removing these toxins, the body recovers faster, cognitive sharpness returns, and immune function strengthens.

The modern world presents a new wave of environmental threats that impact long-term health, yet very few people are actively testing for them. Microplastics, pesticides, and herbicides are now ubiquitous in the food supply and water sources, slowly accumulating in the body and disrupting endocrine function. These hidden pollutants are linked to hormonal imbalances, metabolic dysfunction, and inflammation— yet most individuals are unaware of their presence. The ultra-wealthy and elite performers prioritize testing for environmental toxins, taking action to remove contaminants and fortify their detoxification pathways. Those who eliminate these disruptors experience greater metabolic efficiency, reduced disease risk, and increased longevity.

Comprehensive hormone testing is another non-negotiable for those who operate at the highest level. Hormones govern energy production, mental focus, strength, and recovery, yet many people go years without assessing their hormonal status. Suboptimal testosterone, estrogen, or thyroid levels can create chronic fatigue, weight gain, mood instability, and cognitive decline. By optimizing hormone function, individuals gain a massive edge in performance, motivation, and resilience. Many of the world's most accomplished leaders undergo routine hormone optimization therapy to ensure they maintain youthful vitality well into their later years.

Cognitive dominance is not just about intelligence—it is about neurotransmitter balance. Decision-making, stress resilience, emotional regulation, and creativity are all governed by neurotransmitters like dopamine, serotonin, and acetylcholine. Neurotransmitter imbalances can result in brain fog, impulsivity, mood swings, and mental fatigue, impairing performance at critical moments. Testing neurotransmitter levels allows for precision-based cognitive enhancement, using targeted nutrition, supplementation, and lifestyle strategies to create mental clarity, focus, and sustained motivation.

The secret to long-term success is not just working harder—it is working smarter by optimizing the biological foundation that fuels peak performance. Those who take their health seriously recognize that it is the ultimate competitive advantage. Energy, mental sharpness, and physical resilience determine who succeeds and who struggles to keep up. In a world where stress, toxicity, and metabolic dysfunction are becoming the norm, the elite few who prioritize precision-based health strategies will always stay ahead.

The future of high performance is not in waiting for disease to appear—it is in systematically removing hidden obstacles, tracking personal health data, and engineering resilience at every level. Those who commit to this approach will not only live longer but perform at their peak for decades to come. This is not about simply avoiding illness; it is about achieving an elite level of vitality that allows for sustained excellence in every area of life.

Every major success story—whether in business, athletics, or personal development—is underpinned by strong health, clear thinking, and boundless energy. The individuals who consistently outperform their peers do not leave their health to chance. They test, track, optimize, and repeat. This is the winning formula for those who want to stay ahead of the curve.

The next step is clear: schedule your annual labs, start tracking your personal health trends, and commit to data-driven health optimization. By making these strategies a cornerstone of your life, you will not only extend your longevity but ensure that every day is filled with the energy, focus, and resilience needed to achieve your biggest goals. Health is not just a priority—it is the ultimate foundation for success, and those who master it will always be in control of their future.

PART THREE

INTERPRETING & OPTIMIZING YOUR BODY LIKE A BILLION-DOLLAR PORTFOLIO

6

The Most Important Vitamin & Mineral for You is... The One You Need

I magine stepping into a high-performance vehicle and filling it with the cheapest fuel available. The engine sputters, the acceleration lags, and despite the sleek exterior, it struggles to perform at its best. Now, imagine that same vehicle fueled with precision-engineered, high-octane fuel, designed specifically for its engine. The difference is night and day. Your body operates the same way. You can follow generic health advice, take the same multivitamins everyone else is taking, and hope for the best—or you can customize your nutrition, fueling your body with exactly what it needs to perform at peak levels.

For years, the standard approach to health has been built around one-size-fits-all recommendations. Doctors prescribe the same basic guidelines to every patient—take a multivitamin, eat a balanced diet, exercise regularly, and hope it all works out. But hope is not a strategy when it comes to optimizing performance, longevity, and vitality. The real breakthrough in health is personalization—using data, precision testing, and targeted interventions to identify exactly what your body needs rather than relying on guesswork.

Many people believe they are covering their nutritional bases simply by taking a daily multivitamin or following the latest health trends. But what works for one person may not work for another. Some thrive on high-fat diets, while others feel sluggish and inflamed. Some require more magnesium for muscle recovery and sleep, while others need higher levels of B vitamins to support energy production. Without objective data, people are playing a guessing game with their health, hoping to feel better but never truly optimizing their body's potential.

The key to sustained energy, mental clarity, and long-term health lies in understanding and correcting your unique biochemical imbalances. What's missing in your body? What's in excess? Where are the weak points in your system that, if addressed, could unlock a new level of vitality? These are the questions that high achievers, elite athletes, and longevity-focused individuals are now asking—and answering through personalized nutrition and functional medicine.

A growing body of research shows that nutrient status is one of the most significant predictors of overall health and disease prevention. Deficiencies in key vitamins and minerals can contribute to fatigue, cognitive decline, hormonal imbalances, poor immune function, and metabolic dysfunction. Yet, many people are nutrient-deficient without even realizing it. They may feel "fine" but unknowingly operate at a fraction of their full potential. This is why testing and targeted correction are essential.

Personalized health is the future, and those who embrace this approach are the ones who will thrive while others struggle with unexplained fatigue, brain fog, and chronic inflammation. If you've ever felt frustrated by generic health advice that didn't work for you, it's time to shift your perspective. The true key to optimizing your body is not in following what works for the masses—it's in discovering exactly what works for you.

Instead of blindly following trends or assuming that a standard dose of vitamins will meet your needs, the smarter approach is to measure, track, and adjust based on real data. Functional medicine practitioners and forward-thinking doctors have now developed advanced testing methods that reveal hidden deficiencies, absorption issues, and metabolic imbalances. These tests go far beyond the basic panels offered in conventional medicine, providing a blueprint for your body's precise nutritional needs.

The truth is, nutritional status is as unique as a fingerprint. Your genetic makeup, lifestyle, stress levels, diet, and even environmental exposures all play a role in determining your specific vitamin and mineral requirements. A sedentary office worker may require an entirely different set of nutrients than a high-performance athlete, yet conventional medicine often fails to make this distinction. Even more concerning is that many people who appear healthy on the surface are walking around with significant nutrient imbalances that are silently draining their energy, focus, and long-term resilience.

For example, magnesium deficiency is widespread, yet it is rarely tested for in conventional medical settings. Magnesium is critical for muscle recovery, sleep regulation, heart health, and stress resilience, yet most people are unknowingly deficient. Similarly, Vitamin D levels vary significantly among individuals based on genetics, sun exposure, and dietary intake. Some people require three to four times the standard recommended dose to maintain optimal levels, yet they would never know unless they tested. The same applies to B vitamins, omega-3 fatty acids, zinc, and iron—all of which play essential roles in maintaining peak performance.

The biggest mistake people make when it comes to nutrition is assuming that "normal" lab results mean optimal health. Standard blood tests often look at broad reference ranges based on the general population, which includes many unhealthy individuals. Just because a nutrient level falls within a "normal" range does not mean it is optimal for high performance, longevity, or disease prevention. Functional medicine takes a different approach—focusing on what's ideal, not just what's average.

Take fasting blood glucose as an example. Conventional medicine considers anything under 100 mg/dL to be "normal." But optimal levels for peak metabolic function and longevity are closer to 75-85 mg/dL. The same principle applies to cholesterol, inflammatory markers, and even hormone levels. High performers are not interested in simply being "normal"—they want to be at their absolute best.

Personalized health is about precision. It's about removing guesswork and replacing it with real, actionable data that allows you to make informed decisions about your body. It is the difference between hoping you're getting enough nutrients and knowing you are optimizing every system in your body for peak performance.

When done correctly, personalized nutrition can transform everything—from energy levels and cognitive performance to sleep quality, immune function, and disease prevention. Imagine waking up every day with sustained energy, mental clarity, and the confidence that you are fueling your body exactly as it needs. That is the power of precision-based health strategies.

The reality is, the most important vitamin or mineral for you is not the one that's most popular—it's the one you are missing. And the only way to find out what your body truly needs is through testing, tracking, and strategically supplementing based on objective data. This chapter will explore the science behind functional nutrient testing, optimal lab ranges, and how to correct deficiencies with precision-based supplementation.

True health optimization is not about taking more supplements— it's about taking the right supplements in the right doses for your unique biology. It's about understanding what your body needs at any given time and adjusting accordingly. Personalized nutrition is not a luxury—it is a necessity for anyone who wants to operate at their best, avoid premature aging, and maximize their lifespan and healthspan.

Health is not a guessing game. It's time to stop treating it like one. By the end of this chapter, you will have the tools to decode your body's unique needs, correct imbalances, and take control of your health in a way that no generic approach ever could. This is the future of medicine, and those who embrace it will not only live longer but thrive at levels most people never experience.

Imagine waking up every day with boundless energy, clear mental focus, and a body that operates at peak efficiency. Now imagine the opposite—dragging through the day, feeling exhausted despite getting enough sleep, struggling with brain fog, mood swings, and unexplained aches. Many people assume these fluctuations are just part of aging, stress, or genetics. But the truth is, these symptoms are often the result of micronutrient imbalances—deficiencies that are not always severe enough to trigger a medical diagnosis but are powerful enough to impact daily performance, longevity, and well-being.

The key to unlocking optimal health is not found in generic health advice or one-size-fits-all supplementation. What works for one person may be entirely ineffective or even harmful for another. True health optimization begins with understanding individual biological needs, and that requires interpreting personal health data rather than relying on broad, generalized guidelines.

Most people assume that if their doctor says their lab work is "normal," then they must be in good health. This assumption is deeply flawed. Conventional medicine often focuses on broad reference ranges, which are based on statistical averages rather than optimal health markers. These ranges are designed to detect disease, not to optimize well-being. A lab result that falls within a reference range does not necessarily mean it is ideal—it simply means it is not at an extreme enough level to raise concern.

For example, a patient may have magnesium levels that fall within the "normal" range, yet they still experience chronic muscle cramps, poor sleep, and low energy. Their doctor may dismiss these symptoms because their lab numbers are not technically deficient. But functional medicine practitioners recognize that suboptimal magnesium levels— while not classified as a deficiency—can still impair nerve function, muscle recovery, and stress adaptation.

The same is true for vitamin B12, an essential nutrient for nerve health, red blood cell production, and cognitive function. Standard lab ranges for B12 are so broad that many people with low-normal levels still experience symptoms such as fatigue, depression, and brain fog. Functional medicine looks beyond these general guidelines, considering how well the body is actually utilizing a nutrient rather than just whether it is present in the blood.

There is a vast difference between having enough nutrients to survive and having the right nutrients to thrive. Functional medicine shifts the focus from avoiding disease to achieving optimal health by looking at three key factors: ideal nutrient ranges for energy, brain function, and longevity, the body's ability to properly absorb and use those nutrients, and individual metabolic demands based on genetics, lifestyle, and environment.

Many people assume that if they consume a nutrient, they are absorbing it. But gut health, inflammation, and genetics all impact how well the body actually utilizes vitamins and minerals. A person can eat a diet rich in magnesium, for example, yet still be deficient due to poor absorption caused by stress, poor gut function, or excessive caffeine intake. Addressing these underlying issues is just as important as the nutrient itself.

No two bodies are the same, and each person has unique nutritional needs based on stress levels, lifestyle, and biochemical makeup. A high-performing athlete, for example, may have greater needs for electrolytes and B vitamins due to increased metabolic demand, while someone dealing with chronic stress may require higher levels of magnesium, zinc, and adaptogenic herbs to support adrenal function. These factors make it clear that the key to long-term health and peak performance is not just ensuring adequate intake but also personalizing nutrition to each individual's needs.

When nutrient levels are even slightly off, the body begins to compensate. These compensations may not be immediately obvious, but over time, they create a cascade of dysfunction that impacts energy, immune resilience, metabolism, and cognitive performance. An individual with low but technically "normal" vitamin D levels may experience weakened immunity, low mood, and chronic inflammation. Over time, this persistent low-grade inflammation can contribute to fatigue, joint pain, and increased risk for autoimmune disorders. Someone with marginally low iron levels may not have full-blown anemia, but they may experience subtle signs of poor oxygen delivery, such as brain fog, reduced exercise capacity, and brittle nails.

The problem with waiting until a full-blown deficiency develops is that by then, damage has already occurred. The goal is to catch these imbalances early, before they have the chance to disrupt long-term health and performance. Simply taking a multivitamin and hoping for the best is not an effective strategy. Many generic supplements contain inadequate doses, poorly absorbed forms of nutrients, or unnecessary fillers that do little to correct true deficiencies. More importantly, without data, there is no way of knowing whether the nutrients being taken are helping, unnecessary, or even harmful.

Dr. West's proprietary method for correcting imbalances follows a precision-based approach, utilizing functional lab testing to detect deficiencies long before symptoms appear, high-quality bioavailable nutrients tailored to individual absorption capacity, dietary interventions to support natural nutrient replenishment, and lifestyle adjustments that enhance nutrient utilization. If a patient has low magnesium and high stress levels, simply taking magnesium may not be enough. Addressing cortisol regulation, hydration, and gut health ensures that the body absorbs and utilizes magnesium efficiently rather than just passing it through the digestive system.

Patients who have embraced a data-driven approach to their nutrient needs have experienced dramatic improvements in energy, mental clarity, and physical recovery. A middle-aged executive who struggled with chronic fatigue and focus issues found that his B vitamin and zinc levels were critically low, impairing neurotransmitter function and cellular energy production. After correcting these deficiencies with targeted supplementation and dietary changes, his energy returned, mental sharpness improved, and stress resilience increased. An endurance athlete who suffered from frequent injuries and slow recovery discovered that he was deficient in omega-3s, vitamin D, and collagen-building nutrients. By incorporating high-dose fish oil, vitamin D3, and bioavailable protein, he reduced inflammation, improved joint health, and accelerated muscle recovery.

These transformations are not the result of luck or trial-and-error supplementation—they are the direct outcome of testing, identifying, and correcting nutrient imbalances before they manifest as serious health issues. The most important vitamin or mineral is not what is trending on social media or what the latest supplement company is pushing. It is the one your body actually needs.

Every individual has a unique set of requirements based on their genetics, lifestyle, environment, and stress levels. Without data, achieving peak health is guesswork. But with a functional medicine approach, targeted nutrition, and precise supplementation, true health optimization becomes a reality.

Your energy, cognitive function, resilience, and longevity are directly tied to whether or not your body is getting the right nutrients in the right amounts. The difference between merely surviving and truly thriving lies in personalized health data—understanding exactly what your body needs and taking action to meet those needs with precision. This is the future of medicine, and it is the key to unlocking your highest potential.

Health is often viewed in binary terms—either you are sick or you are well. Conventional medicine operates under this framework, categorizing patients based on whether they meet the clinical threshold for disease. However, many individuals who technically fall within the "normal" range for lab tests still suffer from persistent fatigue, brain fog, mood imbalances, and sluggish metabolism. They may not be diagnosed with a disease, but they are far from thriving. This gap in care is where functional medicine excels. Rather than waiting for a patient's health to deteriorate enough to meet diagnostic criteria, functional medicine practitioners focus on identifying and correcting hidden imbalances before they manifest as chronic illness.

One of the most overlooked aspects of modern healthcare is the presence of subclinical nutrient deficiencies—levels of vitamins and minerals that may not be low enough to trigger an official deficiency diagnosis but are insufficient to support optimal function. Standard lab tests are designed to detect severe deficiencies, yet they often fail to flag subtle imbalances that still have profound effects on energy levels, cognitive function, immune resilience, and metabolic efficiency. When individuals experience persistent fatigue, chronic inflammation, mood swings, or weight management difficulties, these symptoms are often attributed to stress, aging, or poor sleep. But in many cases, they are the direct result of long-term micronutrient depletion.

Among the most commonly overlooked nutrient deficiencies are magnesium, B vitamins, vitamin D, omega-3 fatty acids, zinc, and iron. These micronutrients play critical roles in cellular energy production, hormone balance, immune response, and neurological function. A deficiency in any of these can cause subtle but chronic dysfunction that is difficult to detect using conventional lab ranges. Many patients with so-called "normal" lab results continue to struggle with unexplained symptoms, leading them to feel unheard or dismissed by traditional medical providers. Functional medicine takes a different approach, prioritizing optimal ranges rather than just avoiding the lowest acceptable thresholds.

Magnesium is one of the most crucial yet underappreciated minerals in the body. It is involved in over 300 enzymatic reactions, including those that regulate energy production, muscle contraction, and nervous system function. Despite its importance, magnesium deficiency is alarmingly common, largely due to depleted soil quality and the prevalence of processed foods in the modern diet. Individuals with inadequate magnesium levels may experience muscle cramps, anxiety, poor sleep, and chronic fatigue. Because standard blood tests only measure serum magnesium, they fail to reflect the body's actual magnesium stores, leading to undiagnosed deficiencies that persist for years.

B vitamins, particularly B6, B9 (folate), and B12, are essential for brain health, neurotransmitter production, and red blood cell formation. A deficiency in B12, for instance, can cause brain fog, memory issues, and nerve dysfunction, yet conventional testing often misses low levels because the standard reference range is too broad. Many individuals with symptoms of B12 deficiency are told their levels are normal when, in reality, they are far from optimal. Similarly, folate and B6 are crucial for methylation, a biochemical process that affects detoxification, neurotransmitter balance, and DNA repair. When these vitamins are lacking, individuals may experience mood instability, fatigue, and poor stress resilience.

Vitamin D is another critical yet widely deficient nutrient, even in individuals who live in sunny climates. Unlike other vitamins, vitamin D functions more like a hormone, regulating immune function, bone health, and inflammation. Low levels are associated with increased susceptibility to infections, autoimmune conditions, and chronic pain. Many conventional lab tests set the threshold for deficiency too low, meaning individuals with levels in the low-normal range still experience symptoms such as fatigue, depression, and muscle weakness. Functional medicine recognizes that optimal vitamin D levels—far above the standard cutoff—are necessary for robust immune defense and overall vitality.

Omega-3 fatty acids, particularly EPA and DHA, are essential for brain health, cardiovascular function, and inflammation control. Because the body does not produce omega-3s, they must be obtained through diet or supplementation. Many individuals consume an excess of inflammatory omega-6 fats found in processed foods while failing to get enough omega-3s from fatty fish or high-quality supplements. This imbalance leads to chronic inflammation, which contributes to conditions such as joint pain, cardiovascular disease, and neurodegenerative disorders. Conventional medicine rarely tests for omega-3 status, yet deficiency is widespread and contributes to premature aging and cognitive decline.

Zinc is a key mineral for immune function, wound healing, and hormone production, yet it is frequently overlooked in standard lab panels. Individuals with low zinc levels may experience frequent colds, poor skin health, and imbalanced testosterone or estrogen levels. Because zinc plays a role in cellular repair and enzyme function, chronic deficiency can impair digestion, slow metabolism, and contribute to infertility.

Iron is one of the most commonly tested but poorly interpreted nutrients. Many physicians focus solely on hemoglobin levels when assessing iron status, but hemoglobin may remain normal even when iron stores are depleted. Ferritin, a marker of stored iron, provides a more accurate picture of iron levels. Low ferritin is often associated with chronic fatigue, hair loss, and poor exercise endurance, yet it is rarely tested unless anemia is already present. Many individuals suffer from iron depletion long before anemia develops, leading to years of unexplained exhaustion and reduced productivity.

Recognizing these hidden deficiencies is only the first step. Dr. West has developed a precision-based method for restoring nutrient balance, ensuring that individuals receive the exact nutrients they need rather than taking a scattershot approach with generic multivitamins. The first step in this method is comprehensive functional lab testing. Unlike conventional tests that focus on disease detection, functional testing evaluates nutrient levels, inflammatory markers, and metabolic efficiency to identify imbalances before they become clinical problems. This data-driven approach eliminates guesswork, allowing for precise interventions tailored to each individual's needs.

Once deficiencies are identified, the next step is precision-based supplementation. Instead of recommending generic multivitamins, which often contain synthetic or poorly absorbed nutrients, Dr. West utilizes bioavailable forms of vitamins and minerals that the body can efficiently absorb and utilize. For example, magnesium glycinate is preferred over magnesium oxide due to its superior absorption and reduced likelihood of causing digestive discomfort. Similarly, methylated B vitamins are used for individuals with genetic variations that impair folate metabolism. This level of specificity ensures that the body receives nutrients in a form it can actually use.

Restoring balance is not just about supplementation; it also involves strategic dietary and lifestyle interventions. Many nutrient deficiencies are caused by poor absorption rather than inadequate intake. Gut health plays a critical role in nutrient assimilation, and individuals with leaky gut, low stomach acid, or chronic inflammation may struggle to absorb key vitamins and minerals even when consuming a nutrient-dense diet. Addressing gut health through targeted probiotics, digestive enzymes, and anti-inflammatory foods enhances nutrient uptake, allowing the body to restore balance naturally.

Another essential component of Dr. West's method is ongoing monitoring and strategic adjustments over time. The body's needs change due to aging, stress, and lifestyle factors, meaning that a static approach to supplementation is ineffective. By regularly tracking health markers, adjusting dosages, and modifying interventions as needed, patients can maintain optimal nutrient levels and prevent deficiencies from recurring. This dynamic approach ensures that health is continuously optimized rather than addressed reactively when symptoms arise.

The conventional model of healthcare often fails to recognize the profound impact of hidden nutrient deficiencies. Many individuals suffer from chronic fatigue, poor concentration, and sluggish metabolism for years without realizing that these symptoms are rooted in subtle biochemical imbalances. Functional medicine shifts the focus from disease treatment to health optimization, ensuring that individuals achieve not just the absence of illness, but true vitality. By prioritizing functional lab testing, targeted supplementation, and personalized interventions, Dr. West's approach empowers individuals to take control of their health, optimize performance, and unlock their full potential.

The difference between just getting by and truly thriving lies in the details—nutrient balance, metabolic efficiency, and the ability to correct deficiencies before they become disease. The future of medicine is personalized, data-driven, and precision-focused, and those who embrace this approach will experience greater energy, enhanced cognitive function, and long-term resilience. Health is not about waiting for symptoms to appear; it is about proactively creating the conditions for lifelong vitality.

Health is not a one-size-fits-all equation. Every individual has unique nutritional requirements based on genetics, lifestyle, and metabolic function. Yet, conventional health advice often promotes generic solutions—multivitamins with indiscriminate doses, fad diets that claim to work for everyone, and wellness trends that fail to acknowledge the complexity of human physiology. This generalized approach leaves many people feeling frustrated when they do not see results or, worse, when they continue to struggle with fatigue, poor focus, or unexplained health issues despite doing everything "right."

Personalized nutrition is the game-changer that allows individuals to optimize their health by addressing their body's specific needs. The difference between thriving and simply getting by often comes down to understanding and correcting unique nutrient deficiencies. When the body is properly nourished, energy levels soar, cognitive performance improves, and the risk of chronic disease diminishes. The power of personalized nutrition is not theoretical—it is demonstrated every day in the lives of people who take a data-driven approach to health.

One such case involved a successful entrepreneur in his early 40s who, despite following a seemingly perfect diet and exercise routine, felt chronically fatigued. He woke up exhausted, struggled to concentrate throughout the day, and relied on caffeine just to keep functioning. Traditional lab tests showed nothing abnormal, and he was told his symptoms were likely due to stress. Unsatisfied with this vague explanation, he sought functional testing, which revealed critically low levels of magnesium, vitamin B12, and omega-3 fatty acids. These deficiencies were impairing his mitochondrial function, reducing his body's ability to produce energy at the cellular level. By correcting these imbalances through targeted supplementation and dietary adjustments, his energy dramatically improved, his mental clarity returned, and his dependence on stimulants vanished. His case exemplifies why conventional lab results that fall within "normal" ranges are not necessarily optimal for high performance.

Another compelling example is that of a 55-year-old woman who had spent years battling brain fog, joint pain, and mood swings. She was told by various doctors that these symptoms were likely part of aging and that she should "learn to live with them." However, further analysis revealed low vitamin D, zinc, and iron levels, all of which play critical roles in immune function, cognition, and inflammation regulation. Once she began a precise nutrient protocol tailored to her deficiencies, her symptoms resolved within months. She regained mental sharpness, felt stronger in her daily activities, and even noticed improved emotional resilience. This case underscores the transformative power of correcting micronutrient imbalances and highlights how conventional medicine often overlooks the root causes of chronic symptoms.

Another striking case involved a young athlete who trained rigorously but struggled with slow recovery, frequent injuries, and declining endurance. He had followed mainstream advice on nutrition, consuming high amounts of protein and electrolytes, yet he was not seeing improvements. His functional health assessment revealed insufficient vitamin D, inadequate omega-3 intake, and a deficiency in vitamin K2, which is crucial for calcium metabolism and bone health. After adjusting his diet and implementing a precision-based supplementation plan, his injury rate dropped, his stamina improved, and his recovery time was cut in half. This example demonstrates why athletes cannot afford to rely on generic dietary recommendations; their nutritional demands are vastly different from the general population, and even minor deficiencies can significantly impact performance.

These stories illustrate a powerful truth: when the right nutrients are provided in the right amounts, the body responds with resilience, clarity, and vitality. The traditional approach of addressing health concerns only when they reach a crisis point is outdated and ineffective. The future of medicine is precision-based, preventative, and data-driven. By identifying deficiencies before they cause significant dysfunction, individuals can take control of their well-being and prevent a lifetime of unnecessary suffering.

True health optimization means abandoning the mindset of following trends and embracing the concept of creating a personalized health blueprint. There is no single "best" vitamin, supplement, or diet. The best approach is the one tailored to the body's unique biochemistry. What works for one person may be ineffective for another, which is why testing, tracking, and fine-tuning nutrients is the key to sustained wellness.

This level of precision is what separates those who merely feel "okay" from those who operate at their highest level. People who take their health seriously do not wait for symptoms to appear—they measure, analyze, and optimize. They treat their bodies as high-performance machines, ensuring that every system is functioning at its best. Whether it is optimizing hormone balance, improving brain function, increasing energy, or preventing disease, personalized nutrition is the tool that allows individuals to unlock their greatest potential.

The best investment anyone can make is in understanding their own body's needs. Supplements should not be taken blindly, diets should not be followed without consideration for individual metabolism, and health decisions should not be based on assumptions. The key to long-term vitality is precision, not trends. Those who embrace this philosophy will not only extend their lifespan but will also ensure that every day is filled with the energy, clarity, and resilience needed to live life at its fullest.

For those who have spent years wondering why they feel sluggish despite doing everything "right," the answer lies in taking a closer look at nutrient imbalances and biochemical individuality. The journey to optimal health begins with a commitment to testing, analyzing, and correcting deficiencies. This approach does not just improve how a person feels today—it creates the foundation for lasting vitality, disease prevention, and peak performance for years to come.

The time to take control of health is now. Ignoring the body's needs only leads to declining performance and preventable illness. The solution is not found in generic health recommendations but in a personalized, data-driven strategy that identifies and corrects deficiencies before they impact quality of life. Those who embrace this approach will not only live longer but will thrive in every aspect of their lives. It is not about following the latest health trend; it is about investing in the only thing that truly matters—your own well-being.

7

The Secret to Longevity – Rebuilding & Revitalizing Your Body

Imagine waking up every morning with boundless energy, a sharp mind, and a body that moves with strength and ease—no pain, no fatigue, no signs of slowing down. Imagine living each decade with the same vitality and resilience as you had in your youth, free from the chronic conditions that many accept as an inevitable part of aging. Now, imagine knowing that this reality is not just possible but entirely achievable with the right approach to health. Longevity is not just about adding years to life; it is about ensuring that those years are filled with vitality, strength, and clarity.

Modern medicine has made extraordinary advancements in treating acute illness and managing disease, but it often fails when it comes to preventing degeneration before it starts. The conventional model focuses on intervention only after symptoms appear, prescribing medication to suppress issues rather than addressing the root causes. For decades, people have been conditioned to believe that aging means an inevitable decline in health, function, and quality of life. This outdated approach overlooks one fundamental truth: the human body is designed to regenerate, heal, and thrive when given the right support. The key to long-term health is not reactive treatment but proactive care—nourishing the body at a cellular level before dysfunction sets in.

Dr. West has spent the last 25 years refining a clinical formula for long-term health success. This formula is not built on temporary fixes or pharmaceutical dependence but on the foundations of cellular repair, rejuvenation, and biological optimization. Through a combination of essential vitamins and minerals, powerful phytonutrients, organ-specific regenerative compounds, and cutting-edge peptide therapies, this approach represents the next evolution of functional medicine. It is a system designed to rebuild and revitalize the body from within, slowing the aging process while enhancing strength, cognitive function, and metabolic efficiency.

One of the most critical distinctions between conventional medicine and this functional approach is the focus on prevention versus reaction. While traditional medicine waits for symptoms to emerge before addressing them, functional medicine works ahead of time, identifying and correcting imbalances before they lead to disease. Every chronic illness, from cardiovascular disease to neurodegenerative disorders, begins at the cellular level. Cellular aging, inflammation, and nutrient deficiencies accumulate over time, eventually leading to dysfunction. By targeting these processes early, it is possible to not only extend lifespan but improve the quality of every year lived.

The foundation of this formula starts with essential vitamins and minerals, the non-negotiable elements required for cellular function, detoxification, and energy production. Many people assume they are getting enough nutrients through diet alone, but modern food sources are often depleted of key vitamins and minerals. Soil degradation, processed foods, and poor absorption contribute to widespread deficiencies that impact everything from immune function to hormone balance. Without proper micronutrient support, the body is unable to repair damaged cells, regulate inflammation, or maintain metabolic efficiency.

Beyond basic micronutrients, phytonutrients and herbal medicine provide nature's answer to pharmaceuticals. These plant-based compounds have been used for thousands of years in traditional medicine systems, yet they are only now being validated by modern science. Polyphenols, flavonoids, and adaptogenic herbs offer powerful antioxidant and anti-inflammatory properties, helping to protect the body from oxidative stress and cellular damage. These compounds support brain function, cardiovascular health, and immune resilience, offering a natural and effective way to maintain long-term vitality.

One of the most revolutionary aspects of Dr. West's longevity formula is the use of protomorphogens, the cellular building blocks for organ repair and regeneration. Unlike standard supplements that merely support organ function, protomorphogens work at the structural level, stimulating tissue healing and renewal. This approach has been shown to restore adrenal, thyroid, liver, and kidney health, reversing years of accumulated damage and dysfunction. While conventional medicine often assumes that organ degeneration is irreversible, this therapy challenges that notion by providing the body with the raw materials it needs to rebuild itself.

At the cutting edge of longevity science are peptides, the next frontier in age-reversal and performance optimization. Peptides are short chains of amino acids that act as messengers in the body, triggering processes such as tissue repair, immune enhancement, and cognitive regeneration. They have been found to increase growth hormone levels, accelerate recovery, and improve metabolic function, making them a key component in the future of anti-aging medicine. Peptides like BPC-157, Thymosin Beta-4, and Epitalon have shown remarkable results in reducing inflammation, enhancing neurological function, and even extending lifespan. As science continues to explore the potential of peptides, they are becoming an essential tool for those looking to not just live longer, but thrive at every stage of life.

The combination of these therapies represents a powerful, multi-faceted approach to longevity—one that goes beyond simply avoiding disease and instead focuses on rebuilding, regenerating, and optimizing every system in the body. This is not about following health trends or relying on pharmaceutical interventions. It is about understanding the body's natural ability to heal and using science-backed strategies to support that process.

True longevity is not measured in years alone, but in the quality of those years. Many people today live well into their 80s and 90s, but how many of them maintain strength, mental clarity, and independence? The goal is not just to extend lifespan, but to extend healthspan—the years spent living in peak condition. The difference between those who age well and those who decline rapidly is not genetics alone. It is lifestyle, nutrient sufficiency, cellular resilience, and the ability to counteract the effects of time with proactive interventions.

The future of medicine is shifting away from the outdated notion that aging is synonymous with decline. Longevity is not about luck, nor is it determined solely by genetics. It is the direct result of how well the body is nourished, protected, and supported throughout life. Those who take control of their health now—who commit to cellular repair, inflammation control, and strategic nutrient optimization—will be the ones who live with vitality, clarity, and strength in their later years.

The decision to invest in longevity starts today. Every choice made—every meal eaten, every supplement taken, every lifestyle habit adopted—either contributes to or detracts from long-term health. Waiting until disease appears is no longer an option. The key to a long, vibrant life is taking proactive steps now, building the foundation for lasting wellness through science, strategy, and commitment to cellular renewal.

Dr. West's 25-year clinical formula offers a blueprint for longevity, integrating proven natural therapies with cutting-edge advancements in regenerative medicine. This is not a quick fix or a temporary solution. It is a system designed for lifelong vitality, preventing disease before it begins, and allowing individuals to live at their highest potential for decades to come. The time to take charge of health and longevity is now. The only question that remains is: how long do you want to thrive?

Health and longevity are built at the cellular level, and the most fundamental requirement for cellular function is the presence of essential vitamins and minerals. These nutrients serve as the raw materials for every biological process, from energy production to detoxification, immune response, and metabolic efficiency. Without adequate levels of these critical micronutrients, the body struggles to repair itself, maintain homeostasis, and protect against the onset of chronic disease. Conventional medicine often overlooks the importance of micronutrient optimization, focusing instead on diagnosing and treating disease after it has already taken hold. Functional medicine takes a different approach, recognizing that deficiencies in key vitamins and minerals contribute to premature aging, impaired immunity, and decreased energy production.

The modern lifestyle makes micronutrient deficiencies alarmingly common. Depleted soil conditions, processed food consumption, chronic stress, and environmental toxins all contribute to the erosion of essential nutrients from the body. Many individuals unknowingly operate at suboptimal levels, suffering from fatigue, brain fog, weakened immune function, and slow recovery without realizing that these issues stem from nutritional imbalances. Addressing these deficiencies is not about simply preventing disease; it is about restoring vitality, optimizing performance, and ensuring that every cell functions at its highest capacity.

Magnesium is one of the most crucial minerals for human health, yet it is also one of the most commonly deficient. It plays a role in over three hundred enzymatic reactions, including energy production, muscle function, nerve transmission, and detoxification. Magnesium is essential for the conversion of food into cellular energy, and without sufficient levels, mitochondria—the powerhouses of the cell—become inefficient. This inefficiency leads to chronic fatigue, muscle cramps, poor stress adaptation, and even cardiovascular issues. Conventional medicine rarely tests for magnesium levels, and when it does, it often measures serum magnesium, which is a poor indicator of total body stores. Functional medicine practitioners understand that intracellular magnesium levels are a far more accurate reflection of overall magnesium status and that replenishing this vital mineral can improve everything from sleep quality to insulin sensitivity and cardiovascular health.

Zinc is another indispensable mineral that plays a vital role in immune function, hormone production, wound healing, and cognitive health. The body does not store zinc efficiently, making regular intake essential. Deficiencies are increasingly common due to modern agricultural practices that deplete zinc from the soil, as well as the widespread consumption of processed foods that lack bioavailable forms of this mineral. Low zinc levels impair immune resilience, making individuals more susceptible to infections, prolonged illnesses, and poor recovery. Zinc is also crucial for testosterone production, making it particularly important for both men and women in maintaining hormonal balance. Beyond its role in immunity and hormones, zinc is a key player in neurological function, influencing memory, learning, and neuroplasticity. A lack of zinc contributes to brain fog, mood disorders, and cognitive decline, further reinforcing the need for optimal levels.

Vitamin D, often referred to as the "sunshine vitamin," is actually a hormone that influences a vast array of biological functions. It is essential for calcium absorption and bone health, but its impact goes far beyond skeletal strength. Vitamin D regulates immune function, modulates inflammation, and plays a critical role in mood stability and cognitive function. Deficiencies in vitamin D are linked to an increased risk of autoimmune diseases, depression, cardiovascular disorders, and even cancer. Despite its importance, vitamin D deficiency is widespread, particularly in individuals who live in northern latitudes, work indoors, or have darker skin pigmentation, which reduces the body's ability to synthesize vitamin D from sunlight. Conventional medicine sets the threshold for vitamin D deficiency far too low, failing to recognize that while a level of thirty nanograms per milliliter may prevent rickets, it is far from optimal for immune function and disease prevention. Functional medicine prioritizes levels between fifty and eighty nanograms per milliliter, ensuring that individuals not only avoid deficiency but achieve the full spectrum of benefits that vitamin D provides.

B vitamins are a family of water-soluble nutrients that are essential for energy metabolism, brain function, and red blood cell production. Each B vitamin serves a unique function, yet they work synergistically to support cellular repair and neurological health. Vitamin B12, for example, is crucial for the formation of myelin, the protective sheath around nerves, and a deficiency in B12 can lead to neuropathy, fatigue, and cognitive decline. Many people who experience memory loss, mood imbalances, or difficulty concentrating are unknowingly deficient in B12, particularly if they follow vegetarian or vegan diets, as B12 is primarily found in animal products. Folate, or vitamin B9, is necessary for DNA synthesis and cell division, making it especially important for pregnant women and individuals recovering from illness. Low folate levels are linked to elevated homocysteine, a marker of cardiovascular disease and neurodegenerative conditions. Vitamin B6 is required for neurotransmitter synthesis, and inadequate levels can contribute to anxiety, depression, and poor stress resilience. Despite their significance, B vitamin deficiencies are often missed by conventional lab testing, which does not account for methylation efficiency or individual genetic variations that affect B vitamin metabolism.

The conventional approach to nutrition sets dangerously low benchmarks for vitamin and mineral intake. The Recommended Daily Allowance (RDA) was originally established to prevent acute deficiency diseases such as scurvy and rickets, but these guidelines do not reflect the levels needed for optimal health and disease prevention. Functional medicine practitioners recognize that nutrient needs vary from person to person based on genetics, lifestyle, stress levels, and environmental exposures. A standardized approach fails to account for individual variations in nutrient metabolism and absorption. The goal should not be to simply avoid deficiency but to achieve the highest levels of health and performance possible.

The impact of optimal vitamin and mineral intake extends beyond basic health maintenance. These nutrients influence how well individuals age, how efficiently their bodies repair damaged cells, and how resilient they are against chronic disease. Inflammation, one of the primary drivers of aging and degenerative disease, is significantly influenced by nutrient status. Magnesium, zinc, and vitamin D all have anti-inflammatory properties that help regulate immune responses and prevent excessive oxidative stress. When these nutrients are present at optimal levels, the body is better equipped to repair cellular damage, maintain metabolic balance, and sustain long-term vitality.

The depletion of essential vitamins and minerals does not happen overnight. It is a gradual process that occurs over years of poor diet, chronic stress, environmental toxin exposure, and suboptimal supplementation. The symptoms of micronutrient deficiencies are often dismissed as signs of aging or stress when in reality, they are the body's way of signaling that it is running on empty. Addressing these deficiencies with a functional approach ensures that cells have everything they need to function optimally, reducing the risk of disease and enhancing overall quality of life.

The future of healthcare lies in precision-based nutrition. The days of generic multivitamins and one-size-fits-all dietary recommendations are coming to an end. Individuals must take control of their health by identifying and addressing their unique nutrient needs. Functional lab testing offers a deeper insight into where deficiencies exist, allowing for targeted supplementation and dietary interventions that restore balance at the cellular level. Investing in optimal vitamin and mineral status is not just about preventing disease—it is about maximizing energy, cognitive function, immune strength, and longevity.

For those seeking to optimize their health, the answer is not found in waiting for symptoms to appear or relying on outdated nutrient recommendations. The solution is found in a proactive, data-driven approach that prioritizes cellular repair, metabolic efficiency, and immune resilience. The human body is designed to thrive, but only when given the essential raw materials it requires. By embracing the principles of functional medicine and prioritizing optimal nutrient levels, individuals can reclaim their vitality, slow the aging process, and build a foundation for lifelong health. The time to take action is now—because the key to longevity begins with what fuels the body at its most fundamental level.

For centuries, nature has provided the foundation for healing, long before the advent of synthetic pharmaceuticals. Traditional medicine systems across the world have relied on plant compounds to prevent disease, promote longevity, and restore balance to the body. Today, scientific research is confirming what ancient healers have known for millennia—phytonutrients and herbal compounds possess powerful anti-inflammatory, antioxidant, and regenerative properties that support health at the cellular level. These plant-derived compounds are not only effective in reducing oxidative stress and inflammation but also play a critical role in disease prevention and longevity.

Modern medicine has often overlooked the healing power of nature in favor of pharmaceuticals that target symptoms rather than underlying causes. While pharmaceutical drugs can be life-saving, they often come with side effects and fail to address the root imbalances that contribute to chronic disease. In contrast, phytonutrients and herbal medicines work synergistically with the body, promoting natural healing processes and enhancing resilience against environmental and biological stressors.

One of the primary benefits of phytonutrients is their ability to reduce oxidative stress, a major driver of aging and disease. Oxidative stress occurs when there is an imbalance between free radicals—unstable molecules that damage cells—and the body's ability to neutralize them with antioxidants. When left unchecked, oxidative stress accelerates cellular aging, contributes to chronic inflammation, and increases the risk of diseases such as cancer, cardiovascular disorders, and neurodegenerative conditions.

Polyphenols and flavonoids, two major classes of phytonutrients, are among the most potent antioxidants found in nature. Polyphenols are widely distributed in plant-based foods, including berries, green tea, and dark chocolate, and have been shown to combat oxidative stress at a cellular level. Flavonoids, found in citrus fruits, onions, and cocoa, have strong anti-inflammatory effects and help protect cells from damage. These compounds have been extensively studied for their ability to enhance vascular health, improve immune function, and even support cognitive longevity by protecting neurons from degeneration.

Adaptogenic herbs, another class of powerful plant compounds, have been used for centuries in traditional medicine to enhance resilience to stress and support energy balance. Adaptogens such as ashwagandha, rhodiola, and ginseng help regulate the hypothalamic-pituitary-adrenal (HPA) axis, which controls the body's stress response. Chronic stress leads to elevated cortisol levels, which can weaken the immune system, disrupt metabolism, and accelerate aging. Adaptogens help modulate cortisol production, allowing the body to recover from stress more efficiently while preventing the long-term damage that chronic stress inflicts on cells and tissues.

Traditional medicine systems, including Ayurveda, Chinese medicine, and Western herbalism, have long recognized the profound impact of plant compounds on human health. Ayurveda, an ancient system of medicine from India, classifies herbs based on their energetic properties and their ability to balance the body's three doshas—Vata, Pitta, and Kapha. Herbs like turmeric, tulsi (holy basil), and triphala are revered for their anti-inflammatory, detoxifying, and rejuvenating effects. Turmeric, in particular, has been extensively studied for its active compound, curcumin, which has potent anti-inflammatory and antioxidant properties. Curcumin has been shown to modulate inflammatory pathways, support liver detoxification, and protect against neurodegenerative diseases such as Alzheimer's.

Chinese medicine has a rich history of using herbal formulations to restore harmony within the body. Herbs such as reishi mushroom, astragalus, and ginseng have been used for thousands of years to strengthen the immune system, increase vitality, and promote longevity. Reishi, known as the "mushroom of immortality," has been studied for its ability to enhance immune function, reduce inflammation, and protect against cancer. Astragalus is another key herb in Chinese medicine that supports immune resilience and has been shown to activate telomerase, an enzyme that protects the integrity of DNA and slows cellular aging.

Western herbalism has also contributed to the understanding and application of plant-based medicine. The use of elderberry for immune support, milk thistle for liver detoxification, and echinacea for respiratory health are just a few examples of how herbal medicine has been integrated into modern wellness practices. Many of these herbs have undergone rigorous scientific evaluation, confirming their efficacy and mechanisms of action.

Recent scientific breakthroughs have validated the powerful effects of specific phytonutrients in promoting longevity and preventing disease. Curcumin, the active compound in turmeric, has been found to inhibit nuclear factor-kappa B (NF-kB), a key regulator of inflammation. By suppressing NF-kB activity, curcumin helps protect cells from chronic inflammation, which is a major contributor to degenerative diseases. Studies have also shown that curcumin enhances the production of brain-derived neurotrophic factor (BDNF), a protein that supports neuronal growth and cognitive function.

Resveratrol, a polyphenol found in red grapes and berries, has gained attention for its ability to activate sirtuins, a family of proteins involved in cellular repair and longevity. Sirtuins play a crucial role in regulating metabolic processes, reducing inflammation, and promoting DNA stability. Resveratrol has been studied for its potential to extend lifespan by mimicking the effects of calorie restriction, a well-known intervention that has been shown to enhance longevity in multiple species.

Quercetin, a flavonoid found in apples, onions, and capers, is another phytonutrient with remarkable health benefits. It has been shown to have strong antiviral, anti-inflammatory, and immune-modulating effects. Quercetin inhibits histamine release, making it an effective natural remedy for allergies and immune hypersensitivity. Research has also suggested that quercetin can reduce the risk of cardiovascular disease by improving endothelial function and reducing arterial inflammation.

Medicinal mushrooms, including reishi, lion's mane, and chaga, offer another layer of protection against aging and disease. Lion's mane has been extensively researched for its neuroprotective properties, with studies showing that it stimulates the production of nerve growth factor (NGF), which is essential for the survival and function of neurons. NGF levels decline with age, contributing to cognitive decline and an increased risk of neurodegenerative disorders such as Alzheimer's and Parkinson's. By enhancing NGF production, lion's mane supports brain plasticity, memory retention, and overall cognitive longevity.

Chaga mushroom, often referred to as the "king of medicinal mushrooms," is rich in antioxidants and beta-glucans, which support immune function and protect against oxidative stress. Studies have found that chaga extracts possess anti-cancer properties, potentially inhibiting tumor growth by modulating immune system activity.

These scientific findings underscore the immense potential of phytonutrients and herbal medicine in promoting longevity, preventing chronic disease, and supporting overall well-being. Unlike synthetic pharmaceuticals that often target isolated pathways, plant compounds work in a holistic manner, addressing multiple biological processes simultaneously. This makes them particularly valuable for long-term health maintenance, as they do not merely suppress symptoms but instead restore balance at a foundational level.

The resurgence of interest in herbal medicine and phytonutrients is a testament to their effectiveness and the growing recognition that nature offers solutions that modern pharmaceuticals cannot always provide. Integrating these plant-based compounds into daily health practices can lead to profound improvements in vitality, resilience, and longevity. With ongoing scientific advancements, the potential for phytonutrients to revolutionize healthcare is becoming increasingly evident, bridging the gap between traditional wisdom and modern medicine.

The future of health and wellness lies in harnessing the power of nature's medicine. Rather than waiting for disease to develop, individuals can take proactive steps to support cellular health, modulate inflammation, and enhance longevity through the strategic use of phytonutrients and herbal compounds. The time has come to shift from a reactive model of healthcare to a proactive approach that empowers individuals to take control of their health with the wisdom of nature and the insights of modern science.

The human body is a remarkable system designed for self-repair and regeneration. Yet, as individuals age or experience chronic stress, poor nutrition, and environmental toxicity, their bodies' ability to heal diminishes. Traditional medicine often focuses on managing symptoms rather than addressing the root cause of organ dysfunction. While many people turn to supplements and dietary changes to support their health, few recognize the power of providing the body with the precise cellular materials it needs to rebuild damaged tissue. Protomorphogens, an advanced yet underutilized therapy in regenerative medicine, offer a revolutionary approach to healing at the cellular level by directly supplying the building blocks required for organ repair.

Protomorphogens represent a fundamental breakthrough in regenerative medicine by targeting damaged or weakened organs and stimulating their ability to rebuild themselves. Unlike standard vitamin and mineral supplementation, which supports general health but does not necessarily encourage direct tissue regeneration, protomorphogens work by providing the body with the exact cellular materials it needs to restore function. These specialized extracts, derived from healthy animal tissues, contain essential nucleoproteins and peptides that serve as templates for cellular repair. Rather than merely alleviating symptoms, they work at a foundational level to encourage proper organ function and renewal.

The science behind protomorphogens is rooted in the understanding that all tissues and organs contain specific genetic blueprints that dictate their function and structure. When an organ becomes damaged due to chronic inflammation, autoimmune dysfunction, or toxic exposure, its ability to repair itself is compromised. Protomorphogens act as a form of molecular signaling, instructing the body to initiate repair processes within the affected tissues. By supplying key regulatory factors from healthy tissues, these compounds help restore balance and optimize cellular function.

One of the most remarkable applications of protomorphogens is their ability to support kidney regeneration. The kidneys play a vital role in filtering waste, balancing electrolytes, and regulating blood pressure. When kidney function declines, whether due to chronic disease or acute injury, conventional medicine often focuses on symptom management rather than regeneration. Protomorphogen therapy provides the kidney cells with the necessary structural components to enhance their ability to repair themselves. Patients who have used kidney-specific protomorphogens have reported significant improvements in creatinine levels, reduced proteinuria, and increased energy, demonstrating that this approach has the potential to reverse early-stage kidney dysfunction and slow the progression of more advanced disease.

Liver regeneration is another area where protomorphogens have shown profound success. The liver is a highly resilient organ capable of regenerating even after substantial damage. However, chronic conditions such as fatty liver disease, hepatitis, and toxin exposure can impair its regenerative capabilities over time. Standard liver support supplements, such as milk thistle and glutathione precursors, provide antioxidant benefits but do not directly supply the structural elements required for tissue repair. Protomorphogens offer a more targeted approach by delivering the nucleoproteins necessary for rebuilding liver cells. Patients who have incorporated liver protomorphogen therapy into their health protocols have experienced improvements in liver enzyme levels, enhanced detoxification capacity, and relief from chronic fatigue and digestive issues.

Adrenal function is another critical area where protomorphogens demonstrate remarkable benefits. The adrenal glands are responsible for producing hormones that regulate stress, metabolism, and immune function. In today's world, chronic stress depletes adrenal reserves, leading to fatigue, brain fog, and hormonal imbalances. While adaptogenic herbs and B vitamins can support adrenal resilience, they do not directly rebuild adrenal tissue. Protomorphogens provide adrenal-specific cellular components that help restore glandular function at a much deeper level. Many individuals who have suffered from adrenal burnout have reported significant improvements in energy, mood stability, and immune resilience after using targeted adrenal protomorphogens.

Thyroid health is another area where this therapy has shown extraordinary promise. Thyroid disorders, including hypothyroidism and Hashimoto's thyroiditis, are becoming increasingly common due to environmental toxins, stress, and autoimmune dysfunction. Conventional treatments rely on hormone replacement therapy, which can help manage symptoms but does not restore thyroid function. Protomorphogens offer a different approach by supplying the thyroid with the specific nucleoproteins needed for tissue repair and hormone production. Many patients who have used thyroid protomorphogens alongside functional medicine protocols have reported reductions in fatigue, improved metabolic function, and decreased dependence on synthetic thyroid medications.

The key difference between standard organ support supplements and protomorphogen therapy lies in the method of action. Most supplements provide nutrients that help organs function more efficiently but do not directly contribute to tissue repair. Antioxidants, amino acids, and herbal compounds all play a role in cellular health, but they do not supply the fundamental building blocks necessary for organ regeneration. Protomorphogens, on the other hand, provide tissues with the precise molecular signals required for self-repair. This allows the body to rebuild damaged structures rather than merely compensating for dysfunction.

Another critical advantage of protomorphogens is their ability to support the immune system in cases of autoimmune-related organ dysfunction. Many chronic diseases stem from the immune system mistakenly attacking healthy tissues. This is particularly evident in conditions such as rheumatoid arthritis, multiple sclerosis, and Hashimoto's thyroiditis. Protomorphogens help retrain the immune system by providing organ-specific cellular components that modulate immune responses, reducing inflammation and slowing disease progression. Patients with autoimmune disorders who have integrated protomorphogen therapy into their treatment plans have often experienced significant reductions in symptoms, as well as improvements in overall organ function.

The future of regenerative medicine lies in harnessing the body's innate ability to heal itself. Protomorphogens represent an innovative step forward in this process, offering a precise, natural, and highly effective method for rebuilding organs at the cellular level. As more research emerges on the applications of protomorphogen therapy, it is becoming increasingly clear that this approach has the potential to transform how chronic disease is managed. Instead of merely slowing decline, regenerative medicine seeks to restore function, enhance longevity, and improve quality of life.

For individuals struggling with chronic organ dysfunction, protomorphogen therapy provides a compelling alternative to conventional treatments. Rather than resigning themselves to a lifetime of symptom management, patients now have the opportunity to actively rebuild and rejuvenate their bodies. The ability to supply the body with the exact cellular materials it needs for repair is a game-changer in modern healthcare. Those who incorporate this therapy into their wellness strategies may experience profound improvements in energy, resilience, and overall organ function.

The science of regenerative medicine is evolving rapidly, and protomorphogens are at the forefront of this transformation. The conventional medical model often underestimates the body's ability to heal, relying on medications and interventions that suppress symptoms rather than fostering true recovery. Protomorphogens shift this paradigm by aligning with the body's natural regenerative capabilities, providing the raw materials needed for long-term healing.

The best investment anyone can make in their health is in understanding the mechanisms that drive regeneration and longevity. Protomorphogens offer a direct path toward true healing by rebuilding what has been damaged and restoring function at the most fundamental level. Those who embrace this approach will not only recover from chronic illness but will also experience enhanced vitality, better resilience, and a stronger foundation for long-term health.

Regeneration is not a myth, nor is it something that only happens in extreme cases. The body is constantly repairing itself, and with the right support, it has the potential to rebuild even the most compromised tissues. Protomorphogens are the missing link in achieving this level of healing. By integrating them into a comprehensive wellness plan, individuals can harness the power of true organ repair and experience a new standard of health, vitality, and longevity.

The pursuit of longevity and peak performance has driven medical and scientific advancements for centuries. While traditional approaches to health and aging have focused on lifestyle, diet, and supplementation, the emergence of peptides as powerful biological messengers represents a revolutionary shift in how the body can be optimized for healing, performance, and lifespan extension. Peptides, which are short chains of amino acids, function as molecular signals that regulate a wide range of biological processes. These compounds stimulate cellular repair, enhance immune function, and modulate inflammation, making them a promising tool in age-reversal and disease prevention. As research continues to uncover the vast potential of peptide therapy, their role in regenerative medicine is becoming increasingly clear.

Peptides serve as the body's internal communication system, sending precise instructions to cells to perform specific tasks such as tissue repair, muscle growth, and neurological function. Unlike traditional pharmaceuticals that often work by blocking or altering biochemical pathways, peptides work with the body's natural mechanisms to restore balance and optimize function. This makes them highly effective while minimizing side effects. Their ability to target and enhance fundamental biological processes has made peptides a key area of focus in the fields of anti-aging medicine and performance enhancement.

One of the most exciting applications of peptides is their ability to boost growth hormone production, which plays a crucial role in tissue regeneration, muscle repair, and metabolic efficiency. As people age, growth hormone levels decline, leading to slower recovery from injuries, decreased muscle mass, and increased fat accumulation. Certain peptides, such as CJC-1295 and Ipamorelin, stimulate the release of growth hormone from the pituitary gland, mimicking the natural hormonal rhythms of youth. By enhancing growth hormone production, these peptides promote faster healing, improved physical performance, and overall cellular rejuvenation. Unlike synthetic growth hormone therapy, which can lead to imbalances and side effects, peptide-based growth hormone stimulators support the body's own endocrine function in a natural and sustainable way.

Peptides also play a significant role in tissue repair and inflammation reduction, making them a powerful tool for injury recovery and chronic disease management. BPC-157, a peptide derived from gastric proteins, has been extensively studied for its regenerative properties. It has been shown to accelerate the healing of muscles, tendons, and ligaments while also protecting the gastrointestinal tract from damage. BPC-157 works by promoting angiogenesis, the formation of new blood vessels, which enhances nutrient delivery to damaged tissues. It also modulates inflammatory pathways, reducing swelling and pain while speeding up recovery. Athletes and individuals with chronic musculoskeletal injuries have increasingly turned to BPC-157 as a natural and effective alternative to traditional pain management and rehabilitation strategies.

Another peptide with remarkable healing properties is Thymosin Beta-4, which plays a crucial role in immune modulation, cellular repair, and tissue regeneration. This peptide is naturally produced in the thymus gland and is essential for wound healing and immune system function. Thymosin Beta-4 has been found to promote stem cell migration to sites of injury, enhancing the body's ability to repair damaged tissues. Its role in immune regulation makes it particularly valuable for individuals dealing with chronic inflammatory conditions, autoimmune disorders, and compromised immune function. By reducing excessive inflammation and promoting cellular renewal, Thymosin Beta-4 supports both recovery and long-term health.

The impact of peptides extends beyond physical recovery and muscle regeneration; they also play a pivotal role in cognitive function and neuroprotection. The aging brain is particularly susceptible to oxidative stress, neuroinflammation, and mitochondrial dysfunction, all of which contribute to cognitive decline and neurodegenerative diseases. Peptides such as Epitalon have shown promise in extending lifespan and protecting against neurological deterioration. Epitalon, originally discovered in Russia, is a synthetic tetrapeptide that has been studied for its ability to regulate the pineal gland and increase the production of melatonin. Melatonin not only regulates sleep cycles but also acts as a powerful antioxidant in the brain, reducing neuroinflammation and supporting neuronal function. Epitalon has also been shown to lengthen telomeres, the protective caps at the ends of chromosomes that shorten with age. By preserving telomere length, Epitalon has the potential to slow down cellular aging and improve overall longevity.

The future of peptide therapy lies in its ability to address the underlying mechanisms of aging rather than merely treating symptoms. One of the most exciting frontiers in peptide research is its application in preventing neurodegeneration. Conditions such as Alzheimer's disease and Parkinson's disease are driven by chronic inflammation, mitochondrial dysfunction, and impaired protein clearance in the brain. Peptides that target these specific pathways, such as Cerebrolysin, have shown promise in enhancing cognitive function, promoting neuroplasticity, and reducing the accumulation of toxic proteins that contribute to neurodegenerative diseases. By improving mitochondrial efficiency and reducing oxidative stress, peptides may offer a new strategy for preserving brain health and preventing age-related cognitive decline.

Metabolic health is another area where peptides are demonstrating significant benefits. Insulin resistance, obesity, and metabolic syndrome are major contributors to aging and chronic disease. Peptides such as Tesamorelin and MOTS-c have been shown to enhance mitochondrial function, improve glucose metabolism, and regulate insulin sensitivity. By optimizing metabolic pathways, these peptides help individuals maintain healthy body composition, sustain energy levels, and reduce the risk of developing metabolic disorders. Rather than simply addressing symptoms with pharmaceuticals that often come with side effects, peptide therapy provides a targeted approach to restoring metabolic balance at a cellular level.

The ability of peptides to enhance longevity is not limited to internal physiological processes. Many peptides are now being explored for their impact on skin health, collagen production, and overall aesthetics. Peptides such as GHK-Cu, a copper-binding peptide, have been found to stimulate collagen synthesis, improve skin elasticity, and reduce the appearance of wrinkles. By enhancing cellular regeneration in the skin, peptides provide a natural approach to maintaining a youthful appearance without the need for invasive cosmetic procedures.

As peptide therapy continues to gain recognition, the challenge lies in ensuring accessibility, safety, and regulatory oversight. While peptides have been extensively studied in clinical and laboratory settings, their widespread use in mainstream medicine has been limited due to regulatory hurdles. Unlike pharmaceuticals, peptides are naturally occurring compounds that do not fit neatly into the conventional drug classification system. This has led to a lack of standardized dosing guidelines and inconsistent availability. However, as the demand for evidence-based regenerative therapies grows, the medical community is increasingly recognizing the need for further research and structured implementation of peptide-based interventions.

The future of peptide therapy is promising, offering new solutions for those seeking to optimize performance, reverse aging, and prevent disease. Unlike traditional approaches that focus on symptom management, peptides target the root causes of aging and degeneration at a cellular level. Their ability to enhance growth hormone production, accelerate tissue repair, improve cognitive function, and regulate metabolic health makes them one of the most powerful tools in modern longevity science.

For those looking to take control of their health and optimize longevity, understanding and integrating peptide therapy may be the key to unlocking their full potential. As research continues to evolve, peptides are set to become a cornerstone of regenerative medicine, transforming the way we approach aging, recovery, and overall well-being. The next frontier in healthcare is not just about extending lifespan but about enhancing healthspan—the ability to live longer while maintaining peak physical and mental performance. Peptides offer a pathway to achieving this goal, bridging the gap between science and longevity in a way that has never before been possible.

Longevity is no longer a vague aspiration or a hope for the distant future. The science of aging and regenerative medicine is evolving at an unprecedented rate, offering new tools to restore vitality, slow the aging process, and enhance both physical and mental performance. For decades, conventional medicine has approached health reactively, treating disease only after symptoms appear. But the future of medicine—and the future of true longevity—lies in a proactive approach that focuses on cellular repair, metabolic optimization, and precision-based nutrition. Those who embrace these advancements today will not only extend their lifespan but also ensure that the extra years are filled with energy, resilience, and the ability to thrive.

True longevity is not just about adding years to life but about adding life to years. Too many people spend their later decades battling chronic disease, struggling with fatigue, or living in a state of slow decline. The difference between those who deteriorate with age and those who maintain strength, mental clarity, and vitality is not simply a matter of genetics or luck—it is the result of deliberate choices made decades earlier. By focusing on regenerative therapies and strategic interventions, individuals can dramatically shift the trajectory of their health, delaying or even reversing the processes that lead to physical and cognitive decline.

The foundation of long-term health begins at the cellular level. Every biological function—from energy production to immune defense, detoxification, and tissue repair—is dictated by cellular efficiency. When cells are properly nourished and supported, they function optimally, allowing the body to repair damage, eliminate toxins, and maintain metabolic balance. However, when cellular function deteriorates, inflammation increases, DNA integrity is compromised, and the body becomes vulnerable to premature aging and disease. The secret to longevity lies in addressing these root causes before they become irreversible.

Dr. West's 25-year clinical formula is a roadmap for achieving this goal, blending functional medicine, precision-based nutrition, and cutting-edge regenerative therapies. This approach moves beyond simply managing symptoms and focuses on revitalizing the body from the inside out. It is based on the understanding that aging is not an inevitable decline but a dynamic process that can be influenced, slowed, and even reversed through targeted interventions.

One of the key pillars of longevity is proactive cellular support. Essential nutrients such as magnesium, zinc, vitamin D, and B vitamins are foundational for cellular energy, mitochondrial efficiency, and immune resilience. Deficiencies in these key nutrients accelerate the aging process by impairing detoxification pathways, reducing metabolic flexibility, and increasing systemic inflammation. Conventional medicine often underestimates the impact of subclinical deficiencies, failing to recognize that even mild imbalances can significantly affect long-term health. Functional medicine prioritizes optimal nutrient levels rather than simply avoiding outright deficiencies, ensuring that the body has the raw materials it needs to function at peak capacity for decades to come.

Beyond micronutrients, regenerative therapies play a crucial role in slowing the biological clock. Peptide therapy, for example, has emerged as one of the most promising advancements in anti-aging medicine, offering targeted interventions that enhance tissue repair, boost growth hormone production, and improve cognitive function. Peptides such as BPC-157 and Thymosin Beta-4 accelerate wound healing, reduce inflammation, and support immune function, making them powerful tools for maintaining longevity at the cellular level. Similarly, protomorphogens, the building blocks of organ regeneration, are revolutionizing how the body can restore damaged tissues and reverse degenerative conditions before they become life-threatening.

Precision-based nutrition is another cornerstone of longevity. The one-size-fits-all approach to diet and supplementation is outdated, as individual metabolic needs vary based on genetics, environment, and lifestyle factors. Personalized health assessments allow individuals to identify specific deficiencies, hormonal imbalances, and inflammatory markers, guiding the development of a targeted protocol that enhances metabolic efficiency and prevents age-related decline. This approach not only optimizes energy production and cognitive function but also reduces the risk of chronic conditions such as cardiovascular disease, diabetes, and neurodegenerative disorders.

The most common mistake people make when it comes to longevity is waiting too long to take action. Many assume that because they feel fine today, they do not need to prioritize proactive health strategies. But the truth is, by the time symptoms appear, the body has often been compensating for imbalances for years, if not decades. The key to longevity is not reacting to disease but preventing it through continuous monitoring, strategic adjustments, and early interventions.

The future of longevity is now. The knowledge and technology to extend healthspan and improve quality of life already exist, but they require a shift in mindset. Instead of viewing aging as an inevitable decline, it must be seen as a process that can be actively influenced. Those who embrace this approach will not only live longer but will enjoy more years of strength, vitality, and independence.

The next step is clear. Do not wait for illness to dictate the course of your life. Take charge of your biological future by implementing the principles of cellular repair, metabolic optimization, and regenerative medicine. Start by testing and tracking key health markers, identifying potential deficiencies, and making the necessary changes before disease ever has a chance to develop. Invest in your health now, because the decisions made today will determine the quality of life in the decades ahead.

The difference between merely existing and truly thriving is found in the choices made long before the body begins to decline. By prioritizing longevity now—through precision-based nutrition, regenerative therapies, and proactive cellular support—it is possible to rewrite the aging process. The future belongs to those who take control of their health today. The question is not if longevity can be improved, but whether you will take the steps necessary to make it a reality. The opportunity is here, the science is available, and the time to act is now.

8

The Mind-Body Connection: The Hidden Key to Longevity and Success

Imagine waking up every morning with boundless energy, mental clarity, and a body that moves effortlessly through the day. Picture feeling completely in control of your health, knowing that your mind and body are operating at peak performance. Now, consider the opposite—dragging yourself out of bed, battling fatigue, struggling to focus, and dealing with chronic aches and pains that seem to appear out of nowhere. For far too many people, the latter scenario is their daily reality. The difference between these two experiences is not luck or genetics; it is the result of conscious choices made over time. Health is not something that simply happens—it is an asset that must be actively built, maintained, and protected.

For years, health has been framed in terms of numbers on lab tests, lists of supplements, and dietary fads that promise quick fixes. But the truth is, true wellness goes far beyond lab results. It is not just about what you eat, what you take, or what your blood work shows. It is about how you feel, how you think, and how you take care of yourself. It is about the resilience of your mind, the balance of your emotions, and the daily choices that determine the trajectory of your well-being. It is about recognizing that optimizing your body is no different than managing a billion-dollar portfolio—except that you are the most important investment you will ever make.

The modern world constantly pushes the idea that success is measured by external achievements—money, career milestones, or material possessions. But none of those matter without health. People spend decades building wealth, only to spend that wealth trying to regain their health when it begins to fail. The real secret to long-term success and happiness lies in prioritizing health before it becomes a problem. Longevity, energy, and vitality are not accidental; they are the result of deliberate effort. Investing in your well-being does not just mean preventing illness—it means thriving, having the stamina, mental sharpness, and emotional resilience to fully engage with life at every stage.

One of the biggest misconceptions about health is that it is simply a physical state, dictated by genetics or luck. But in reality, health is a dynamic and holistic system that encompasses far more than physical biomarkers. The state of the mind influences the state of the body, and vice versa. Chronic stress, unresolved emotional trauma, and mental fatigue all take a toll on physical health, increasing inflammation, weakening immune function, and accelerating aging. Optimizing health requires looking beyond nutrition and exercise; it requires acknowledging the role that mental resilience and emotional balance play in long-term well-being.

Mental resilience is one of the most overlooked pillars of health. The ability to adapt, to manage stress, and to maintain a positive, solution-focused mindset directly impacts physical health. Chronic stress floods the body with cortisol, disrupts sleep, and contributes to metabolic dysfunction. When stress is left unchecked, it creates the perfect storm for chronic disease. But resilience—the ability to navigate challenges with confidence and adaptability—can be cultivated through deliberate practices. Meditation, breathwork, and mindfulness are not just relaxation techniques; they are powerful tools for recalibrating the nervous system, improving immune function, and fostering long-term vitality.

Emotional balance is just as critical. Suppressed emotions, unresolved conflicts, and negative thought patterns create physiological stress that wears down the body over time. Studies have shown that people who experience chronic loneliness or emotional distress have higher levels of inflammation, greater risk of cardiovascular disease, and shorter lifespans. Conversely, those who prioritize emotional well-being—through deep social connections, self-awareness, and emotional processing—tend to live longer, healthier lives. Cultivating emotional balance is not a luxury; it is a requirement for optimal health.

Self-care, often dismissed as an indulgence, is actually one of the most strategic investments a person can make. It is the maintenance required to keep the body and mind functioning at peak levels. Sleep, for example, is not just a passive state but a biological reset button that allows for cellular repair, detoxification, and memory consolidation. Yet, in a culture that glorifies overwork, sleep is often sacrificed, leading to a slow but steady decline in metabolic health, cognitive function, and immune resilience. Nutrition, movement, and relaxation are all forms of self-care that fuel longevity, yet they are often treated as optional rather than essential. True self-care is not about occasional treats or spa days; it is about consistently providing the body and mind with what they need to thrive.

One of the biggest barriers to optimal health is the belief that it requires perfection. Many people avoid making changes because they feel overwhelmed by the idea of doing everything "right." But health is not about perfection—it is about progress. Small, consistent improvements lead to exponential gains over time. A single night of good sleep improves immune function. One nutrient-rich meal provides cells with what they need to repair. A few minutes of deep breathing can lower cortisol and recalibrate the nervous system. These small wins, when repeated consistently, create a compounding effect that leads to profound transformation.

The most successful people in the world understand that their health is their most valuable asset. They track their performance, they fine-tune their routines, and they make adjustments based on what their body needs. They do not wait until something is wrong; they take proactive measures to ensure they remain at the top of their game. This is the mindset that separates those who merely survive from those who thrive.

Waiting until symptoms appear before prioritizing health is the biggest mistake people make. By the time an issue is felt, it has often been developing beneath the surface for years. Energy crashes, brain fog, digestive issues, and mood instability are early warning signs that the body is out of balance. These symptoms are not nuisances to ignore but messages that something needs to change. Addressing them before they escalate is the key to avoiding more serious health challenges in the future.

Health is a long-term strategy, not a short-term fix. It requires ongoing adjustments, continuous learning, and a commitment to self-awareness. Just as an investor would never make decisions based on a single stock price but instead evaluates trends over time, a person's approach to health should be based on tracking progress, making data-driven adjustments, and taking a proactive stance toward longevity.

The world is filled with distractions and demands that pull people away from prioritizing their well-being. But the truth remains: nothing matters without health. No achievement, no amount of success, no external validation can replace the ability to wake up every day feeling strong, clear-minded, and energized. The best investment anyone can make is in their own body and mind. The return on this investment is not just more years of life—it is a better quality of life.

The time to take control of health is now. Not tomorrow. Not when life slows down. Not when the next health scare forces action. Now. Because every choice made today determines the trajectory of the future. The decision to prioritize resilience, balance, and self-care is not just about feeling good in the present; it is about ensuring vitality, longevity, and the ability to show up fully in every aspect of life. The future belongs to those who invest in themselves—physically, mentally, and emotionally. The question is, will you make the investment?

At the core of health, longevity, and personal fulfillment is a truth that many people overlook: self-worth is not a luxury but a necessity. Without it, every attempt at self-improvement—whether through diet, exercise, or stress management—becomes a battle against one's own subconscious beliefs. The way a person sees themselves, how they value their own needs, and how much they prioritize their well-being are not just emotional or psychological concerns; they are biological imperatives. The body and mind function optimally when they are supported by a strong foundation of self-worth, yet many individuals continue to place themselves last, believing that prioritizing their health is selfish or indulgent. Nothing could be further from the truth. The first and most critical step in achieving lasting health and longevity is recognizing that you are the most important investment you will ever make.

You are the CEO of your own health. No doctor, coach, or expert can do the work for you. Just as a business leader would never allow their company to run on autopilot without oversight, your body and mind require the same level of attention, strategy, and care. Many people go through life expecting that their health will take care of itself as long as nothing catastrophic happens. But in reality, waiting until a crisis forces change is the exact reason so many people struggle with chronic illness, burnout, and premature aging. Leading a thriving, healthy life requires an active approach, one that involves making conscious choices every day to nourish the body, protect mental well-being, and cultivate emotional resilience.

One of the biggest mindset shifts in the journey to health and longevity is recognizing that self-worth is not arrogance. Many people, conditioned by cultural and social expectations, associate self-care with selfishness. They believe that putting their own needs first is somehow wrong, that prioritizing their physical and mental health makes them self-absorbed. This belief is deeply flawed and is one of the greatest obstacles to achieving lasting health. Liking oneself is not about vanity or self-importance; it is about understanding that you matter. Your body, your mind, and your emotional well-being deserve care, and no one else can provide that for you.

Every time an individual dismisses their own needs, sacrifices rest for productivity, or puts off self-care in the name of being "too busy," they reinforce the belief that they are not a priority. Over time, this mindset erodes not only emotional health but also physical well-being.

Stress accumulates, sleep deprivation takes its toll, and the immune system weakens. People who consistently put themselves last often experience higher levels of chronic inflammation, increased risk of cardiovascular disease, and accelerated aging. The body interprets chronic self-neglect as a sign that it is under constant threat, triggering a physiological stress response that damages cells, disrupts hormone balance, and weakens immune function.

One of the most insidious barriers to self-worth is comparison syndrome. In today's world of social media, curated highlight reels, and relentless competition, it has never been easier to fall into the trap of comparing oneself to others. This constant measurement against external benchmarks is a direct assault on both mental and physical health. Comparison is the thief of joy, but it is also the thief of energy, focus, and longevity. The moment a person starts believing that they are not good enough because they do not measure up to someone else's success, appearance, or achievements, they enter a state of chronic stress that has tangible biological consequences.

Comparison-driven stress activates the same physiological pathways as physical danger. The brain does not differentiate between an immediate threat to survival and the social pressure of feeling inadequate. In response, it releases cortisol, the body's primary stress hormone, which in small doses is useful but in excess becomes toxic. Chronically elevated cortisol levels lead to systemic inflammation, impaired immune function, and disrupted brain chemistry. People who engage in frequent self-comparison experience higher rates of anxiety, depression, and fatigue because their nervous system is in a constant state of fight-or-flight. Over time, this stress contributes to the breakdown of cellular function, increasing the risk of conditions such as metabolic syndrome, neurodegeneration, and autoimmune disorders.

The scientific impact of comparison syndrome extends far beyond emotional distress. Studies have shown that individuals who frequently compare themselves to others exhibit higher levels of pro-inflammatory markers, which accelerate aging and increase vulnerability to disease. Chronic stress triggered by self-comparison can alter the gut microbiome, leading to digestive issues, nutrient malabsorption, and increased susceptibility to illness. The brain also suffers, as stress-induced inflammation disrupts neurotransmitter balance, impairing mood regulation, memory, and decision-making.

Escaping the trap of comparison and reclaiming self-worth is one of the most powerful steps toward long-term health. The antidote to comparison is self-compassion—the ability to see oneself as valuable and worthy without needing external validation. Cultivating self-compassion does not mean avoiding self-improvement; it means approaching personal growth from a place of self-respect rather than self-criticism. Instead of constantly measuring progress against others, it means focusing on individual growth, recognizing strengths, and making peace with imperfections.

Building self-worth is not just about mindset; it requires tangible action. It means creating non-negotiable habits that reinforce the belief that personal well-being is a priority. This includes setting boundaries that protect mental and physical health, making time for activities that nourish the body, and surrounding oneself with people who uplift rather than diminish. It also means re-evaluating the subconscious beliefs that drive behavior. Many people operate under outdated narratives about success, productivity, and self-sacrifice that keep them stuck in cycles of burnout. Recognizing and rewriting these narratives is essential for breaking free from comparison-driven stress and reclaiming control over health.

The true path to longevity and wellness begins with recognizing that health is not something to be earned only after reaching a certain level of success. It is the foundation upon which all success is built. No amount of wealth, achievement, or recognition can replace the ability to wake up every day feeling energized, clear-minded, and physically strong. Prioritizing health is not a reward for hard work; it is the prerequisite for a life of fulfillment, joy, and sustained performance.

The question is not whether self-worth matters—it does. The real question is whether you will take the necessary steps to embody that truth. Will you continue to put yourself last, allowing stress, comparison, and self-doubt to erode your well-being? Or will you make the decision today to invest in yourself, recognizing that prioritizing your health is the most important commitment you will ever make? The future of your health is determined not by external circumstances, but by the choices you make every single day. You are the CEO of your health. No one else can make these decisions for you. The time to take ownership is now. The best investment you will ever make is in yourself.

Success, whether in health, business, or personal fulfillment, is rarely determined by external factors alone. The difference between those who thrive and those who struggle is not just their diet, exercise, or financial strategies, but something deeper—their mindset. The world's healthiest, wealthiest, and most successful individuals have an internal blueprint that governs how they think, react, and adapt to life's challenges. Their habits, self-talk, and beliefs shape their reality, influencing not only their emotional well-being but also their physical health, longevity, and capacity for peak performance.

The foundation of long-term health is built within the mind. While modern medicine focuses largely on physical markers—lab results, genetic predispositions, and biomarkers of disease—there is an undeniable connection between mental resilience and physical vitality. Research consistently shows that stress, negative thought patterns, and unresolved emotional trauma are some of the biggest contributors to chronic disease, premature aging, and even immune suppression. On the other hand, individuals who cultivate emotional intelligence, stress management techniques, and a high-performance mindset often experience faster healing, better energy, and greater longevity.

A strong mental foundation is not just about avoiding anxiety or depression. It is about developing an internal state that supports healing, enhances physical function, and strengthens resilience in the face of adversity. The body follows the mind, and those who master their mental landscape gain an unmatched advantage in both health and life.

One of the most overlooked yet powerful performance enhancers is spirituality and mindfulness. Whether through prayer, meditation, or deep self-reflection, engaging in a practice that strengthens the mind-body connection has been shown to improve immune function, lower inflammation, and enhance cognitive clarity. In a world that glorifies productivity, people often neglect the profound benefits of stillness. Studies reveal that regular meditation can reduce cortisol, improve cardiovascular health, and even slow the aging of the brain. Prayer, when practiced with intention, has similar effects, promoting inner peace and resilience against stress. These are not just esoteric practices reserved for monks or the deeply religious—they are tools for high performance, longevity, and sustainable health.

Breathing techniques are another underestimated tool for optimizing both mental and physical health. While breathwork is often associated with relaxation, its effects extend far beyond simple stress reduction. Controlled breathing influences the autonomic nervous system, shifting the body out of a chronic stress state and into one of regeneration and repair. Techniques such as diaphragmatic breathing, box breathing, and alternate nostril breathing have been used for centuries to regulate heart rate, improve oxygen utilization, and enhance mental clarity. When used strategically, breathwork can sharpen focus, support cardiovascular health, and even boost athletic performance.

Positive self-talk is one of the most transformative habits a person can cultivate. The way individuals speak to themselves on a daily basis has a direct impact on their neurobiology, influencing the release of stress hormones, neurotransmitters, and immune function. Negative self-talk—filled with doubt, fear, or self-criticism—creates a physiological response that weakens the immune system and increases inflammation. In contrast, individuals who reprogram their inner dialogue for confidence, gratitude, and self-empowerment experience greater resilience, better health outcomes, and a more fulfilling life.

The brain is constantly rewiring itself based on repeated thought patterns. This concept, known as neuroplasticity, means that no matter how deeply ingrained certain beliefs or self-perceptions are, they can be changed. By consciously replacing negative thought loops with positive affirmations, individuals can reshape their subconscious mind to support health and high performance. This is not about blind optimism but about choosing thoughts that fuel strength rather than weakness.

Mental and emotional resilience are not inherited traits; they are cultivated skills. The ability to remain calm under pressure, recover from setbacks, and maintain an unwavering belief in one's potential is what separates those who thrive from those who merely survive. Resilient individuals do not crumble under stress because they have trained their minds to respond with clarity rather than panic. They understand that while they cannot always control external circumstances, they can always control their reaction to them.

Physical health and mental resilience are deeply intertwined. Chronic stress leads to inflammation, which is one of the primary drivers of degenerative disease. Anxiety and fear trigger the release of stress hormones that impair digestion, suppress the immune system, and disrupt sleep patterns. Conversely, individuals who cultivate emotional balance through mindfulness, self-awareness, and strategic mental conditioning are able to keep their bodies in a state of repair and regeneration rather than chronic breakdown.

Developing a high-performance mindset requires daily commitment. Just as muscles strengthen with consistent training, mental resilience is built through repeated habits that reinforce a state of balance and strength. Journaling, visualization, and gratitude practices are among the most effective tools for rewiring the brain toward a positive and empowered state. When individuals intentionally focus on what is going well, rather than dwelling on problems, they create a biochemical environment that supports healing and growth.

The most successful individuals do not wait until they are overwhelmed to implement these strategies. They integrate them into their daily routine, making emotional resilience and mental conditioning a non-negotiable part of their lives. They understand that high performance is not just about working harder but about thinking smarter, regulating emotions, and optimizing stress responses.

The true key to long-term success and fulfillment is not found in external achievements but in inner mastery. Those who learn to master their emotions, direct their thoughts, and condition their mindset for resilience gain an advantage in every area of life. They do not let challenges dictate their actions; they dictate how they respond to challenges.

The path to longevity and high performance is not just about physical interventions like nutrition, exercise, or supplements. It is about retraining the mind to operate from a place of strength rather than survival. Every thought, every belief, and every mental habit either moves a person closer to health or further away from it.

Those who prioritize mental and emotional resilience will not only live longer but will experience a richer, more fulfilling existence. They will have the energy to pursue their passions, the strength to navigate adversity, and the clarity to make decisions that align with their highest potential.

The best investment a person can make is not in external assets but in their own mind. This is the blueprint for high performance, resilience, and lifelong vitality. The world's healthiest and most successful individuals understand that the mind is the foundation for everything. Those who choose to cultivate it will always have the advantage.

The human body is designed to adapt, evolve, and overcome challenges. At its core, survival depends on resilience—both physical and mental. In a world where comfort is abundant and stress is often viewed as the enemy, many people have lost touch with the fundamental truth that controlled stress builds strength. The science of hormesis reveals that exposing the body to carefully managed stressors—like cold, heat, and intense physical exertion—forces it to adapt, becoming more resilient, efficient, and energized.

Modern lifestyles are filled with conveniences that shield people from discomfort. Central heating ensures homes remain at a comfortable temperature year-round, food is readily available without the need for physical exertion, and relaxation is prioritized over physical hardship. But the price of this comfort is a body that is less capable, less adaptable, and more vulnerable to disease, inflammation, and fatigue. The answer is not to reject modern convenience but to reintroduce controlled stress into daily life to strengthen the body's natural defenses and restore vitality.

Cold exposure and heat therapy are two of the most powerful and accessible tools for resetting the nervous system, enhancing recovery, and building resilience. Ice baths, cryotherapy, saunas, and red light therapy provide a simple yet profound way to tap into the body's innate ability to heal, adapt, and grow stronger. While they offer measurable physiological benefits—boosting immune function, enhancing circulation, and reducing inflammation—the real power of these therapies lies in what they do for mental toughness.

Few things test the mind and body as instantly as stepping into ice-cold water. The moment cold envelops the skin, the nervous system reacts, triggering an immediate fight-or-flight response. The heart rate spikes, breathing becomes rapid, and every instinct urges an escape from the discomfort. But learning to control that reaction, to breathe through the initial shock and remain calm, is where the magic happens.

Cold exposure is one of the most effective ways to train the vascular system, boost metabolism, and sharpen mental focus. The shock of cold water forces blood vessels to constrict, then dilate upon warming, effectively exercising the vascular system much like lifting weights strengthens muscles. Over time, this improves circulation, enhances cardiovascular health, and increases overall endurance. Ice baths also trigger the release of cold shock proteins, which help protect and repair cells, reducing inflammation and promoting recovery.

Beyond the physical benefits, ice baths cultivate mental resilience. The discipline required to step into the cold, night after night, is a powerful exercise in controlling the mind's response to discomfort. The moment before entering the water, doubt creeps in, every excuse surfaces, and the mind resists. But learning to silence that inner hesitation and commit anyway is a lesson in mental toughness that carries over into every aspect of life.

The Man Up Ice Bath Club was born from this idea—an accountability system built around the power of doing hard things together. A group of like-minded individuals meeting nightly to embrace the discomfort, to push through resistance, and to become tougher, both physically and mentally. The goal is not just physiological health but a daily practice of proving to oneself that they can endure discomfort and emerge stronger.

The ice bath is a reminder that challenges will come, that stress is inevitable, and that overcoming discomfort is not just possible—it is necessary. Every night, stepping into the cold is an act of choosing strength over ease, discipline over avoidance, and growth over stagnation. The true reward is not just improved circulation or faster recovery; it is the knowledge that you are capable of handling anything that comes your way.

While cold exposure forces adaptation through constriction and shock, heat therapy triggers adaptation through relaxation and expansion. The human body thrives on cycles of stress and recovery, and heat provides an essential counterbalance to the intensity of cold exposure. Saunas, infrared heat, and red light therapy activate detoxification pathways, improve cardiovascular function, and support deep relaxation.

The benefits of heat therapy are well-documented. Regular sauna use has been linked to reduced cardiovascular disease, improved circulation, and enhanced muscle recovery. Heat causes blood vessels to expand, increasing blood flow and allowing the body to flush out metabolic waste more efficiently. Sweating is one of the body's most powerful detox mechanisms, helping to eliminate heavy metals, environmental toxins, and inflammatory byproducts.

Red light therapy takes the benefits of heat exposure even further by stimulating cellular repair and energy production. Using specific wavelengths of light, this therapy penetrates deep into the skin, activating mitochondria to produce more ATP—the energy currency of the body. This boost in cellular energy accelerates tissue healing, reduces inflammation, and improves skin health.

Heat therapy is not just about relaxation—it is about training the body to handle stress and recover efficiently. The alternating use of heat and cold forces the nervous system to become more adaptable, more efficient, and more capable of handling physiological and psychological stressors.

The body is constantly responding to signals—some from within, some from the environment. The nervous system controls how stress is managed, how recovery occurs, and how energy is distributed. When the nervous system is overloaded with chronic stress, poor sleep, and environmental toxins, it becomes dysregulated, leading to fatigue, brain fog, and inflammation.

Cold exposure and heat therapy act as a reset button for the nervous system. They teach the body to handle stress more effectively, improving heart rate variability, reducing cortisol levels, and enhancing sleep quality. By repeatedly exposing the body to short, controlled bursts of intense stress, these therapies train the nervous system to recover faster and perform better.

The real reward is not just the physical benefits—it is the transformation that occurs in the mindset. Each ice bath is a lesson in discipline. Each sauna session is an investment in long-term health. Every session of red light therapy is a commitment to cellular regeneration. This process rewires the nervous system to become stronger, more adaptable, and more resistant to both physical and mental fatigue.

Longevity, energy, and mental toughness are not given; they are built. In a world that prioritizes ease and comfort, those who intentionally embrace controlled stress gain an unmatched advantage. The choice to step into discomfort, to train the nervous system, and to push through resistance is not just about health—it is about creating an unbreakable foundation of resilience that carries into every area of life.

The next step is not waiting for stress to break you down. It is choosing to strengthen your body and mind before challenges arise. It is making recovery an intentional practice, not an afterthought. It is about integrating these tools—cold exposure, heat therapy, and nervous system training—into your daily routine. The people who thrive are not those who avoid stress, but those who train themselves to handle it with strength and clarity.

Every night, the ice bath is waiting. Every sauna session is an opportunity. Every choice to embrace discomfort is a step toward becoming tougher, stronger, and more resilient. The question is not whether these tools work. The question is, will you use them? The decision to take control of your health, your mindset, and your resilience begins now.

Modern life glorifies productivity, treating busyness as a badge of honor. Society applauds the relentless grind, rewarding those who sacrifice sleep, rest, and enjoyment in pursuit of their goals. Success, in this framework, is measured not by joy or fulfillment but by external achievements—promotions, financial milestones, and an ever-growing to-do list. The workaholic culture has convinced people that slowing down is a weakness and that leisure is a luxury for the undisciplined. Yet, this mindset is one of the greatest barriers to true health and well-being. The obsession with productivity is not just mentally and emotionally exhausting; it is physically destructive. Constant pushing, stress, and deprivation of joy prevent true healing, disrupt the nervous system, and accelerate the very burnout that so many high achievers work tirelessly to avoid.

The idea that healing is only about nutrition, exercise, and medical interventions is incomplete. While those elements are critical, they fail to address a deeper truth: the human body and mind thrive not just on discipline but on joy, connection, and play. The science of longevity, resilience, and peak performance consistently demonstrates that those who incorporate play, creativity, and leisure into their lives outperform those who drive themselves into exhaustion. The very activities that seem frivolous—laughing, painting, playing music, engaging in sports for fun rather than competition—are the ones that optimize brain function, regulate stress hormones, and support recovery at the deepest level.

The workaholic trap is a powerful and seductive illusion. It convinces people that they are just one more task away from success, that if they can push a little harder, they will finally achieve the freedom, recognition, or stability they crave. This mentality creates a never-ending cycle of striving, where no accomplishment is ever enough because there is always something more to do. Many high achievers fall into this trap, believing that their worth is directly tied to their output. They ignore the warning signs—fatigue, irritability, loss of motivation—until their bodies force them to stop. Chronic stress leads to hormonal imbalances, suppressed immune function, and neurological dysfunction, yet people continue to push forward, mistakenly believing that rest will set them back rather than propel them forward.

Healing requires a shift in mindset. It is not about doing more but about doing what truly matters. It is about understanding that rest, joy, and creativity are not indulgences but biological imperatives. The nervous system, which governs everything from digestion to immune response, operates in two primary states: fight-or-flight and rest-and-repair. Constant stress keeps the body in a heightened state of alertness, flooding the system with cortisol and adrenaline while suppressing the body's ability to regenerate. Play and creativity act as counterbalances to this stress response, activating the parasympathetic nervous system, which is responsible for recovery and cellular repair.

The science of play is profound. When people engage in hobbies and activities that bring them joy, the brain releases a cascade of neurotransmitters, including dopamine, serotonin, and oxytocin. These chemicals regulate mood, reduce inflammation, and enhance cognitive function. Play has been shown to improve problem-solving skills, boost creativity, and strengthen neural pathways that enhance adaptability and resilience. Engaging in creative activities, such as painting, writing, or playing an instrument, stimulates neuroplasticity, allowing the brain to form new connections that improve mental agility and emotional well-being. Studies have demonstrated that those who engage in regular creative pursuits show lower levels of stress, better immune function, and even increased longevity.

High achievers who recognize the power of play and rest do not just live longer; they perform better. The misconception that rest is the enemy of success is one of the most damaging myths of modern life. Some of the most successful individuals in history—scientists, entrepreneurs, artists, and athletes—have understood that their best ideas and greatest breakthroughs often come not from working harder but from stepping away, allowing their minds to wander, and giving themselves the space to recharge.

Albert Einstein, one of the greatest minds in history, often spoke of the importance of play and curiosity. He credited much of his scientific insight to his ability to think like a child, to engage in playful exploration rather than rigid problem-solving. His breakthroughs were not born from relentless struggle but from a mind that was free to imagine and create. Similarly, many of the most successful entrepreneurs build play and leisure into their schedules, understanding that their ability to innovate depends on maintaining a state of mental flexibility and joy.

Athletes, too, understand the power of recovery. The best in the world do not train at full intensity every single day. They incorporate active rest, play, and mental relaxation into their routines because they know that growth happens in recovery, not just in exertion. The same principle applies to anyone striving for high performance in any field. Without rest, without moments of joy, the body and mind break down.

Yet, despite the overwhelming evidence, many people resist integrating play and creativity into their lives. They believe that taking time for themselves is selfish or unproductive. They feel guilty for doing something that is not directly tied to their goals. But this guilt is misplaced. The truth is that rest is not a break from progress; it is part of progress. When people allow themselves to experience joy, when they engage in activities that make them feel alive, they are not losing time—they are extending it. They are preventing burnout, optimizing their health, and ensuring that they can continue to show up fully for the things that matter most.

True success is not achieved by grinding until there is nothing left to give. It is achieved by cultivating a lifestyle that supports longevity, creativity, and resilience. Those who integrate fun, play, and creativity into their lives do not just feel better; they achieve more. They make better decisions, solve problems more effectively, and maintain a level of energy and focus that those stuck in the workaholic trap can never sustain.

The challenge is not simply to work less; it is to work better. It is to understand that health is a holistic system that requires nourishment on every level—physical, mental, emotional, and spiritual. The lost art of fun must be reclaimed, not just as a concept but as a fundamental part of a healthy life. Play is not a waste of time. Creativity is not a distraction. Joy is not optional. These are the elements that make life worth living, and they are also the elements that make healing and high performance possible.

The invitation is simple. Step away from the endless cycle of busyness. Give yourself permission to engage in something purely for the joy of it. Let your mind wander, let your body move freely, let yourself experience life beyond your obligations. The more you embrace fun, the more you will realize that it was never a luxury—it was always a necessity. The key to longevity, healing, and true success is not in working yourself to the bone but in understanding that play is one of the most powerful tools for transformation.

The most important investment you can make is in your well-being, and that includes making space for joy. The question is not whether you have time for play, creativity, and leisure. The question is whether you can afford not to. The cost of ignoring this truth is too high. The time to reclaim the lost art of fun is now.

The foundation of health extends beyond nutrition, exercise, and medical interventions. True well-being is a reflection of the mind-body connection, a delicate balance between mental resilience, emotional stability, and daily self-care rituals that nourish both the brain and the nervous system. The ability to manage stress, cultivate gratitude, engage in restorative practices, and set boundaries is as critical to longevity as any supplement or laboratory test. In a world filled with distractions, external pressures, and relentless digital stimulation, building a mental and emotional wealth plan is not just beneficial—it is essential.

Health is often measured in physical terms—blood markers, energy levels, and organ function—but the state of the mind directly influences the state of the body. Chronic stress weakens the immune system, unchecked anxiety fuels systemic inflammation, and emotional distress depletes energy at a cellular level. When mental and emotional well-being are neglected, even the best physical health strategies will fall short. The mind is not separate from the body; it is the command center that dictates everything from metabolic function to immune resilience. Without a structured approach to mental and emotional well-being, long-term vitality is unsustainable.

One of the most powerful ways to cultivate a strong mind-body connection is through the practice of morning gratitude and visualization. How the mind is primed in the first few minutes of the day sets the tone for everything that follows. Neuroscientific research has shown that practicing gratitude shifts brain chemistry, enhancing dopamine and serotonin levels while reducing stress hormones like cortisol. When the mind begins the day focused on abundance and possibility, it creates a ripple effect, influencing energy levels, cognitive function, and emotional stability. Visualization amplifies this process by activating the brain's reticular activating system, a network of neurons responsible for filtering and prioritizing information. By visualizing success, health, and a state of calm, the brain begins to seek and reinforce those outcomes, turning thoughts into reality through neuroplasticity.

Breathwork and meditation serve as powerful tools for stress management and focus. Breath is one of the few bodily functions that can be controlled consciously, and through intentional breathing techniques, the nervous system can be regulated in profound ways. Shallow, erratic breathing is a marker of stress, triggering the sympathetic nervous system, also known as the fight-or-flight response. In contrast, deep, controlled breathing activates the parasympathetic nervous system, shifting the body into a state of repair, digestion, and relaxation. Practices such as diaphragmatic breathing, box breathing, and alternate nostril breathing have been shown to lower blood pressure, reduce inflammation, and increase heart rate variability—a key indicator of resilience and longevity.

Meditation further enhances mental clarity, emotional regulation, and stress resilience. Contrary to common misconceptions, meditation is not about clearing the mind but rather about training attention and awareness. By regularly engaging in meditation, the prefrontal cortex—the region responsible for decision-making, focus, and emotional control—becomes stronger, while the amygdala—the part of the brain that triggers fear and anxiety—becomes less reactive. This shift enhances the ability to respond to challenges with composure rather than reactivity. Even a few minutes of meditation per day can rewire neural pathways, creating lasting changes in mental and emotional health.

The body thrives when it is exposed to adaptive stressors, challenges that force it to become stronger and more resilient. One of the most effective ways to reset the nervous system is through controlled exposure to extreme temperatures. Ice baths, sauna therapy, and nature walks are three powerful methods for recalibrating the body's stress response, enhancing circulation, and boosting neurochemistry.

Cold exposure through ice baths or cold showers has been widely studied for its ability to increase norepinephrine levels, a neurotransmitter that enhances mood, focus, and resilience. Cold therapy also stimulates the vagus nerve, which plays a crucial role in regulating the parasympathetic nervous system. Over time, regular exposure to cold improves stress tolerance, lowers systemic inflammation, and strengthens mental discipline.

Sauna therapy offers complementary benefits by promoting detoxification, increasing circulation, and triggering heat shock proteins that aid in cellular repair. The cardiovascular benefits of regular sauna use have been compared to moderate exercise, and research has shown that sauna therapy reduces the risk of cardiovascular disease, neurodegeneration, and premature aging. Beyond its physiological effects, heat exposure creates a mental shift, forcing the body into a state of deep relaxation and release.

Spending time in nature further reinforces emotional balance and nervous system regulation. The Japanese practice of forest bathing, or shinrin-yoku, has demonstrated significant benefits for reducing cortisol levels, improving immune function, and enhancing mental clarity. Nature exposure recalibrates the body's circadian rhythms, promotes deep sleep, and counteracts the overstimulation caused by urban environments and digital screens. Time spent in natural settings is not a luxury but a necessity for maintaining optimal mental and emotional well-being.

Journaling is one of the most effective tools for maintaining emotional balance. The act of writing down thoughts, emotions, and reflections provides a structured outlet for processing experiences, identifying patterns, and gaining insight into mental and emotional states. Expressive writing has been shown to reduce symptoms of anxiety and depression, improve immune function, and strengthen cognitive processing. Journaling helps to bridge the gap between subconscious emotions and conscious awareness, allowing individuals to cultivate self-awareness and resilience. Whether used for gratitude, problem-solving, or self-reflection, the practice of writing enhances mental clarity and emotional stability.

Creativity plays a crucial role in brain health and emotional well-being. Engaging in fun and creative activities stimulates neuroplasticity, the brain's ability to adapt and form new connections. Creative pursuits such as painting, playing music, dancing, or even solving puzzles activate the default mode network, a region of the brain associated with insight, imagination, and problem-solving. These activities provide a break from linear, task-oriented thinking, allowing the brain to enter a state of flow, which is associated with increased dopamine release and overall well-being. Creativity is not just a form of entertainment but an essential component of a resilient and high-functioning brain.

One of the most important yet overlooked aspects of mental and emotional well-being is the ability to set boundaries. In a world that demands constant connectivity, the ability to protect personal time, energy, and mental space is a skill that determines long-term health outcomes. Digital stimulation, excessive work hours, and the inability to disconnect lead to chronic stress, burnout, and cognitive overload. Setting boundaries with work and technology is essential for protecting mental clarity and emotional resilience.

Creating structured time away from screens, implementing digital detox days, and establishing work-life separation are key strategies for maintaining focus and preventing decision fatigue. The brain was not designed to process endless streams of notifications, emails, and social media updates. Continuous exposure to digital stimuli hijacks dopamine pathways, reducing attention span, increasing stress, and impairing deep thinking. Protecting cognitive bandwidth requires intentional boundary-setting, prioritizing offline moments of stillness, reflection, and deep engagement with the present moment.

A strong mind-body connection is not achieved through a single practice but through a holistic system of daily rituals that reinforce mental clarity, emotional stability, and resilience. The compounding effects of gratitude, breathwork, cold exposure, journaling, creative expression, and boundary-setting create a biochemical environment that supports longevity, cognitive health, and overall well-being.

The difference between those who struggle with stress, fatigue, and emotional imbalance and those who maintain long-term resilience and vitality is not luck but deliberate action. Investing in mental and emotional wealth is just as important as investing in physical health. The brain and nervous system dictate how well the body adapts, recovers, and thrives.

The future of health is not just about what you eat or how much you exercise. It is about how well you regulate stress, how deeply you connect with yourself, and how intentionally you engage in practices that nourish your mind and emotions. True wellness is built from the inside out, and the most valuable investment you can make is in the habits that strengthen your mental and emotional foundation.

Health is a lifelong journey, and the mind-body connection is the key to sustaining energy, clarity, and emotional resilience. The decisions made today will determine not only the quality of life in the present but the trajectory of well-being in the years to come. Prioritizing mental and emotional wealth is not optional—it is the foundation of a thriving, fulfilled, and high-performance life.

Health and wealth are often viewed as separate pursuits, but they are deeply intertwined. True success is not just about financial gains or career achievements; it is about having the physical, mental, and emotional capacity to enjoy those accomplishments. The reality is that without health, wealth loses its meaning. A thriving business, a strong investment portfolio, or professional accolades mean little if the body is constantly exhausted and the mind is overstressed. High performance in any arena—whether in business, athletics, or personal development—requires more than just physical endurance.

It demands mental resilience, emotional stability, and the ability to recover efficiently.

The world glorifies productivity, pushing the idea that doing more leads to greater success. The culture of overwork has conditioned people to believe that rest is a sign of weakness, that pushing harder is always the answer, and that burnout is an unavoidable side effect of ambition. But this mindset is fundamentally flawed. The highest performers do not just work harder; they recover better. They understand that optimal performance is not about endlessly increasing output but about balancing effort with restoration. Without proper recovery, even the most disciplined individuals will eventually hit a wall—physically, mentally, or emotionally.

Training the mind and emotions is just as crucial as training the body. Mental resilience allows individuals to navigate challenges, make better decisions under pressure, and maintain clarity in the face of uncertainty. Emotional intelligence ensures that stress does not spiral into chronic anxiety, that setbacks do not turn into self-doubt, and that relationships—both personal and professional—remain strong. These are not secondary concerns; they are foundational elements of sustainable success. The most successful individuals are not just physically fit; they have mastered their internal state. They are calm under pressure, adaptable in the face of change, and capable of maintaining focus despite distractions.

The ability to recover effectively is often what separates those who sustain long-term success from those who burn out. Recovery is not just about sleep, though sleep is a critical component. It is about actively engaging in practices that replenish mental and emotional reserves. Meditation, breathwork, and mindfulness are not luxuries reserved for monks and spiritual practitioners; they are essential tools for anyone operating at a high level. These practices reduce stress hormones, improve cognitive function, and increase emotional regulation, allowing for better decision-making and greater resilience in the face of challenges.

The misconception that success requires constant effort leads many people to neglect the very things that would allow them to sustain high performance. Rest is not wasted time. Mental stillness is not laziness. Recovery is not optional—it is a strategic necessity. The best athletes in the world do not train at maximum intensity every day; they build recovery into their routine to ensure their bodies and minds remain strong over time. The same principle applies to anyone striving for success in any field. Without recovery, even the most talented individuals will eventually see diminishing returns.

The best investment anyone can make is not in stocks, real estate, or business ventures. It is in themselves—their health, their peace of mind, and their personal fulfillment. Wealth without health leads to regret. Health without emotional balance leads to dissatisfaction. Success without internal peace leads to emptiness. The ultimate goal should not be just to accumulate financial wealth, but to build a life that is rich in energy, clarity, and purpose.

Many people chase external success, believing that once they achieve a certain level of income or recognition, they will finally feel fulfilled. But external success does not fix internal imbalances. Money does not eliminate stress. Career achievements do not automatically create peace of mind. The real work of fulfillment happens internally. It is in mastering thoughts, regulating emotions, and creating a lifestyle that prioritizes both achievement and well-being. The individuals who experience the deepest levels of success are not just financially wealthy; they are mentally clear, emotionally balanced, and physically strong.

In a world that constantly demands more, the real challenge is learning to do less—not in terms of ambition, but in terms of unnecessary strain. Working harder is not always the answer. Sometimes, the key to greater success is learning to recover, recharge, and realign with what truly matters. Sustainable success comes not from depletion but from balance. The most powerful individuals are not the ones who sacrifice everything for success; they are the ones who understand that success and well-being are not mutually exclusive.

The future belongs to those who take control of their health—not just their physical health, but their mental and emotional well-being. If the goal is to perform at the highest level, then training the mind and emotions must be given the same priority as training the body.

High performance is not about pushing endlessly—it is about knowing when to push and when to pull back, when to take action and when to allow space for recovery.

Now is the time to shift the mindset around success. The future is not just about working harder—it is about living smarter. Investing in health, emotional balance, and recovery is the ultimate strategy for longevity, fulfillment, and peak performance. Those who recognize this will not only achieve more but will enjoy the journey along the way. The best investment one can make is not in external achievements, but in mastering the internal state that allows for sustainable success. The time to take action is now. Health, wealth, and fulfillment are not separate pursuits—they are part of the same equation. Prioritize them, and everything else will follow.

PART FOUR

THE HIGH-PERFORMANCE LIFESTYLE FOR LONGEVITY & SUCCESS

9

The Longevity Secrets of Ultra-Successful Individuals

I magine standing at the peak of your success—your mind sharp, your body strong, and your energy boundless. Now imagine watching it all slip away, not because of lost ambition or dwindling opportunity, but because your health could no longer keep up with the demands of your life. The sad reality is that most people don't realize that success is only as sustainable as the body and mind supporting it. The world's highest achievers—those who build legacies, disrupt industries, and remain at the top of their game for decades—know that longevity is not just about extending life. It's about maintaining peak performance over time.

The difference between those who thrive well into their later years and those who burn out too soon isn't just about genetics or luck. It's about strategy. The highest performers in the world approach their health the same way they approach their careers—intentionally, systematically, and with a commitment to optimization. They understand that their mind and body are their greatest assets, and they invest in them accordingly. They don't wait for illness to strike or energy to fade before taking action. They take proactive steps to ensure that they are not just surviving, but thriving—decade after decade.

Longevity is often misunderstood. It is not simply about living to an old age; it is about the quality of those years. It is the ability to keep doing what you love, to keep creating, building, and innovating without being held back by fatigue, pain, or cognitive decline. For those who aim to outlive and outperform their competition, longevity is a strategic advantage. It allows them to continue making an impact long after their peers have faded into the background.

Over the past twenty-five years, I have worked with high-performing individuals—from elite athletes and Fortune 500 executives to industry leaders and innovative entrepreneurs—who understand that their edge in life is directly tied to how well they take care of their health. They seek more than just standard medical advice; they seek the most effective strategies for extending their healthspan, optimizing their physiology, and ensuring that they remain at the top of their game. They recognize that modern medicine, while excellent at handling acute illness and emergencies, is reactive by design. It waits until something is broken before stepping in to fix it. But the world's top performers do not wait for problems to arise. They take a preventative, data-driven, and highly strategic approach to their health, ensuring that they remain strong, clear-minded, and high-functioning well into their later years.

The human body is not designed to simply decay with age; it is designed to adapt, repair, and regenerate. The key is knowing how to support and enhance those natural processes. The traditional medical model tells us that aging comes with inevitable decline—slower metabolism, reduced cognitive function, decreased muscle mass, and a higher risk of chronic disease. But those who are serious about longevity know that these changes are not inevitable; they are preventable and, in many cases, reversible.

The world's most successful individuals do not just rely on conventional wisdom when it comes to their health. They use advanced strategies and biohacks that keep them operating at their highest level for longer than anyone else. They harness the power of cellular regeneration, strategic fasting, metabolic flexibility, targeted supplementation, and cutting-edge regenerative therapies to slow aging, reduce inflammation, and optimize cognitive and physical function. They understand that small, consistent interventions can yield exponential results over time.

One of the greatest mistakes people make when thinking about longevity is assuming that they can focus on it later, that they can wait until they start to feel the effects of aging before making it a priority. But by the time energy declines, brain fog sets in, and chronic aches become a daily reality, the body has already been operating at a deficit for years. True longevity requires early intervention. It requires taking action now, when you feel good, so that you continue to feel even better decades from now.

Another misconception is that longevity is simply about avoiding disease. While preventing illness is certainly important, the real goal is performance optimization. It's not just about staying alive; it's about staying sharp, strong, and fully engaged in life. It's about being able to wake up with energy, to push through challenges without burnout, to think clearly and act decisively, and to recover quickly from stressors. It's about designing a life where your body and mind are working for you, not against you.

The elite performers I work with do not view health as a passive outcome; they see it as something they build, maintain, and optimize. They treat their body as a high-performance machine, fine-tuning every system to operate with maximum efficiency. They take advantage of medical advancements that allow them to measure and track their biological markers, ensuring that they are constantly making informed adjustments to their health strategy. They do not wait for symptoms to appear before taking action—they stay ahead of the curve.

They also recognize that longevity is about balance. It is not just about pushing harder, training more, or constantly striving. It is about recovery, restoration, and renewal. The highest achievers know that performance is only sustainable when recovery is prioritized. Sleep, stress management, and nervous system regulation are just as important as physical fitness and nutrition. The mind must be trained, the emotions must be balanced, and the nervous system must be supported to handle the demands of a high-pressure lifestyle.

This is why I take a holistic approach to longevity with my clients. It's not just about the right diet, the best supplements, or the most advanced therapies—it's about a total lifestyle approach that optimizes every aspect of well-being. Physical health, mental clarity, emotional resilience, and deep recovery are all essential pieces of the longevity puzzle.

The future of longevity is no longer a mystery. Science has given us the tools to extend lifespan while increasing healthspan—the number of years we remain fully functional and thriving. The question is no longer whether it's possible to outlive and outperform the competition; the question is whether you are willing to take the necessary steps to make it happen.

If you are serious about sustaining your success, about remaining mentally sharp, physically strong, and fully engaged in your life for decades to come, the time to act is now. Longevity is not something that happens by chance. It is a result of the choices you make today. Will you be one of the few who takes control of their health, optimizes their body, and sets themselves up for long-term success? Or will you wait until it's too late, hoping that you can reverse years of neglect once the damage has already been done? The choice is yours. Your future depends on it.

Success is built on strategy, and longevity is no exception. The world's most successful individuals understand that maintaining peak performance, mental clarity, and sustained energy well into their later years is not a matter of chance but of meticulous planning and execution. Just as they apply precision to business ventures, financial investments, and personal development, they bring that same level of commitment to their health. Longevity is not simply about living longer—it is about thriving for as long as possible, ensuring that every year is filled with vitality, resilience, and capability.

For too long, society has viewed health as something to be addressed only when problems arise. The traditional medical model is built around a reactive approach, where disease is treated only after it has manifested in symptoms. This mindset is deeply flawed. By the time most people seek medical attention, their body has been in a state of dysfunction for years, sometimes even decades. The ultra-successful recognize that waiting for a crisis to take action is a losing game. Instead, they proactively build a foundation for health, investing in regenerative medicine, advanced diagnostics, and preventative strategies to ensure that they are always one step ahead of illness and degeneration.

The key to longevity is adopting a preventative mindset. Just as an elite athlete does not wait for an injury to start rehabilitative training, those who aim for long-term health do not wait for symptoms before making adjustments. They recognize that their body, like a high-performance vehicle, requires constant fine-tuning, high-quality fuel, and preventative maintenance. Every decision made today impacts the body's ability to function optimally in the future. Health is not a static state; it is a dynamic, ever-evolving system that must be monitored, adjusted, and optimized over time.

One of the most significant shifts in modern medicine is the transition from a reactive healthcare model to a proactive and regenerative approach. Traditional medicine focuses primarily on managing disease, prescribing medications, and alleviating symptoms. Functional and regenerative medicine, however, focus on identifying the root causes of dysfunction, reversing early imbalances, and enhancing the body's ability to repair and regenerate itself. This shift is not just about preventing illness but about optimizing the body's natural ability to thrive.

Regenerative medicine offers cutting-edge tools that allow individuals to restore function, repair damage, and extend longevity at the cellular level. Therapies such as peptide treatments, stem cell therapy, hormone optimization, and advanced nutrient protocols provide the body with the precise materials needed to sustain peak performance. These treatments do not simply mask symptoms; they restore balance, enhance cellular communication, and create a biological environment that resists aging and disease. The best in the world do not wait until they are sick to explore these strategies—they implement them long before their body starts to show signs of decline.

The mindset of longevity requires thinking beyond the present. It means shifting focus away from short-term relief and toward long-term resilience. Those who succeed in maintaining lifelong health understand that every small action taken today compounds over time. Just as financial investments grow with consistent contributions, health investments—whether in nutrition, exercise, sleep, or advanced medical interventions—create exponential returns in terms of energy, mental clarity, and disease resistance.

One of the biggest mistakes people make is assuming that feeling fine today means they are in optimal health. The reality is that disease does not appear overnight. Most chronic conditions develop over years, often silently, without obvious symptoms. Inflammation, nutrient deficiencies, hormone imbalances, and metabolic dysfunctions can be brewing beneath the surface, slowly eroding the body's ability to function at peak levels. The individuals who stay ahead of these issues track their biomarkers, analyze trends, and make adjustments before imbalances become irreversible.

Monitoring key health markers is not about paranoia—it is about intelligent strategy. The same way a business owner would never operate without reviewing financial reports, those who prioritize longevity routinely assess their biological data. They optimize blood sugar levels, inflammatory markers, metabolic function, and cellular repair mechanisms, ensuring that their internal environment supports long-term performance. This level of detail is what separates those who live reactively from those who engineer their health for success.

Beyond physical health, longevity is also deeply tied to mental resilience, emotional well-being, and stress management. The body and mind are intricately connected, and chronic stress accelerates aging at a cellular level. High-achieving individuals understand that optimizing longevity is not just about diet and exercise; it requires strategies to manage mental load, cultivate emotional balance, and develop psychological resilience.

Stress is one of the most significant accelerators of aging. Chronic stress floods the body with cortisol, weakens the immune system, disrupts sleep, and promotes inflammation. Those who truly master longevity implement strategies to regulate stress, improve nervous system function, and enhance cognitive resilience. They practice mindfulness, engage in restorative activities, and use biochemical interventions such as adaptogens, nootropics, and neurotransmitter support to balance the brain's chemistry.

Sleep is another non-negotiable. The most successful people do not treat sleep as optional; they prioritize high-quality, deep sleep as a fundamental pillar of long-term health. Sleep is when the body repairs DNA, detoxifies the brain, and restores hormone balance. Those who understand longevity protect their sleep as fiercely as they protect their business deals. They invest in circadian rhythm optimization, high-performance sleep protocols, and biohacking strategies to ensure their body gets the most regenerative rest possible.

The mindset of longevity also means embracing lifelong learning and adaptation. The landscape of medicine is evolving rapidly, and those who stay ahead are constantly integrating the latest research, therapies, and technologies. Longevity is a moving target, and what works today may need to be refined tomorrow. The most successful individuals remain students of their own health, continuously refining their approach based on new data, emerging therapies, and their body's evolving needs.

Perhaps the most important realization is that longevity is not about merely avoiding death—it is about maximizing life. It is about having the energy, strength, and mental sharpness to engage fully with the world, pursue passions, and continue growing long past what society considers the "prime years." Those who adopt a longevity mindset do not accept the traditional model of aging. They do not believe that decline is inevitable or that they must surrender their physical or cognitive abilities to time. They actively build their future with the same intensity and precision they apply to every other area of success.

The time to take control of longevity is not someday—it is now. The choices made today dictate the quality of life in the decades to come. Waiting until something goes wrong is no longer an option. Those who understand this do not wait for symptoms to dictate their health decisions—they take action before issues arise. They invest in advanced testing, track biomarkers, optimize nutrition, and implement regenerative therapies years before conventional medicine would even consider intervention.

Longevity is the ultimate investment. The returns are measured in years of strength, energy, and clarity. The greatest wealth is not money, but time spent in a body that functions optimally. The most successful individuals already know this, and they are taking steps today to ensure that their future is one of vitality, not decline.

The question is not whether longevity can be improved—the science is already there. The real question is who will take action and who will wait until it is too late. The answer lies in shifting perspective, thinking beyond the present, and embracing the mindset that longevity is not something that happens—it is something that is built, engineered, and optimized over time. The future belongs to those who take ownership of their health today.

The key to longevity is not found in a one-size-fits-all diet or a trendy nutrition plan promoted by the latest wellness influencer. The world's top performers—those who outlive and outperform their peers—do not follow mainstream nutritional trends. They understand that nutrition is as individual as a fingerprint, and the only way to truly optimize health is through a data-driven, personalized approach. Nutrition is not just about eating well; it is about feeding the body precisely what it needs to function at peak capacity while minimizing the internal stressors that accelerate aging.

For years, the conventional approach to diet has been based on generalized recommendations, designed to prevent nutrient deficiencies rather than to optimize human performance. While this approach may keep people from developing severe malnutrition, it does not support longevity, resilience, or sustained cognitive and physical excellence. The individuals who consistently function at the highest levels—whether in business, athletics, or personal development—take a completely different approach. They do not guess what their body needs; they test and adjust based on their own biomarkers, allowing them to fine-tune every aspect of their nutritional intake. This level of precision allows them to reduce inflammation, support cellular repair, enhance metabolic flexibility, and ultimately extend their healthspan.

Strategic fasting has become one of the most effective tools for longevity and vitality. The practice of fasting is not new; it has been embedded in human evolution for thousands of years. The body was designed to function efficiently in both fed and fasted states, yet modern eating patterns have shifted toward constant consumption. Frequent eating, especially of processed and refined foods, keeps the body in a perpetual state of digestion and glucose metabolism, which over time leads to insulin resistance, chronic inflammation, and metabolic dysfunction. Strategic fasting allows the body to shift into repair mode, activating autophagy, a process where cells remove damaged components and regenerate new, healthier ones.

The most successful individuals incorporate fasting into their lifestyle in a way that suits their metabolic needs. Some follow intermittent fasting, which involves a daily eating window of six to eight hours, while others practice longer fasts to enhance deep cellular detoxification. Fasting is not just about caloric restriction; it is about giving the body the opportunity to reset, clear out dysfunctional cells, and optimize energy production. When done correctly, fasting improves insulin sensitivity, enhances brain function, and promotes mitochondrial efficiency, all of which are critical for longevity and sustained high performance.

Metabolic flexibility is another essential principle for those looking to extend their lifespan while maintaining high levels of energy and focus. Most people are metabolically inflexible, meaning their bodies are dependent on a constant intake of carbohydrates to function. This reliance on glucose prevents the body from efficiently using fat for fuel, leading to energy crashes, sugar cravings, and difficulty maintaining stable weight. The ability to switch between fuel sources—using carbohydrates when needed and relying on fat when necessary—is a hallmark of metabolic health.

Achieving metabolic flexibility requires intentional dietary strategies, including intermittent fasting, low-carbohydrate periods, and the strategic use of healthy fats. Those who prioritize longevity train their bodies to burn fat efficiently, reducing inflammation and stabilizing blood sugar levels. When the body becomes metabolically flexible, it can access stored energy more efficiently, resulting in better cognitive function, improved physical endurance, and protection against age-related metabolic disorders.

Nutrient timing is another factor that plays a significant role in optimizing longevity. The timing of food intake affects everything from hormone regulation to digestion and energy levels. Eating at the right times ensures that nutrients are absorbed efficiently and utilized optimally by the body. One of the most important aspects of nutrient timing is aligning eating patterns with the body's natural circadian rhythms. Late-night eating, for example, disrupts sleep cycles and interferes with insulin sensitivity, while eating earlier in the day aligns with the body's peak digestive function, promoting better metabolism and energy balance.

Top performers use nutrient timing to enhance their physical and cognitive performance. Many front-load their nutrients earlier in the day, prioritizing protein and healthy fats in the morning to fuel brain function while avoiding high-carbohydrate meals late at night to prevent metabolic dysfunction. Some use strategic carbohydrate intake to enhance recovery after workouts, while others rely on periods of protein fasting to activate cellular repair mechanisms. Understanding how and when to eat is just as important as what to eat, and those who master nutrient timing gain a significant advantage in maintaining vitality and longevity.

Precision-based supplementation is an essential part of any longevity-focused nutritional strategy. While whole foods should always be the foundation of a healthy diet, the reality is that modern agriculture, soil depletion, and environmental stressors have made it nearly impossible to get all essential nutrients from food alone. Even those who eat an organic, nutrient-dense diet often have micronutrient deficiencies that impact their overall health.

The world's top performers do not take generic multivitamins; they use targeted supplementation based on their individual needs. Functional lab testing reveals precise deficiencies, allowing for a customized approach to nutrient optimization. Magnesium, for example, is a mineral that is involved in over 300 enzymatic reactions in the body, yet the majority of the population is deficient. A lack of magnesium contributes to poor sleep, increased stress, muscle cramps, and metabolic dysfunction. Individuals who optimize their magnesium intake experience improved recovery, better sleep quality, and enhanced resilience to stress.

Vitamin D is another critical nutrient that is often overlooked. It is essential for immune function, bone health, and inflammation control, yet deficiencies are rampant, even in sunny climates. Functional testing allows for the precise dosing of vitamin D to ensure optimal levels, rather than relying on generic recommendations that may be insufficient for high-performance individuals. Omega-3 fatty acids, B vitamins, zinc, and iodine are also commonly deficient in those who have not optimized their supplementation based on personal data.

Another key component of precision-based supplementation is the use of bioavailable forms of nutrients. Many standard supplements contain synthetic or poorly absorbed versions of vitamins and minerals, leading to suboptimal results. Those who prioritize longevity seek out highly bioavailable forms that are readily absorbed and utilized by the body. Instead of relying on cheap multivitamins with synthetic fillers, they use medical-grade supplements tailored to their body's specific needs.

The secret to lifelong vitality is not found in restrictive diets or following mainstream nutritional advice. It is found in a personalized approach that is based on testing, tracking, and adjusting. The world's top performers understand that their nutritional needs evolve over time, and they continuously refine their strategies to stay ahead of aging and metabolic decline. What works for one person may not work for another, and the key to success is precision—eliminating guesswork and using real data to make informed choices.

The future of health and longevity belongs to those who take control of their nutrition. It is no longer enough to follow general dietary guidelines or rely on outdated recommendations. The individuals who outlive and outperform their peers are those who invest in their health before problems arise, rather than waiting for symptoms to dictate action. The science of longevity is advancing rapidly, and those who take advantage of these breakthroughs today will be the ones who experience the greatest benefits in the decades to come.

Now is the time to shift the approach to nutrition from reactive to proactive. The key to lifelong vitality lies in metabolic flexibility, strategic fasting, nutrient timing, and precision-based supplementation. The body has an extraordinary ability to repair, regenerate, and function at peak levels—but only if given the right tools. Those who understand and implement these strategies will not only live longer but will thrive, remaining strong, clear-minded, and resilient well into their later years.

The time to take action is now. Investing in advanced nutritional strategies today is the key to preventing disease, enhancing longevity, and optimizing every aspect of life. Those who take their health seriously do not leave their nutrition to chance—they test, refine, and personalize their approach to ensure they are always operating at their absolute best. The question is not whether these strategies work—the question is, will you use them to take control of your future?

Longevity is not simply the art of adding more years to life. It is the science of ensuring that every year is filled with vitality, clarity, and strength. While many people fear aging as an inevitable decline, the reality is that the choices made today dictate the trajectory of future health. The ultra-successful understand this better than anyone. They do not leave their wealth, their businesses, or their investments to chance—so why would they leave their health to chance? The strategies they employ are not secret; they are simply proactive. They prioritize long-term health in the same way they prioritize long-term financial success.

The idea that aging equals suffering is a myth built on outdated medical models that focus on disease treatment rather than prevention. The truth is that the body is designed to regenerate, adapt, and remain resilient when given the right conditions. The challenge is that modern life works against this natural longevity. Poor nutrition, chronic stress, environmental toxins, and sedentary lifestyles accelerate the aging process, leading to premature degeneration of the body and mind. However, just as a financial portfolio can be strategically managed to build long-term wealth, health can be actively cultivated to ensure extended performance and quality of life.

One of the most important investments anyone can make is in their cellular health. Every function in the body—from energy production to cognitive processing, immune defense, and tissue repair—relies on optimal cellular function. Mitochondria, the powerhouses of the cell, are responsible for generating energy, but they decline with age if not properly supported. The ultra-successful take steps to preserve and enhance mitochondrial function through targeted nutrition, supplementation, and regenerative therapies. This is why they maintain high energy levels and sharp cognitive function long past the age when most people begin to experience fatigue and mental decline.

Nutrition is a cornerstone of longevity. What a person eats today determines how well their body will function in the future. The standard diet, filled with processed foods and inflammatory ingredients, is a leading contributor to chronic disease. In contrast, those who live long, active lives focus on nutrient-dense, anti-inflammatory foods that nourish the body at the cellular level. They emphasize metabolic flexibility, ensuring that their bodies can efficiently use both carbohydrates and fats for fuel. They incorporate fasting protocols that reduce oxidative stress and promote autophagy, the body's natural process of cellular cleanup and repair. They do not eat just to satisfy hunger; they eat strategically to fuel longevity.

The world's top performers also understand that stress is the silent killer. Chronic stress is not just an emotional burden; it is a physiological disruptor. Elevated cortisol levels wreak havoc on the nervous system, increase inflammation, and accelerate aging at the cellular level. Managing stress is not a luxury—it is a necessity for long-term health. Those who outperform their peers incorporate stress-reduction techniques into their daily routines. They engage in practices like breathwork, meditation, and structured recovery periods to reset their nervous system and ensure sustained high performance. They prioritize sleep, recognizing that deep, restorative sleep is where the real healing and regeneration occur.

Physical movement is another non-negotiable. The body was designed to move, and stagnation is one of the fastest ways to deteriorate health. Exercise is not about aesthetics; it is about preserving muscle mass, optimizing circulation, and maintaining functional strength well into later years. The strongest predictors of longevity are not cholesterol levels or genetics but rather grip strength, muscle mass, and cardiovascular endurance. The ultra-successful train with longevity in mind. They incorporate resistance training to maintain muscle integrity, engage in cardiovascular activity to support heart health, and use mobility exercises to prevent injuries. They do not stop moving as they age; they adapt their training to continue thriving.

Regenerative therapies are the next frontier of longevity. Medical advancements in peptide therapy, ozone therapy, hyperbaric oxygen, and IV nutrient therapy provide powerful tools to enhance recovery, reduce inflammation, and stimulate cellular repair. These therapies are not just for the elite; they are becoming more accessible and will be a standard part of proactive healthcare in the future. The smartest individuals do not wait until their bodies break down to seek these treatments; they integrate them into their health strategy before dysfunction sets in.

Longevity is also deeply tied to hormonal balance. As people age, hormone levels fluctuate, impacting everything from metabolism to cognitive function, mood, and energy levels. The ultra-successful monitor their hormonal health and make necessary adjustments to ensure their bodies continue functioning optimally. They understand that declining testosterone, estrogen imbalances, and thyroid dysfunction are not just inconveniences but major contributors to premature aging. Through hormone optimization strategies—whether natural or bioidentical—they ensure that their biological age does not dictate their performance.

Cognitive longevity is just as critical as physical longevity. A sharp mind is the greatest asset a person can have, yet neurodegenerative diseases like Alzheimer's and cognitive decline are becoming increasingly common. The ultra-successful do not just focus on preventing brain disease; they focus on enhancing cognitive function. They use nootropic compounds to improve focus, engage in brain-training exercises to maintain neuroplasticity, and consume high-quality fats and antioxidants to protect against oxidative damage. They view brain health as a lifelong investment, ensuring that their decision-making, creativity, and mental acuity remain strong no matter their age.

The biggest mistake most people make when it comes to longevity is waiting until something is wrong. By the time symptoms appear, damage has already accumulated. The best approach is preventative and proactive. The difference between those who deteriorate in their later years and those who thrive is simple—one group ignored their health until it became a problem, and the other treated it as their most valuable asset. Longevity is not about chasing youth; it is about maximizing healthspan, the years lived in full function, without disease or limitation.

The time to invest in longevity is not in ten years or when health starts to decline—it is now. The body is an adaptive, resilient system, but it requires the right inputs to function at its best. Nutrition, movement, stress management, regenerative medicine, and cognitive optimization are not optional for those who want to extend their prime years. The people who will dominate in the future—whether in business, athletics, or personal fulfillment—are those who invest in their health today.

The ultra-successful prove that health is the greatest wealth. Every decision made about food, movement, sleep, and recovery is an investment—one that will either compound into long-term vitality or decline into premature aging. The most powerful realization is that longevity is a choice. It is not dictated by genetics alone but by daily habits, proactive interventions, and a commitment to never settling for mediocrity in health.

The call to action is simple: start now. Begin tracking health markers, refining nutritional strategies, incorporating recovery protocols, and seeking cutting-edge therapies that will support long-term performance. Do not wait for a crisis to force action. Those who take control of their biological future today will reap the benefits for decades to come. The future of longevity is not in waiting—it is in engineering a life of strength, clarity, and resilience. The best investment a person can make is in themselves. The decision to prioritize health today will determine not just how long one lives, but how well one lives.

10

The Ultimate Blueprint for Energy, Resilience & Performance

Imagine waking up every morning with an unstoppable sense of energy, clarity, and drive. Picture a body that moves effortlessly, a mind that remains sharp under pressure, and a level of endurance that carries you through even the most demanding challenges. This is not a luxury reserved for the genetically gifted or the exceptionally lucky. It is the result of deliberate choices—an engineered approach to energy, resilience, and peak performance.

The world's most successful individuals do not leave their performance to chance. They understand that sustained high performance is not an accident—it is a strategy. Every decision, from the way they sleep to the way they eat, move, and recover, is designed to optimize function. These are not random habits or generic health trends; they are carefully curated protocols backed by science, experience, and results. Those who consistently perform at the top of their field, whether in business, athletics, or creative endeavors, do so because they have mastered the fundamentals of physiology, cognition, and recovery.

In today's fast-paced, high-demand world, energy is the ultimate currency. Without it, even the most talented individuals struggle to execute their vision, maintain focus, or push through the inevitable obstacles that come with ambitious goals. Resilience—the ability to recover quickly from stress, setbacks, and fatigue—is equally crucial. Without it, burnout is inevitable. Peak performance, then, is not just about working harder; it is about creating a biological foundation that allows for sustained success over time.

Most people make the mistake of viewing health as a reactive measure—something to think about only when they begin to feel tired, sick, or burned out. The ultra-successful operate differently. They treat their bodies and minds like a high-performance machine, taking action before problems arise. They do not wait for their energy levels to crash before prioritizing sleep. They do not wait for cognitive decline before fueling their brains with the right nutrients. They do not wait until their bodies break down before integrating recovery protocols. Instead, they proactively optimize every aspect of their physiology to sustain focus, endurance, and resilience for the long haul.

The reality is that most people are performing far below their potential. Chronic fatigue, brain fog, erratic energy levels, poor sleep, and slow recovery are not just normal parts of aging or high achievement. They are symptoms of suboptimal biological function— signs that the body and brain are being pushed beyond their capacity without the necessary support to repair and regenerate. When ignored, these small imbalances compound over time, leading to accelerated aging, chronic disease, and a loss of both mental and physical vitality. The good news is that this decline is not inevitable. It can be prevented—and even reversed—through strategic lifestyle interventions.

Optimizing performance starts with a fundamental shift in mindset. It requires moving away from short-term fixes and embracing a long-term strategy for sustainable energy production, cellular resilience, and cognitive longevity. It requires understanding that health is not something that happens by default—it is something that must be built, reinforced, and protected.

The blueprint for high performance begins with four essential pillars: sleep, movement, nutrition, and detoxification. These are not optional extras; they are the foundation upon which all success is built. Neglect one, and the entire system begins to fail. The best performers in the world do not merely dabble in these areas—they master them. They approach sleep with the same discipline as their business meetings. They view movement as a necessity, not an inconvenience. They fuel their bodies with precision, ensuring that every meal enhances cognition and stamina. They prioritize detoxification and recovery, understanding that removing what does not belong is just as critical as adding what does.

The first pillar, sleep, is the single most important yet most neglected performance enhancer. In a culture that glorifies hustle, sleep is often sacrificed in the pursuit of productivity. But the truth is, without high-quality sleep, nothing else functions optimally. The brain cannot consolidate information, the immune system cannot repair, and hormones become dysregulated, leading to chronic fatigue, impaired focus, and increased susceptibility to illness. The highest performers treat sleep as a non-negotiable asset—a tool for enhancing memory, creativity, emotional regulation, and physical recovery. They optimize their circadian rhythms, create structured nighttime routines, and leverage science-backed strategies to achieve deep, restorative sleep that fuels peak performance.

Movement is equally crucial. The body was never designed to sit for hours on end, yet modern lifestyles have turned physical inactivity into a silent epidemic. Lack of movement is not just bad for the body; it is detrimental to the brain. Regular exercise increases blood flow, enhances neuroplasticity, reduces stress, and improves emotional resilience. The most successful individuals do not just work out for aesthetics; they train for longevity, strength, and cognitive sharpness. They incorporate a strategic mix of resistance training, cardiovascular conditioning, and mobility work, ensuring that their bodies remain strong, agile, and capable of handling the demands of their high-performance lives.

Fueling the body with nutrient-dense foods is another non-negotiable. Food is not just calories—it is information for the cells. Every bite either enhances or diminishes performance. The ultra-successful do not eat for convenience; they eat for functionality. They understand that stable energy levels, mental clarity, and immune resilience all depend on what they put into their bodies. They focus on whole, nutrient-dense foods that optimize metabolism, reduce inflammation, and provide the raw materials needed for cellular repair and recovery. They eliminate foods that drain energy and disrupt cognitive function, replacing them with strategic nutrition protocols that enhance longevity and sustained peak performance.

The final pillar, detoxification and recovery, is perhaps the most overlooked yet most powerful key to maintaining high performance over time. The body is constantly bombarded by toxins—environmental pollutants, processed foods, chronic stress, and even overtraining can accumulate biological waste that slows down function. The highest achievers recognize that removing what harms the body is just as important as adding what strengthens it. They use targeted detoxification methods—infrared saunas, cold exposure, lymphatic drainage, and fasting protocols—to ensure that their cells remain clean, energized, and free from toxic burden.

The combination of high-quality sleep, movement, strategic nutrition, and detoxification creates a system that is designed to thrive. This is not a quick fix or a temporary hack—it is a blueprint for lifelong vitality. Those who integrate these principles into their daily lives do not just extend their lifespans; they extend their healthspans—the years in which they remain strong, sharp, and fully functional.

The future belongs to those who take control of their biological performance. The difference between those who achieve and sustain success versus those who burn out and deteriorate is not luck or genetics—it is strategy. Those who invest in these fundamental pillars of health will outperform, outlast, and outlive their peers.

This chapter provides the blueprint for maximizing both physical and mental performance. It is not about doing more—it is about doing the right things consistently. The strategies outlined here are not just theories; they are science-backed, real-world tested protocols that have helped top performers sustain success over time.

The time to take action is now. High performance is not something that happens someday—it is something that is engineered daily. Every decision matters. Every habit compounds. Those who commit to mastering their energy, resilience, and recovery will redefine what is possible in their lives.

Sleep is the foundation of human performance, yet it remains one of the most overlooked and misunderstood aspects of health. In a world that glorifies productivity, hustle culture, and the ability to function on minimal rest, sleep is often sacrificed in the pursuit of success. This is a fundamental mistake. The truth is, without quality sleep, nothing else works as it should. Energy production declines, cognitive function deteriorates, immune resilience weakens, and decision-making becomes impaired. The highest achievers—the individuals who consistently outperform their peers—understand that optimizing sleep is not a luxury but a necessity. They treat sleep as an essential pillar of performance, just as critical as nutrition, movement, and mental resilience.

Modern society places a premium on doing more, working harder, and pushing through exhaustion. Sleep deprivation has become a badge of honor, a misguided symbol of dedication. But the reality is that operating on insufficient sleep does not enhance productivity—it destroys it. A fatigued brain is slower, less creative, and more prone to errors. A body deprived of rest struggles to recover, leading to inflammation, metabolic dysfunction, and accelerated aging. The most successful people in the world do not sacrifice sleep to get ahead; they leverage it as a performance-enhancing tool that gives them a competitive edge.

One of the greatest misconceptions about sleep is that it is simply a passive state of rest. In reality, sleep is an active, highly coordinated biological process that regulates nearly every function in the body. During sleep, the brain undergoes essential maintenance, clearing out toxins, consolidating memories, and strengthening neural connections. The immune system launches repair mechanisms, fighting off infections and reducing systemic inflammation. Hormones are balanced, ensuring that metabolism, appetite, and energy levels remain stable. Skimping on sleep disrupts these vital processes, leading to a cascade of negative effects that impact every aspect of health and performance.

Sleep deprivation is one of the most insidious threats to long-term success. Even a single night of poor sleep can impair cognitive function, reducing attention span, problem-solving ability, and emotional regulation. Chronic sleep deprivation compounds these effects, leading to persistent fatigue, mood instability, and impaired decision-making. Studies have shown that individuals who consistently get less than six hours of sleep per night experience higher levels of stress hormones, increased inflammation, and a greater risk of metabolic disorders. Sleep is not just about feeling rested—it is about optimizing the body's ability to function at its highest level.

One of the most significant ways sleep impacts performance is through its effect on metabolism. Poor sleep disrupts blood sugar regulation, increasing insulin resistance and making it more difficult for the body to maintain stable energy levels. This is why sleep-deprived individuals often crave sugar, caffeine, and processed foods—quick energy sources that temporarily mask fatigue but ultimately lead to further crashes. Over time, chronic sleep deprivation contributes to weight gain, metabolic syndrome, and an increased risk of type 2 diabetes. The body's ability to efficiently process and utilize fuel is directly tied to the quality of sleep it receives.

Inflammation is another critical factor influenced by sleep. Poor sleep triggers an inflammatory response in the body, increasing levels of stress hormones like cortisol and disrupting the delicate balance of the immune system. Chronic inflammation is a key driver of nearly every major disease, including heart disease, cancer, and neurodegenerative disorders. High achievers understand that inflammation is not just a health concern—it is a performance killer. When the body is inflamed, energy production suffers, recovery slows, and mental clarity declines. Prioritizing sleep is one of the most effective ways to reduce inflammation and maintain peak physical and mental performance.

Perhaps the most alarming consequence of sleep deprivation is its effect on brain function. The brain requires deep, restorative sleep to perform essential maintenance tasks. During sleep, the glymphatic system—a specialized waste clearance system in the brain—flushes out toxins that accumulate throughout the day. One of these toxins, beta-amyloid, is a protein associated with Alzheimer's disease. Research has shown that chronic sleep deprivation impairs the glymphatic system, allowing toxic waste to build up and increasing the risk of cognitive decline over time. This is why sleep-deprived individuals often experience memory problems, difficulty concentrating, and slower reaction times. Optimizing sleep is one of the most powerful tools for preserving cognitive function and ensuring long-term brain health.

Achieving deep, restorative sleep requires more than simply spending more time in bed. Sleep quality matters just as much as sleep quantity. The body's natural sleep-wake cycle, known as the circadian rhythm, plays a crucial role in determining how well a person sleeps. The circadian rhythm is regulated by light exposure, meal timing, and lifestyle habits. Disrupting this rhythm—by staying up late, exposing the body to artificial light at night, or eating at irregular times—can interfere with the body's ability to enter deep sleep. One of the most effective strategies for improving sleep quality is aligning daily habits with the body's natural rhythms.

Optimizing the sleep environment is another key factor in achieving deep sleep. Light exposure at night suppresses melatonin production, making it harder to fall asleep and stay asleep. Blue light from screens—phones, computers, and televisions—is particularly disruptive. High performers take sleep hygiene seriously, minimizing artificial light exposure in the evening, using blackout curtains to create a dark sleep environment, and maintaining a cool room temperature to support optimal sleep cycles. Small adjustments in the sleep environment can make a significant difference in sleep quality and overall performance.

In addition to environmental factors, strategic recovery techniques can further enhance sleep quality. Breathwork, meditation, and relaxation exercises activate the parasympathetic nervous system, reducing stress levels and preparing the body for deep sleep. Magnesium supplementation, adaptogenic herbs, and amino acids like glycine and L-theanine can help regulate the nervous system and improve sleep depth. The most successful individuals do not rely on pharmaceutical sleep aids that disrupt natural sleep architecture; they use science-backed recovery strategies that support the body's ability to enter deep, regenerative sleep naturally.

Prioritizing sleep is not about sacrificing productivity—it is about enhancing it. Those who optimize their sleep experience higher energy levels, better cognitive performance, improved emotional regulation, and enhanced resilience to stress. They are more creative, more focused, and more capable of making high-impact decisions. They recover faster, train harder, and sustain peak performance longer than their sleep-deprived counterparts. The difference between those who struggle to keep up and those who thrive at the highest levels is often determined by the quality of their sleep.

The path to sustainable high performance begins with a commitment to mastering sleep. It requires rejecting the outdated belief that sleep is a passive state of rest and embracing the reality that sleep is an active, essential process that fuels every aspect of human function. It demands the same level of discipline and strategy as any other area of health optimization.

The most successful individuals in the world do not view sleep as an inconvenience. They see it as a performance-enhancing tool that gives them the energy, clarity, and resilience to dominate in their fields. They prioritize sleep not because they have to, but because they understand that without it, nothing else works as it should.

The future of peak performance belongs to those who are willing to take control of their sleep. It is not about doing more—it is about doing what is necessary to operate at the highest level. The decision to prioritize sleep is not a passive choice; it is a deliberate, strategic move toward sustained success. Those who master their sleep master their performance. Those who neglect it will always be playing catch-up. The choice is clear. The time to act is now.

In the relentless pursuit of performance, longevity, and vitality, most people focus on what they can add to their lives. They chase the latest superfoods, optimize their supplement regimens, and engage in high-intensity training in hopes of achieving peak energy and resilience. But what if the key to sustained high performance is not just about what is added, but also about what is removed? The human body is an extraordinary system, capable of repair, regeneration, and optimal function—but only when it is not burdened by the toxic load of modern life. Detoxification and recovery are not simply wellness buzzwords; they are fundamental processes that dictate cellular efficiency, mitochondrial function, and the ability to produce energy. Those who fail to address toxicity accumulation inevitably experience fatigue, inflammation, and premature aging.

Detoxification is a biological necessity, a process that allows the body to remove metabolic waste, environmental toxins, and cellular debris that interfere with optimal function. Every day, the body encounters pollutants from air, water, and food, as well as internal byproducts from stress, poor digestion, and metabolic inefficiencies. While the liver, kidneys, and lymphatic system work around the clock to neutralize and eliminate these toxins, modern exposure has surpassed the body's natural ability to keep up. As a result, cellular health is compromised, mitochondrial energy production declines, and inflammation becomes a chronic state rather than a temporary response to injury or illness. The result is an insidious decline in physical and cognitive function, often mistaken for aging, stress, or simply the consequence of a busy life.

Mitochondria, the microscopic power plants inside every cell, are directly impacted by toxic burden. These organelles are responsible for generating ATP, the body's primary energy currency, but they are highly sensitive to environmental and internal stressors. Heavy metals, pesticides, processed foods, and chemical-laden personal care products all introduce toxins that disrupt mitochondrial efficiency. When mitochondria become damaged, energy production falters, leading to fatigue, brain fog, muscle weakness, and reduced recovery capacity. Many individuals suffering from chronic fatigue and unexplained energy depletion are not deficient in motivation or discipline—they are drowning in toxic overload that is robbing them of their biological potential.

Inflammation, often referred to as the silent killer, is another consequence of poor detoxification. While short-term inflammation is a necessary immune response, chronic inflammation is a persistent state that erodes health at every level. It damages blood vessels, impairs cognitive function, contributes to metabolic dysfunction, and accelerates the aging process. Toxins fuel inflammation, creating a cycle in which the body's immune system is in constant overdrive, attempting to neutralize the biochemical stressors that continue to accumulate. The longer this cycle persists, the greater the toll on longevity and resilience. True recovery does not happen until the inflammatory burden is reduced, allowing the body to shift from a state of survival to one of regeneration.

Detoxification and recovery are the missing links for those who feel stuck in a perpetual cycle of exhaustion and underperformance. Traditional medicine often ignores the role of toxicity in disease and dysfunction, focusing instead on symptom management. But functional medicine and longevity science recognize that health is restored not just by adding more interventions but by systematically removing what is causing harm. By integrating strategic detoxification and advanced recovery techniques, individuals can dramatically improve their energy levels, enhance mental clarity, and unlock their full biological potential.

One of the most effective detoxification strategies is the use of infrared saunas. Sweating is one of the body's natural pathways for eliminating heavy metals, chemicals, and stored toxins, but modern lifestyles often suppress this process. Infrared sauna therapy penetrates deep into tissues, mobilizing toxins from fat stores and facilitating their elimination through sweat. Unlike traditional saunas, which primarily heat the air around the body, infrared wavelengths directly stimulate cellular detoxification, increasing circulation, enhancing lymphatic flow, and supporting mitochondrial repair. Regular sauna use has been shown to reduce systemic inflammation, support cardiovascular health, and improve recovery by allowing the body to eliminate biochemical stressors that impair function.

Cold therapy, another powerful recovery tool, works in contrast to heat therapy but is equally effective in promoting cellular renewal. Ice baths, cryotherapy, and cold showers activate a physiological response that reduces inflammation, enhances mitochondrial biogenesis, and improves resilience to stress. When exposed to cold temperatures, the body initiates a survival mechanism that not only reduces inflammation but also stimulates the production of brown adipose tissue, a metabolically active type of fat that enhances energy expenditure and mitochondrial efficiency. Elite athletes and high performers have long used cold therapy for muscle recovery, but its benefits extend far beyond physical resilience—it also sharpens mental clarity, strengthens the immune system, and supports long-term health by reducing chronic stress load.

The lymphatic system, often overlooked in conventional health strategies, plays a critical role in detoxification and recovery. Unlike the cardiovascular system, which has the heart to pump blood throughout the body, the lymphatic system relies on movement, breath, and external stimulation to circulate lymph fluid. This system is responsible for removing cellular waste, transporting immune cells, and maintaining fluid balance, yet many people suffer from lymphatic stagnation due to sedentary lifestyles and chronic inflammation. Techniques such as lymphatic drainage massage, dry brushing, and rebounding on a mini-trampoline can dramatically enhance lymphatic flow, accelerating the removal of toxins and supporting immune function. Those who integrate lymphatic activation into their routine experience improved recovery, reduced swelling, and greater overall resilience.

Beyond physical detoxification, functional medicine protocols offer targeted interventions to support cellular repair and metabolic health. Nutritional detoxification strategies, such as fasting and liver-supportive supplementation, help the body break down and eliminate harmful compounds. Intermittent fasting and extended fasting protocols trigger autophagy, a process in which the body identifies and removes damaged cells, allowing for tissue rejuvenation and enhanced mitochondrial efficiency. Certain nutrients, including glutathione, activated charcoal, and milk thistle, support liver detox pathways, ensuring that harmful substances are efficiently processed and eliminated rather than recirculated in the bloodstream.

Detoxification and recovery are not passive processes; they require intentional action. The body is constantly working to repair and restore itself, but when overwhelmed by toxins and inflammation, it loses the ability to do so effectively. Those who prioritize cellular renewal through detoxification experience not only increased energy and mental sharpness but also greater longevity and disease resistance. True health is not simply the absence of disease; it is the presence of abundant energy, resilience, and the ability to perform at one's highest capacity.

The future of high performance and longevity does not lie solely in cutting-edge supplements, advanced medical treatments, or complex biohacking protocols. It lies in the fundamentals—removing what does not belong so that the body can function as it was designed to. Those who commit to regular detoxification and structured recovery will not only feel better in the short term but will also extend their healthspan, maintaining peak function well into their later years.

The call to action is clear: it is time to shift the focus from constantly adding more to optimizing what is already within. Energy, resilience, and longevity are not reserved for a select few—they are available to anyone who takes the necessary steps to remove the barriers standing in their way. Detoxification is not an occasional cleanse or a temporary fix; it is a lifestyle. Recovery is not just about rest; it is an active process of restoring the body to its full potential. Those who master these principles will not only reclaim their energy but will redefine what is possible for their health, performance, and longevity. The time to start is now.

Energy is the foundation of everything. It is the force that drives success, the fuel that sustains ambition, and the currency that determines how much one can accomplish in a lifetime. It is not simply about feeling good for a few hours or having bursts of motivation. True energy is sustainable, repeatable, and resilient. It allows individuals to show up every single day with focus, strength, and clarity, regardless of external pressures or challenges. The highest performers in every field understand this truth. They know that mastering energy is not about relying on caffeine, stimulants, or willpower—it is about structuring life in a way that allows for consistent high output without burnout.

Most people operate under the false assumption that energy is something that comes and goes randomly, dictated by genetics, luck, or circumstances. In reality, energy is something that is built, maintained, and protected. It is not an accident; it is a science. Those who sustain peak function for decades, thriving in both their professional and personal lives, are not simply working harder—they are working smarter by taking control of their biological performance.

The key to unlocking this level of energy and resilience lies in mastering the fundamentals. The body is an incredibly sophisticated machine, designed to function at a high level when given the right inputs. These inputs are not complicated. They do not require extreme diets, endless hours in the gym, or an expensive regimen of supplements and treatments. Instead, they require consistency in the essentials: sleep, movement, nutrition, and recovery. These are the four pillars of sustainable high performance. They determine how well the body functions, how quickly it repairs itself, and how much energy it can generate on demand.

Sleep is the most underrated component of performance. It is often sacrificed in the name of productivity, yet the truth is that without quality sleep, nothing else works optimally. Sleep is when the body repairs itself, when the brain consolidates memories and learning, and when the nervous system resets. Chronic sleep deprivation does not just lead to fatigue; it disrupts metabolism, increases inflammation, impairs cognitive function, and accelerates aging. The highest achievers in the world do not treat sleep as an inconvenience—they treat it as a performance tool. They structure their routines to ensure deep, restorative sleep, because they understand that more energy, better focus, and improved resilience all begin with mastering sleep.

Movement is the second pillar of long-term energy. The human body was designed to move, yet modern lifestyles have turned physical inactivity into the norm. Sedentary behavior slows metabolism, weakens muscles, and reduces circulation, leading to a gradual decline in vitality. The most successful individuals do not exercise just for aesthetics; they train for strength, longevity, and cognitive sharpness. They understand that physical activity is not just about burning calories—it is about enhancing blood flow, stimulating the nervous system, and maintaining structural integrity. They prioritize strength training to preserve muscle mass, cardiovascular exercise to optimize heart health, and mobility work to maintain flexibility and prevent injuries. Movement is not something they fit in when they have time—it is something they make time for, because they know it is an essential component of sustained energy.

Nutrition is another critical factor in energy production. The food consumed every day is not just fuel—it is information for the body. Every meal either enhances energy levels or depletes them. The difference between those who experience sharp, sustained focus and those who suffer from energy crashes and brain fog is the quality of their nutrition. The most effective individuals do not rely on quick fixes or processed foods to get through the day. They eat in a way that supports stable blood sugar, reduces inflammation, and provides the necessary micronutrients for optimal function. They understand the importance of protein for muscle repair, healthy fats for brain function, and fiber for gut health. They avoid the foods that drain them and prioritize the ones that enhance their energy, focus, and longevity.

Recovery is the final, yet often most overlooked, pillar of sustained high performance. The world conditions people to push harder, do more, and grind longer, but this approach leads to burnout, breakdown, and exhaustion. The key to long-term success is not just exertion—it is recovery. The best performers in the world do not just train hard; they recover just as hard. They incorporate rest, relaxation, and structured recovery methods that allow the body to regenerate. They use sauna therapy to stimulate circulation, cold exposure to reduce inflammation, breathwork to reset the nervous system, and strategic downtime to enhance cognitive resilience. They do not view recovery as a weakness; they see it as a strategic advantage.

All four of these pillars work together to create an energy blueprint that is sustainable, repeatable, and scalable. This is what separates those who thrive from those who struggle to keep up. When sleep is optimized, the brain functions at its highest level. When movement is a daily habit, the body remains strong and adaptable. When nutrition is dialed in, energy levels remain stable throughout the day. When recovery is prioritized, resilience becomes effortless. It is not about one single factor—it is about the synergy of these elements working in unison.

The mistake many people make is believing that energy is something that decreases with age or is dictated by genetics. In reality, energy is a product of choices. The people who sustain high performance for decades do so because they control the variables. They do not let modern life dictate their energy levels; they engineer their environment, routines, and habits to ensure they remain at their best.

The ultimate advantage in business, life, and longevity belongs to those who take control of their biological performance. In a world where burnout is common and fatigue is normalized, the ones who master energy will always rise to the top. They will outthink, outlast, and outperform their peers—not because they are working harder, but because they are working smarter.

The time to start is now. Energy is not something to be wished for; it is something to be built, protected, and optimized. The blueprint is clear. The tools are available. The only question is who will take action. Those who invest in sleep, movement, nutrition, and recovery today will be the ones who dominate in the future. High performance is not a mystery—it is a choice. And that choice begins with taking control of energy before energy takes control of you.

PART FIVE

THE HEALTH-WEALTH
LEGACY PLAN

11

How to Make Your Health Your Most Valuable Asset for Life

There is a moment in every high achiever's life when the realization hits—without health, nothing else matters. It does not matter how much wealth has been accumulated, how many businesses have been built, or how much power has been attained if the body is failing, energy is dwindling, and the mind is clouded. The harsh truth is that success, in any form, is meaningless if one does not have the physical and mental capacity to enjoy it. While many chase financial gains, power, and prestige, the wealthiest and most successful individuals have come to a profound conclusion: health is the only investment that guarantees both longevity and fulfillment.

The idea that health is an investment, rather than an expense, is not new. However, it has taken decades for society to recognize that the same principles applied to building financial wealth should also be applied to maintaining and optimizing health. The concept of compounding—where small, consistent investments yield massive returns over time—is just as applicable to physical well-being as it is to a financial portfolio. The choices made today, from nutrition and exercise to sleep and stress management, directly dictate the quality of life in the years to come. Yet, for many, health is treated as an afterthought, something to be addressed only when a problem arises. This mindset is not only flawed but dangerous.

The ultra-successful understand this at a deep level. They know that health is not a reactive pursuit; it is a strategic, proactive investment that pays dividends in energy, longevity, and resilience. Unlike money, which can be lost and regained, time and vitality are irreplaceable. This is why the wealthiest individuals in the world are shifting their focus away from mere material accumulation and toward longevity and vitality. They recognize that the true measure of success is not just how long they live, but how well they live.

The problem with traditional views on health is that they focus almost entirely on disease management rather than prevention and optimization. Conventional medicine is designed to address problems after they occur, treating symptoms rather than building resilience. The new paradigm, embraced by those who prioritize longevity, focuses on preventative and regenerative medicine—strategies that do not just extend life but enhance its quality. This means shifting from a passive approach to an active one, where every decision made is an intentional step toward a stronger, more capable, and more vibrant body and mind.

Energy, resilience, and peak performance are not the results of luck or genetics; they are cultivated. The people who remain sharp and physically strong well into their later years are not simply fortunate— they are disciplined in the way they approach their health. They structure their lives to support their well-being, understanding that health is not something that can be delegated or outsourced. It must be built from the inside out. This means making time for movement, eating with intention, prioritizing recovery, and optimizing stress management techniques that allow them to remain at their best.

The compounding effect of health is one of the most powerful forces in human performance. Just as a financial investment grows exponentially over time, so do the benefits of consistent health optimization. A person who starts prioritizing nutrition, movement, and recovery early in life does not just prevent disease; they build a body that is highly resistant to illness, stress, and aging. Small daily habits—such as maintaining stable blood sugar levels, engaging in strength training, improving sleep quality, and reducing inflammation—may seem insignificant in the moment, but over years and decades, they create an undeniable advantage. Conversely, neglecting these fundamentals leads to a gradual decline that becomes increasingly difficult to reverse.

There is a reason why the world's most powerful people are now investing in their health like never before. The ultra-wealthy are not just buying luxury cars and real estate; they are funding cutting-edge research in longevity science, accessing personalized health programs, and leveraging biohacking technologies to extend both lifespan and healthspan. They recognize that wealth means little if their bodies and minds deteriorate too quickly to enjoy it. Longevity clinics, IV therapy centers, peptide treatments, and regenerative medicine are no longer fringe concepts—they are becoming the gold standard for those who refuse to accept decline as an inevitable part of aging.

The most significant shift in recent years is the realization that success is not just about external accomplishments but internal optimization. The wealthiest individuals do not just accumulate assets; they optimize their physiology to sustain peak function for as long as possible. They are not merely seeking to live longer; they are ensuring that every additional year is one of strength, clarity, and vitality. They do not wait until problems arise to take action. Instead, they track biomarkers, fine tune nutrition, and implement recovery strategies that allow them to stay ahead of decline.

The irony is that many people spend their lives chasing financial security, sacrificing their health in the process, only to later spend their wealth trying to regain what was lost. The richest individuals in the world have learned from this mistake. They are shifting their focus from short-term gains to long-term sustainability—understanding that wealth without health is meaningless. They structure their businesses, investments, and daily routines around a health-first philosophy because they know that success without vitality is an empty victory.

The lesson here is clear: investing in health is not an option; it is the only path to true success. It is not something to be postponed until later in life or something to prioritize only after a health scare. The best time to invest in longevity is now. Those who make their health a priority today will enjoy compounded benefits in the future, while those who neglect it will find themselves scrambling to recover what they lost.

The ultimate investment is not a stock, a business, or a real estate portfolio. It is the body and mind—the foundation upon which everything else is built. Energy, resilience, and longevity are the true measures of wealth. Those who recognize this early will not only live longer but live better. The world is shifting toward a new paradigm where health is no longer an afterthought but a primary focus for those who understand its value. The question is not whether to invest in health but how soon one will start. The time is now. The choice is clear. Those who prioritize their well-being will lead the future of high performance, success, and longevity.

Health is the one investment that compounds in ways money never can. It is the silent force behind productivity, mental clarity, emotional stability, and the ability to perform at the highest level. Every decision made today regarding health—what to eat, how to move, how much to sleep, and how to manage stress—determines not only the quality of the next day but the trajectory of the next several decades. Like financial wealth, health accumulates over time, either growing stronger and more resilient with consistent investment or deteriorating rapidly with neglect. The difference between those who thrive well into old age and those who face premature decline is not genetics or luck but the accumulation of daily habits that either fortify the body or weaken it.

The human body is an adaptive, self-healing system, but it requires the right inputs to function at its best. Many people assume that aging is synonymous with decline, but that belief is rooted in outdated thinking. What is often perceived as a natural consequence of growing older— low energy, joint pain, cognitive decline, metabolic dysfunction— is frequently the result of years of unchecked inflammation, poor nutrition, lack of movement, and chronic stress. The truth is that the earlier one begins to invest in health, the greater the long-term payoff.

Small, consistent choices—choosing nutrient-dense foods, prioritizing high-quality sleep, engaging in regular exercise, and managing stress effectively—yield exponential benefits over time. These choices dictate how well the body functions in its 40s, 50s, 60s, and beyond.

Neglecting health, on the other hand, does not result in a linear decline. It leads to exponential deterioration. The first warning signs of dysfunction—fatigue, brain fog, weight gain, digestive issues—are often ignored, dismissed as the inevitable stressors of life. But these small disruptions accumulate. The body compensates for nutritional deficiencies and metabolic imbalances for years until it can no longer keep up. At some point, the tipping point is reached, and what was once a minor issue becomes a chronic condition. High blood pressure, insulin resistance, joint degeneration, and cognitive decline do not appear overnight. They are the result of years of compounding damage from unaddressed lifestyle habits. By the time symptoms are severe enough to warrant medical intervention, reversing the damage becomes far more difficult.

Health is often treated as an afterthought, something to be managed only when problems arise. This approach is akin to ignoring a financial portfolio until bankruptcy is imminent. No one would expect to build wealth without strategic planning, consistent contributions, and smart investments. Yet, when it comes to health—the most valuable asset of all—many operate with a short-sighted mindset, assuming that they can undo years of neglect with a crash diet, a few months of exercise, or a handful of supplements. True health cannot be achieved through quick fixes. It requires a long-term commitment to daily habits that support longevity, resilience, and vitality.

The earlier health becomes a priority, the more control one has over long-term well-being. The compounding effect of health means that a 30-year-old who prioritizes sleep, movement, and nutrition is not just improving their present-day energy levels but also preventing the chronic conditions that might otherwise develop in their 50s or 60s. A 40-year-old who focuses on metabolic health today is ensuring that they can remain strong, active, and mentally sharp well into their later years. Investing in health early creates a buffer against disease, allowing the body to function optimally for decades rather than deteriorating prematurely.

One of the greatest advantages of prioritizing health early is the ability to sustain high performance over time. Many people sacrifice their well-being in pursuit of success, believing that long hours, stress, and minimal rest are necessary for achievement. However, this approach is unsustainable. Burnout, cognitive fatigue, and declining physical health eventually erode productivity, making it impossible to maintain peak performance. The most successful individuals recognize that health is not a distraction from ambition—it is the foundation of it. Optimal energy levels, mental clarity, and emotional resilience allow for better decision-making, higher levels of creativity, and the stamina required to sustain long-term success.

Happiness and fulfillment are also deeply tied to health. Chronic pain, fatigue, and disease rob individuals of their ability to fully engage with life. The ability to travel, play with grandchildren, pursue passions, and remain independent well into old age is determined by how well the body is cared for today. Health is not just about longevity; it is about maintaining a high quality of life. Those who take control of their well-being early on do not just live longer; they live better.

The notion that prioritizing health requires significant sacrifice is a misconception. Investing in well-being does not mean giving up enjoyment—it means enhancing it. Eating nutrient-dense foods is not a burden; it is a way to fuel the body for sustained energy and mental clarity. Regular movement is not a chore; it is a tool for maintaining strength, flexibility, and cardiovascular health. High-quality sleep is not wasted time; it is the foundation of recovery, memory consolidation, and hormonal balance. The choices that support long-term health are not restrictive; they are empowering. They provide the freedom to live without limitations, to pursue ambitions without being held back by physical or mental fatigue.

Those who understand the compounding effect of health recognize that small, consistent efforts yield extraordinary results over time. Every meal, every workout, every night of sleep is an investment that pays dividends in longevity, resilience, and vitality. Those who neglect their health will find that the cost of ignoring it increases exponentially, leading to a future filled with doctor visits, medications, and a diminished ability to enjoy life.

The time to invest in health is now. Waiting until symptoms appear or until life slows down is a dangerous gamble. The body is remarkably adaptable, but it thrives when given the right conditions. The best way to ensure a future of strength, energy, and mental acuity is to take action today. Those who commit to making health their top priority will experience the benefits not just in years to come but in their day-to-day lives. They will wake up feeling energized, move through life with ease, and approach challenges with a sharp and focused mind. They will not be burdened by the weight of preventable disease or the regret of not having taken better care of themselves. They will have the freedom to live fully, without limitations.

Health is not an expense; it is the most valuable investment one can make. It is the one asset that determines how all other aspects of life unfold. Success, wealth, relationships, and happiness are all built on the foundation of physical and mental well-being. Those who take charge of their health today will have the advantage in every area of life, ensuring not only longevity but a future filled with energy, resilience, and purpose.

The greatest illusion in modern success culture is the belief that professional achievement and wealth accumulation must come at the cost of personal health. The world glorifies the grind—the long hours, the endless meetings, the late-night work sessions—all in the name of progress. Yet, beneath the surface, many of the most driven individuals are burning out, running on fumes, and sacrificing their well-being for short-term gains. The truth is that health is not a sacrifice that must be made for success; rather, it is the foundation upon which true, lasting success is built.

The wealthiest and most accomplished individuals are waking up to this reality. They are realizing that a health-first philosophy is not just an idealistic notion—it is a strategic advantage. The body and mind are the greatest assets anyone possesses, and how they are maintained determines not only the length of life but also the quality of that life. High performance is not sustainable if it is constantly eroded by exhaustion, stress, and neglect. Those who rise to the top and stay there for decades do not do so by pushing themselves to the breaking point; they do it by mastering the art of energy management, resilience, and long-term vitality.

A career or business should not be an obstacle to health but rather an extension of it. The old paradigm that demanded success at the cost of well-being is rapidly being replaced by a new way of thinking—one that acknowledges that a thriving body and mind lead to sharper decision-making, greater creativity, and higher productivity. The best leaders, entrepreneurs, and visionaries are no longer simply chasing wealth; they are designing their lives in a way that ensures they can enjoy that wealth for as long as possible.

The first shift required in adopting a health-first approach is the restructuring of daily routines. High achievers who sustain their success for decades do not leave their health to chance. They do not view exercise, sleep, or nutrition as optional—they see them as non-negotiable investments. Their calendars reflect this mindset. Just as meetings with investors, clients, and key stakeholders are scheduled with precision, so are their workouts, recovery periods, and health protocols. They do not view these as distractions from their work but as essential components of their performance strategy.

The reason this shift is so powerful is that health is not static. It is a dynamic force that either compounds in one's favor or works against them. Small, consistent investments in well-being create a compounding effect that leads to sustained energy, mental clarity, and resilience. Conversely, neglecting health, even in small ways, accumulates into a slow but inevitable decline. The difference between those who sustain high performance and those who fade out is often found in how well they manage the daily fundamentals of health.

This is where biohacking and regenerative medicine come into play. The most successful individuals do not just maintain their health—they optimize it. They understand that modern science provides tools that can enhance energy, accelerate recovery, and slow the aging process. They invest in cutting-edge therapies such as peptide treatments, intravenous nutrient therapy, hormone optimization, and hyperbaric oxygen therapy to keep their bodies operating at peak levels. They leverage data-driven approaches, using functional lab testing, genetic analysis, and continuous health tracking to ensure they are always making the right adjustments to their protocols.

Longevity is no longer a passive hope—it is an active pursuit. The wealthiest individuals on the planet are investing in their biological future just as they would invest in stocks, real estate, or emerging markets. The global rise of longevity clinics, private medical optimization centers, and personalized health programs is evidence of a paradigm shift. Health is no longer something to be managed only when problems arise—it is something to be proactively cultivated, refined, and protected with the same diligence that one would apply to growing a financial portfolio.

Avoiding burnout is another cornerstone of the health-first philosophy. The misconception that working longer equals working better has been disproven time and time again. Chronic stress, sleep deprivation, and overwork do not lead to higher output—they lead to diminished cognitive function, reduced creativity, and a greater likelihood of costly mistakes. The individuals who perform at the highest level do so because they have learned how to strategically rest, recover, and recalibrate. They integrate restorative practices such as cold exposure, sauna therapy, meditation, breathwork, and structured downtime into their routines—not because they are lazy, but because they understand that sustained energy requires periods of renewal.

The key is designing a lifestyle that does not force one to choose between success and health. Instead, the most effective leaders and business minds are structuring their careers and investments in a way that actively supports their well-being. They eliminate unnecessary stressors, delegate tasks that drain their time and energy, and build businesses that allow for flexibility rather than rigid, high-stress structures. They are not looking to simply accumulate wealth; they are looking to create a life where wealth, health, and fulfillment coexist.

The most successful individuals also understand that health is not just about physical well-being—it is about mental and emotional mastery. A strong body means little if the mind is plagued by anxiety, self-doubt, or chronic stress. Emotional resilience is just as important as physical resilience, and those who thrive in high-pressure environments are the ones who have cultivated the ability to manage stress, adapt to challenges, and maintain mental clarity even in uncertainty. They do not simply train their bodies; they train their minds through mindfulness, psychological conditioning, and deep self-awareness practices.

The health-first philosophy is about playing the long game. It is about realizing that short-term sacrifices for the sake of immediate gains often come at the cost of long-term sustainability. Those who build their careers around their health instead of against it will be the ones who continue to dominate in their fields decades from now. The future of high performance is not in working harder—it is in working smarter, recovering better, and optimizing every variable that influences physical and mental energy.

This shift is happening now. The leaders of tomorrow will not be those who burned themselves out in pursuit of success; they will be the ones who understood that health is the ultimate form of wealth. They will be the ones who engineered their lifestyles in a way that maximized both their productivity and their longevity. They will not simply be the wealthiest individuals—they will be the ones who still have the energy, clarity, and strength to enjoy their success.

The call to action is clear: health cannot be an afterthought. It must be integrated into every decision—how time is spent, how businesses are built, and how investments are structured. The ones who make this shift now will not only extend their lifespan but will redefine what it means to live and work at the highest level. Health is not just a personal responsibility—it is the greatest strategic advantage in life and business. Those who embrace this reality will lead the future.

For centuries, success has been measured in financial terms. Wealth accumulation has long been considered the ultimate goal, the defining achievement of those who rise to the top. Yet, in recent years, something remarkable has shifted among the world's most elite and powerful individuals. The wealthiest people on the planet are no longer solely chasing greater financial returns; they are investing in something far more valuable—their health, longevity, and quality of life.

Money, status, and material success mean little if the body begins to break down, if energy levels plummet, if cognitive function declines, or if disease forces an early retirement from life itself. Those who have built massive fortunes and led industries to success now recognize a simple but profound truth: wealth without health is meaningless. A billionaire confined to a hospital bed, suffering from preventable illness or chronic fatigue, would trade everything for the ability to restore their body to its prime. This realization has led to a dramatic shift in priorities. Instead of seeking to accumulate more material wealth, the world's most successful individuals are redirecting their resources toward extending lifespan, reversing aging, and maintaining peak physical and mental performance for as long as possible.

This shift is not just a passing trend. It is a movement fueled by cutting-edge science, medical breakthroughs, and a deeper understanding of what it means to truly thrive. The new frontier of high-net-worth investment is not stocks, real estate, or businesses—it is private longevity clinics, personalized medicine, and anti-aging research. The wealthiest individuals are funding projects aimed at extending human lifespan, optimizing cellular function, and unlocking the biological secrets to sustained vitality. They are not waiting for traditional medicine to catch up; they are leading the way, pioneering new approaches to health that go beyond disease treatment and focus on preventing degeneration before it begins.

One of the most profound realizations driving this shift is the fact that aging is no longer viewed as an inevitable decline—it is now seen as a process that can be slowed, and in some cases, reversed. The elite are pouring millions into longevity research, seeking ways to extend not just lifespan, but healthspan—the number of years spent in full function, free from disease and frailty. Technologies such as stem cell therapy, peptide treatments, regenerative medicine, and advanced genetic testing are now standard tools in the health regimens of billionaires who understand that maintaining youth and vitality is the ultimate advantage.

Private longevity clinics have become the modern-day equivalent of Swiss bank accounts for the elite. These exclusive medical centers offer a level of care and precision that goes far beyond traditional healthcare systems. Here, elite individuals undergo comprehensive health assessments that map genetic predispositions, metabolic efficiency, cellular age, and inflammatory markers—all with the goal of creating hyper-personalized health strategies. The goal is not just to treat illness, but to optimize the body for peak function at every stage of life.

In these clinics, cutting-edge therapies once considered experimental are now routine. Patients receive intravenous nutrient infusions tailored to their specific deficiencies, ensuring that their cells receive precisely what they need for repair and regeneration. They undergo hormone optimization protocols to maintain youthful energy levels, muscle mass, and mental clarity. They utilize advanced imaging and AI-driven diagnostics to detect potential health risks long before symptoms emerge. This level of precision medicine ensures that their bodies are not just surviving, but thriving.

The growing interest in longevity is not just about avoiding death—it is about maintaining the ability to continue creating, leading, and experiencing life at the highest level. The ultra-wealthy understand that the brain is the most valuable asset of all. Cognitive decline is one of the greatest threats to long-term success, which is why many of the most powerful individuals in the world are now investing heavily in neuroprotective strategies. From nootropic compounds that enhance mental clarity to transcranial magnetic stimulation for cognitive optimization, these individuals are sparing no expense when it comes to maintaining peak brain function well into their later years.

Elite performers are also prioritizing metabolic health as a key factor in longevity. They understand that poor metabolic function is one of the leading drivers of aging and chronic disease. Rather than waiting for conditions like diabetes, cardiovascular disease, or neurodegenerative disorders to develop, they are taking proactive measures to optimize insulin sensitivity, mitochondrial function, and inflammatory response. Advanced fasting protocols, ketogenic cycles, and metabolic flexibility training are standard components of their daily regimens. They do not just eat for pleasure; they eat strategically to ensure sustained energy, cellular repair, and longevity.

Perhaps one of the most telling signs of this shift is the way billionaires now talk about wealth itself. Increasingly, those who have achieved financial success are warning others not to make the same mistakes they once did—sacrificing health in the pursuit of money, only to realize too late that no amount of wealth can buy back lost vitality. Jeff Bezos, Peter Thiel, and Elon Musk are among the many high-profile figures who have redirected significant resources toward longevity research and health optimization. They are not looking for a way to get richer—they are looking for a way to live longer, stronger, and sharper.

The ultimate realization among the ultra-wealthy is that money can always be made, but time is the one resource that cannot be replaced. Yet, with the right approach, time can be extended, enhanced, and optimized. Those who invest in their health today will reap the benefits not just in the form of additional years, but in the quality of those years. They will experience more clarity, more stamina, more resilience, and more joy in the process of living.

This shift in priorities is not just relevant for billionaires—it is a model for anyone who wants to build a life of lasting success and fulfillment. The truth is that you do not need extreme wealth to apply the principles of longevity science. The same strategies that are being used in private longevity clinics can be adapted to everyday life. Precision nutrition, sleep optimization, movement-based longevity practices, and stress reduction techniques are available to everyone who chooses to make their health their greatest investment.

The time to take action is not in the future. It is now. The sooner health becomes a top priority, the greater the long-term returns. Those who continue to operate under the outdated assumption that aging is inevitable and disease is unavoidable will find themselves falling behind—not just in lifespan, but in quality of life. Those who take control of their biological future today will experience more than just an extended lifespan—they will experience a heightened state of existence, where every day is lived at peak capacity.

The message is clear: health is the new wealth. The most successful individuals in the world are no longer satisfied with simply making money—they are investing in their ability to enjoy it, sustain it, and extend their prime years for as long as possible. The opportunity to do the same is available to anyone who chooses to make longevity, vitality, and resilience their highest priority. The question is no longer how much wealth can be accumulated, but how well can life be lived. Those who take charge of their health today will not just add years to their life—they will add life to their years, ensuring that they remain at their peak for decades to come.

Success without health is an illusion. A person can spend decades accumulating wealth, power, and influence, yet if they neglect their physical and mental well-being, the value of that success becomes meaningless. The true measure of success is not just the size of a bank account but the ability to wake up every day with boundless energy, a sharp mind, and a body that allows full engagement in life. Too many high achievers spend their best years sacrificing health in the pursuit of financial freedom, only to realize too late that without vitality, wealth is nothing more than a number on a balance sheet.

The most valuable asset any individual possesses is not their business, investments, or career—it is their body and mind. The ultra-successful are beginning to recognize this truth, shifting their focus away from purely material gains and toward a future where healthspan matters more than lifespan. The goal is no longer just to live longer but to remain fully functional, independent, and capable of peak performance at every stage of life. Those who understand this early have a distinct advantage. They will not only accumulate financial success but will have the energy, cognitive power, and resilience to enjoy it for decades to come.

The problem lies in how society has conditioned people to think about success. There is a prevailing belief that in order to achieve wealth, health must be sacrificed. Long hours, high stress, poor sleep, and quick, nutrient-deficient meals have been normalized in high-performance environments. The grind mentality, glorified in entrepreneurship and executive culture, leads individuals to ignore their biological limits until they are forced to confront them through burnout, disease, or sudden physical decline. The truth is, it does not have to be this way. The most intelligent and forward-thinking individuals are proving that wealth and health are not mutually exclusive. In fact, they are deeply connected, each reinforcing the other when approached strategically.

Building a strong, resilient body and mind is not just about avoiding disease—it is about enhancing every aspect of life. A person with optimized energy levels accomplishes more in a day than someone running on exhaustion and stimulants. A sharp mind, fueled by proper nutrition, deep sleep, and stress management, makes better financial decisions and navigates challenges with ease. A well-functioning body, free from chronic pain and inflammation, does not just add years to life but life to those years. This is not about merely surviving; it is about thriving at the highest level.

The difference between those who sustain long-term success and those who experience decline is not luck or genetics. It is the conscious choice to invest in health as aggressively as one would invest in business, assets, or skills. Just as financial wealth compounds over time, so does health—either in a positive or negative direction. Small daily habits create exponential benefits or irreversible consequences. The earlier a person commits to optimizing their well-being, the greater their long-term advantage.

The compounding effect of health is real. Just as money invested wisely grows over time, consistent attention to sleep, movement, nutrition, and recovery yields powerful returns. Every meal that fuels the body properly contributes to cellular regeneration and longevity. Every night of deep, restorative sleep enhances cognitive function and immune resilience. Every workout strengthens the heart, muscles, and nervous system, ensuring that physical decline is postponed as long as possible. Every stress-management practice fortifies mental resilience, preventing burnout and emotional exhaustion. These are not small, insignificant actions; they are long-term investments in sustained high performance.

Neglecting health, on the other hand, leads to a different kind of compounding effect—one that steals energy, focus, and ultimately, years of life. Chronic stress, poor diet, and sleep deprivation do not just cause temporary setbacks; they accelerate aging, increase inflammation, and create conditions ripe for disease. The cost of neglect is not just measured in medical bills—it is measured in lost opportunities, reduced productivity, and the gradual erosion of quality of life. The mistake most people make is believing that they can postpone health investments until later, assuming they will have time to fix things when the symptoms become too obvious to ignore. But by the time warning signs appear, the damage has often been done. The only way to prevent decline is to stay ahead of it.

The wealthiest and most successful individuals are now prioritizing longevity because they recognize that true freedom comes from having a body and mind capable of enjoying the fruits of success. They are no longer waiting for health problems to appear before taking action. Instead, they are proactively investing in longevity clinics, regenerative medicine, biohacking, and personalized nutrition plans. They track biomarkers, optimize their hormone levels, and implement cutting-edge recovery protocols. They understand that every decision they make about their health today determines their capacity for wealth creation, leadership, and innovation tomorrow.

This shift in mindset is the defining factor between those who stay at the top and those who burn out. The people who dominate their industries for decades are not just financially savvy; they are biologically optimized. They take care of their mitochondria, their gut health, their cognitive function, and their nervous system with the same diligence they apply to scaling a business. They treat their bodies as the most important asset they will ever own, knowing that no amount of external success can compensate for the decline of physical and mental capabilities.

The choice between building wealth or building health is a false choice. The real question is how to do both simultaneously. Prioritizing health does not mean sacrificing success—it means enhancing it. The most effective leaders, entrepreneurs, and visionaries are proving that investing in well-being is not a cost but a competitive advantage. They have more energy, greater focus, and the ability to sustain high performance for years longer than their peers who operate under a self-destructive model of overwork and neglect.

The best time to invest in health is now. There is no ideal future date to begin optimizing sleep, nutrition, movement, and recovery. There is only the present moment and the decisions that compound into either a life of sustained energy and success or a slow decline into fatigue and dysfunction. Those who prioritize their well-being today will lead the future of high performance, wealth, and longevity. They will be the ones making an impact, creating meaningful work, and living with the kind of energy and vitality that others only wish they had.

The ultimate advantage does not belong to those who work the hardest but to those who work the smartest by integrating health as the foundation of everything they do. The future will be shaped by individuals who refuse to accept the outdated idea that success requires self-sacrifice. Instead, they will redefine what it means to be successful, fulfilled, and truly alive.

The call to action is clear: start now. Take control of your biological performance with the same level of intensity and commitment as your financial investments. Build a life where energy is abundant, resilience is effortless, and longevity is the natural result of strategic action. The decision to prioritize health is not just about adding years to life—it is about adding life to those years. Those who understand this truth will not just achieve more; they will experience the full potential of what life has to offer.

12

The Investment Professional's Roadmap to Financial & Physical Longevity

There is a common belief that success comes at a cost—that to build wealth, one must sacrifice health, that long hours, stress, and relentless ambition are the price of financial security. Society has long glorified the image of the overworked executive, the entrepreneur who burns the candle at both ends, the investor so consumed by the pursuit of wealth that they neglect the very foundation that allows them to enjoy it. But what if this model is flawed? What if true success is not about choosing between financial security and physical vitality, but about integrating the two?

The reality is that wealth means little without the health to enjoy it. What good is a thriving business or an expansive investment portfolio if the body is too worn down to experience the rewards? The future belongs to those who recognize that longevity is not just about extending lifespan but about extending healthspan—the number of years spent in peak physical and cognitive condition. The richest individuals in the world are no longer focused solely on accumulating assets; they are turning their attention toward investing in their biology with the same precision they apply to their financial decisions.

The paradigm is shifting. The idea that one must grind through decades of stress, only to attempt to repair the damage in retirement, is no longer acceptable. The most forward-thinking professionals are rewriting the script, designing lives where wealth and health grow together, where financial independence is matched by physical resilience. They understand that true success is not measured by dollars alone but by the ability to wake up each day with energy, clarity, and a body capable of supporting the mind's ambitions.

The compounding effect of health is just as powerful as the compounding effect of wealth. Small, strategic investments in nutrition, movement, recovery, and stress management yield exponential returns over time. Just as an investor would not ignore early signs of market instability, those who prioritize longevity do not ignore the subtle signs of physical or cognitive decline. They take proactive measures, treating their bodies as the ultimate asset—one that must be protected, optimized, and continually strengthened.

For too long, people have viewed health as a secondary concern, something to be addressed only when symptoms appear, when productivity begins to wane, or when the first real warning signs of aging set in. But by then, the cost of repair is exponentially higher than the cost of prevention. The smartest investors know that early intervention is the key to long-term security—both financially and physically. They monitor biomarkers as closely as they monitor financial statements, tracking trends, identifying risks, and making adjustments long before small issues turn into crises.

Longevity is no longer an abstract concept reserved for biohackers or medical futurists. It is the new frontier of high-performance living, a science-backed strategy for ensuring that the best years are not just in the past but still ahead. Those who embrace this mindset do not just extend their careers; they extend their capacity for impact, innovation, and adventure. They remain mentally sharp, physically capable, and emotionally resilient long after their peers have begun to slow down.

The new definition of financial freedom is not just about the ability to retire comfortably. It is about the ability to sustain independence, strength, and vitality for as long as possible. It is about making choices today that guarantee the ability to continue leading, creating, and thriving well into the later decades of life. The most successful people are not those who simply accumulate wealth but those who design lives worth living—where energy remains high, bodies remain strong, and minds remain sharp.

The intersection of wealth and longevity is where the future of success is being redefined. The smartest individuals no longer see health as a cost but as an investment. They are aligning their financial strategies with biological optimization, ensuring that their most valuable asset—themselves—remains strong and fully functional for the long term. They know that the greatest return on investment is not just in stocks, real estate, or businesses, but in a body and mind that allow them to experience life at the highest level.

The path forward is clear. The opportunity is now. The choice is not between wealth and health but between short-term thinking and long-term success. Those who understand this will not only build financial legacies but will also create lives filled with boundless energy, resilience, and vitality. True wealth is not just about money; it is about the freedom to live fully, for as long as possible.

Wealth is often considered the pinnacle of success, but without health, financial success is an empty achievement. The world's most successful individuals are now recognizing that the ability to enjoy wealth over the long term depends entirely on the sustainability of their physical and mental well-being. A thriving investment portfolio is meaningless if a person is too exhausted, too sick, or too cognitively impaired to enjoy the fruits of their labor. The smartest investors are not just those who accumulate assets—they are those who invest in themselves as their most valuable asset.

Financial planning and health planning are deeply connected, operating on the same fundamental principles. A wise investor does not make impulsive, high-risk decisions; they focus on long-term, sustainable growth through compounding, risk management, and diversification. The same principles apply to maintaining health and longevity. A person who prioritizes consistent, healthy habits over time will experience a compounded return in the form of increased energy, cognitive sharpness, and disease resistance. Those who take calculated risks in business also understand the need to mitigate biological risks by making proactive health choices, preventing long-term damage that could undermine their success. And just as a well-diversified portfolio provides stability in unpredictable markets, a well-rounded approach to health—including nutrition, movement, recovery, and mental resilience—ensures sustained high performance through life's inevitable stressors.

The greatest investors take a long-term view of wealth accumulation, understanding that success is not built overnight but through consistent, strategic action. The same is true for longevity. Health is not about quick fixes or temporary improvements—it is about creating a compounding effect that leads to long-term gains. Small, daily health investments—getting high-quality sleep, eating nutrient-dense foods, managing stress, and maintaining physical activity—accumulate into a body and mind that remain strong and resilient over time. Just as an investor would never neglect their portfolio for years and expect it to grow, one cannot ignore health for decades and expect to maintain peak function. The earlier one begins prioritizing health, the greater the return.

Risk management is another essential parallel between wealth and longevity. Investors do not simply chase high rewards without assessing potential downsides. They analyze market conditions, diversify their assets, and hedge against risks. Health must be approached in the same way. The body is constantly exposed to stressors—environmental toxins, inflammatory foods, chronic stress, and poor lifestyle habits. Those who ignore these risks, assuming that they will not impact long-term health, are setting themselves up for catastrophic failure later in life. High achievers who manage their health like they manage their investments seek early detection and intervention, identifying biological weaknesses before they develop into major problems. Instead of reacting to disease once it appears, they proactively fortify their bodies, ensuring that their foundation remains strong regardless of external circumstances.

Diversification is another shared principle between finance and longevity. A successful investor does not put all their resources into a single stock or asset class; they spread their investments across various sectors to create balance and security. The same approach must be applied to health. Relying solely on one strategy—whether extreme dieting, excessive exercise, or aggressive supplementation—leads to imbalance and potential breakdown. True longevity requires a diversified approach, incorporating multiple dimensions of health: a well-rounded diet, movement protocols that support strength and endurance, mental training for cognitive resilience, and regenerative recovery methods to repair and rejuvenate the body. The most successful individuals integrate these strategies seamlessly into their daily lives, ensuring that no single area of their well-being is neglected.

A crucial aspect of both financial and health longevity is the role of high-performance habits. Success is not determined by singular, dramatic actions but by consistent behaviors repeated over time. Those who build financial wealth understand that small, disciplined actions—automating savings, making strategic investments, and reinvesting profits—lead to massive gains over the years. The same is true for health. The individuals who remain strong, sharp, and resilient do not rely on genetic luck or occasional health trends; they maintain structured habits that ensure long-term vitality. They sleep with precision, recognizing that high-quality rest enhances memory, decision-making, and recovery. They fuel their bodies with intention, avoiding foods that cause metabolic dysfunction while prioritizing nutrients that optimize energy and cognitive function. They move daily, understanding that physical stagnation leads to premature aging and decreased performance. They manage stress effectively, preventing chronic inflammation and nervous system overload from eroding their longevity.

The true test of longevity is not just in physical health but in cognitive sharpness and decision-making power over time. The best investors know that mental clarity is their greatest asset. Financial independence means nothing if one cannot think clearly, process information rapidly, and make sound decisions under pressure. Cognitive function is directly tied to lifestyle choices, and those who take their longevity seriously recognize that maintaining brain health requires continuous effort. They prioritize neuroprotective habits, such as consuming essential fatty acids to support brain structure, engaging in regular learning to enhance neuroplasticity, and practicing mindfulness techniques to regulate emotional responses. They avoid the neurological decline associated with chronic inflammation, insulin resistance, and excessive stress, ensuring that their minds remain as sharp at 70 as they were at 40.

Longevity is not just about adding years to life—it is about adding life to those years. The greatest wealth is not money but the ability to fully experience life at the highest level. Those who merge financial intelligence with health intelligence set themselves up for a future in which they can continue creating, innovating, and leading for decades beyond their peers. The world is shifting, and the most forward-thinking individuals are recognizing that health is no longer an afterthought—it is the foundation of sustainable success.

There is no future in waiting for health problems to arise before taking action. The best time to invest in longevity is now. Just as an investor does not wait until retirement to start saving, one cannot afford to wait until illness appears to start prioritizing health. The decisions made today will determine the trajectory of the next several decades. Those who take ownership of their biological performance will experience an extended runway of high achievement, while those who neglect it will face premature decline.

The choice is clear. The smartest investors do not simply chase financial gains—they ensure that they have the energy, vitality, and cognitive power to enjoy their success for a lifetime. By aligning wealth-building strategies with longevity strategies, they create a future in which they do not just survive, but thrive. The greatest return on investment is not in a stock portfolio or a business empire—it is in a body and mind that remain strong, capable, and full of life for as long as possible. The time to start is now.

Freedom has long been defined as financial independence, the ability to retire comfortably, and the security of knowing that wealth will provide for all future needs. However, this definition is rapidly evolving. The world's most successful individuals are realizing that financial freedom without physical independence is a hollow victory. What good is wealth if the body is too fragile to travel, too weak to experience adventure, or too foggy to engage in meaningful conversations? True independence is not just about having money; it is about maintaining the energy, strength, and cognitive clarity to fully enjoy life's rewards. The future belongs to those who recognize that health is an asset just as valuable as wealth and that investing in physical longevity is just as critical as building financial security.

A growing movement among high-net-worth individuals is shifting the focus from wealth accumulation to longevity-focused investing. The wealthiest people in the world are not just investing in stocks, real estate, or business ventures—they are investing in themselves. They are pouring resources into regenerative medicine, biohacking, and cutting-edge health optimization strategies, understanding that the greatest return on investment is a body that continues to function at peak performance for decades beyond conventional expectations. They have realized that longevity is not just about extending life—it is about extending healthspan, the number of years lived in full vitality.

Traditional models of success have often required individuals to sacrifice health in pursuit of wealth. The long hours, high stress, and relentless demands of business and finance have led many to neglect sleep, nutrition, exercise, and recovery, assuming they can repair the damage later. But modern science is revealing a hard truth: the damage accumulates, and waiting too long to prioritize health drastically reduces the chances of reversing it. Chronic inflammation, metabolic dysfunction, and neurodegenerative processes do not emerge overnight; they build over years of neglect. The most successful investors and entrepreneurs are no longer making the mistake of postponing health. They are treating physical independence as a key metric of wealth, just as important as net worth.

The rise of longevity-focused investing is not a trend—it is a revolution. Advances in regenerative medicine are making it possible to repair and rejuvenate the body at a cellular level, extending peak performance far beyond previous limits. Biohacking is allowing individuals to fine-tune their physiology, enhance cognitive function, and optimize recovery with scientific precision. From stem cell therapy to personalized nutrition and epigenetic reprogramming, the frontier of longevity is expanding, and those who invest early stand to gain the most. The ultra-successful are not waiting until they experience decline to seek these treatments. They are actively working to prevent aging, optimize performance, and sustain resilience at every stage of life.

The foundation of this new paradigm is a shift in priorities. Where past generations viewed retirement as the ultimate goal, today's high performers recognize that retirement is meaningless if it coincides with physical and mental deterioration. The goal is not to simply stop working but to continue thriving in all aspects of life for as long as possible. Travel, adventure, deep relationships, creative endeavors, and meaningful contributions to society require energy, strength, and cognitive clarity. The wealthiest individuals are designing their lives around these principles, ensuring that their later years are not defined by decline but by continued expansion and enjoyment.

Time, energy, and health are now seen as the greatest currencies of all. Money can be lost and regained, but time is irreversible. The most forward-thinking individuals are investing in systems that protect and enhance their biological capital, recognizing that no financial asset can replace lost years of mobility, vitality, or mental sharpness. They structure their routines to optimize sleep, movement, and recovery, leveraging the best of modern science to ensure that their bodies and minds remain in peak condition. They do not view longevity as luck but as a strategic investment that requires discipline and action.

One of the most striking shifts in this new paradigm is the way investment strategies are evolving to align with longevity. Just as financial portfolios are diversified to mitigate risk, longevity-focused individuals are diversifying their health strategies. They are incorporating preventative medicine, targeted supplementation, functional movement training, and advanced recovery protocols into their daily lives. They recognize that waiting until disease appears is an outdated model, and that the real advantage lies in staying ahead of potential issues before they manifest.

This approach is not about fear of aging—it is about embracing the possibility of thriving well beyond conventional expectations. The belief that decline is inevitable has been challenged by breakthroughs in regenerative therapies, metabolic science, and neuroplasticity research. The world's top performers are proving that aging does not have to mean slowing down. They are demonstrating that with the right interventions, it is possible to extend youthfulness, sustain energy levels, and maintain sharp cognition for decades beyond what was once thought possible.

The financial industry itself is beginning to reflect this shift. Longevity-focused funds, biotech investments, and health optimization ventures are becoming some of the most lucrative opportunities available. The recognition that people will soon be living longer, healthier lives is driving innovation in pharmaceuticals, medical technology, and personalized wellness services. The ultra-successful are not just investing in their own longevity; they are investing in the future of health itself.

The question is no longer whether people can afford to prioritize their health—it is whether they can afford not to. The wealthiest individuals have come to a stark realization: money cannot buy back time, and it cannot reverse decades of neglect. The only way to ensure that financial success translates into a life well-lived is to treat health as the most important investment of all. Those who wait too long to shift their priorities often find themselves wealthy but unable to enjoy the freedom that wealth was meant to provide.

The decision to align financial independence with physical independence is the most valuable choice any individual can make. Those who start now will gain an unmatched advantage in both longevity and quality of life. The future belongs to those who refuse to accept decline as inevitable. It belongs to those who choose to integrate cutting-edge health optimization with strategic financial planning, ensuring that they do not just live longer but live better.

The time to act is now. Every decision about sleep, movement, nutrition, and recovery compounds over time, just like financial investments. Those who prioritize their well-being today will be the ones who lead the future of high performance, wealth, and longevity. The ultimate measure of success is not just what is accumulated in a bank account, but how much energy, strength, and clarity remains to enjoy it. The new paradigm is clear: financial freedom is meaningless without physical independence. The most powerful investment anyone can make is the one that ensures they are not just alive in the future, but thriving in it.

The pursuit of wealth has long been regarded as the ultimate measure of success. Across industries, high achievers dedicate their lives to accumulating financial security, believing that money equates to freedom, power, and influence. But an undeniable truth is emerging: wealth without health is a fleeting illusion. The most successful individuals in the world are now realizing that financial prosperity means little if it is not accompanied by the physical ability to enjoy it. The ability to travel, innovate, create, and engage in meaningful work is dependent not just on financial resources but on a body and mind capable of sustaining high performance over time.

For decades, the traditional approach to success has emphasized the sacrifice of health in the name of financial gain. Long hours, chronic stress, poor nutrition, and sleep deprivation have been glorified as necessary evils on the path to building a business, climbing the corporate ladder, or expanding an investment portfolio. Many high achievers operate under the assumption that health can always be reclaimed later, that once financial independence is secured, they will have the time and resources to fix the damage done. But this mindset is flawed. By the time the consequences of neglect begin to surface—chronic fatigue, cognitive decline, metabolic disorders, or premature aging—the cost of recovery is exponentially higher than the cost of prevention.

True financial independence is not just about having enough money to retire comfortably. It is about having the physical and mental capacity to continue engaging with the world, to take on new challenges, to explore opportunities, and to sustain energy and resilience well into later years. Without health, the dream of financial freedom becomes a cruel paradox. A person may reach a point where they have all the wealth they ever desired, but if their body is failing, if their mind is sluggish, if they are burdened by disease or dysfunction, what was the point of the sacrifice?

The smartest investors understand the principle of compounding. They know that wealth grows over time when managed wisely, with small, consistent efforts leading to exponential returns. What many fail to recognize is that the same principle applies to health. Every decision—what to eat, how to sleep, how to manage stress, how to move the body—compounds over time, either in a positive or negative direction. A person who invests in their health early and consistently will experience an entirely different trajectory of aging and performance than one who ignores it until problems arise.

Longevity is not just about extending lifespan; it is about extending healthspan. The goal is not simply to live longer but to remain vibrant, strong, and mentally sharp for as many years as possible. This is why the world's wealthiest individuals are now shifting their priorities. Instead of focusing solely on financial gains, they are investing in regenerative medicine, functional health, and performance optimization. They are undergoing comprehensive testing to assess their metabolic health, nutrient levels, and inflammatory markers. They are implementing longevity strategies that include biohacking, advanced supplementation, fasting protocols, and stress resilience training. They are beginning to recognize that the highest return on investment is not in stocks, real estate, or business ventures—it is in the preservation and enhancement of their biological systems.

The future of success belongs to those who understand that time, energy, and health are the most valuable currencies. The ability to sustain high performance, to make sound decisions, to innovate, to lead with clarity—these all depend on biological optimization. It is no longer enough to accumulate financial resources while letting the body deteriorate. The high achievers of the next generation will not just be the wealthiest; they will be the most physically and mentally resilient.

Financial independence and physical independence must go hand in hand. It is no longer acceptable to prioritize one at the expense of the other. Those who continue to operate under the outdated belief that health can wait will find themselves in a position where their wealth is useless to them. The idea that success requires grinding to exhaustion is being replaced by a new paradigm—one that emphasizes intelligent recovery, strategic nutrition, and movement as non-negotiable components of a high-performing life.

The misconception that achieving peak health requires extreme measures prevents many from taking action. Health optimization is not about complex protocols or expensive interventions. It is about mastering the fundamentals—sleep, movement, nutrition, and recovery. It is about making daily choices that enhance energy rather than deplete it. It is about recognizing that every decision contributes to either long-term resilience or long-term dysfunction. The wealthiest individuals who are thriving in both business and life are not simply lucky; they have adopted a mindset that prioritizes health as the foundation for all success.

The compounding effect of health means that small, consistent investments yield extraordinary returns over time. A person who prioritizes deep, restorative sleep will experience sharper cognition, better metabolic health, and enhanced emotional resilience. A person who fuels their body with nutrient-dense foods rather than processed convenience meals will sustain higher energy levels, optimize hormone function, and prevent chronic disease. A person who incorporates movement into their daily routine will maintain muscle mass, improve circulation, and support brain function well into their later years. These are not abstract concepts—they are measurable, tangible strategies that create undeniable advantages in both longevity and performance.

Neglecting health is the most expensive mistake a person can make. It results in lost productivity, increased healthcare costs, and diminished quality of life. It robs individuals of years of vitality and the ability to fully experience the rewards of their hard work. The irony is that those who delay investing in their health often end up spending more in the long run—on medical treatments, medications, and interventions that could have been prevented with a proactive approach.

The most powerful decision any investor can make is to treat health as a non-negotiable investment. The strategies for building financial wealth—discipline, long-term thinking, risk management, and intelligent diversification—are the same principles that must be applied to health. Just as no investor would blindly throw money into a high-risk venture without a clear strategy, no high achiever should blindly expect their body to sustain peak function without intentional care. The future belongs to those who take control of both their financial and physical longevity.

The time to act is now. Health is not something that can be postponed indefinitely without consequences. Every day that passes is either an opportunity to build resilience or a missed chance to prevent decline. Those who take responsibility for their well-being today will be the ones who lead the future—fully present, mentally sharp, physically strong, and capable of experiencing life at the highest level.

This is not about adding years to life; it is about adding life to those years. It is about creating a reality where success is not just measured in financial statements but in the ability to wake up every morning feeling energized, focused, and fully engaged. It is about rejecting the notion that burnout is a requirement for achievement and embracing a model where success is sustainable, fulfilling, and deeply rewarding. The choice is clear. Those who prioritize their well-being today will enjoy the highest returns in every area of life. The future belongs to those who understand that true wealth is not measured in dollars, but in the strength, vitality, and energy to fully live.

As you reach the end of this book, I want to pause and tell you something important: I'm proud of you. Most people never get this far. Most people stay stuck in the cycle of chasing success while sacrificing the very thing that makes success meaningful—their health. But not you. You've chosen awareness. You've chosen knowledge. You've chosen a better way forward.

Learning is only the beginning. Transformation comes from action—consistent, strategic, and intentional. By now, you understand that health isn't a side project or a luxury. It's the foundation of every meaningful success. You can have all the money, influence, and accolades in the world, but if you don't have the energy, strength, or clarity to enjoy them... what's the point? You've seen the problem. Now, here's what you can actually do about it.

At the West Clinic, we've developed a comprehensive strategy that helps people reclaim their health and elevate their life—whether they're burned out, dealing with chronic illness, or simply ready to play at a higher level. It starts with getting your body the tools it needs to repair and regenerate, and we've made it accessible no matter where you are in the world.

One of the most important things you can do is get started with what we call the Foundational Three—a supplement stack that Dr. West recommends for nearly every patient who walks through our doors. This includes a broad-spectrum, medical-grade vitamin and mineral formula to rebuild your depleted reserves, a high-potency essential fatty acid blend to support your brain, heart, and cellular health, and targeted organ support—like adrenal, liver, or kidney formulas—to strengthen the systems that sustain long-term vitality.

These supplements are custom-compounded to Dr. West's exact clinical standards. They are not generic shelf products. They are designed to absorb efficiently, support deep cellular repair, and create momentum in your healing process. You can access these physician-grade supplements directly through our online store at www.westcliniconline.com, where we ship nationwide. In addition to foundational supplementation, we offer personalized protocols based on your lab results, symptoms, and goals. Whether you're navigating hormonal imbalance, cognitive decline, immune dysfunction, or chronic fatigue, we tailor solutions to support your body exactly where it needs it most.

For those ready to dive deeper, we offer at-home testing kits to measure food sensitivities, hormone levels, inflammation markers, heavy metal toxicity, and gut health indicators. These insights allow us to create your Health Independence Blueprint—a personalized plan of action to help you reclaim and optimize your body's potential.

If you're seeking a more aggressive or accelerated transformation, we invite you to experience our in-office therapies Intravenous IV nutrient therapy to flood your cells with bioavailable vitamins, minerals, and antioxidants. Ozone therapy to reboot mitochondrial energy and stimulate immune resilience. Neural therapy to reset the autonomic nervous system and address hidden injury patterns. Peptide therapy to activate natural tissue regeneration, hormone optimization, and anti-aging pathways.

These therapies aren't future promises—they are proven, evidence-based tools available right now, helping people reclaim their lives every single day. If you're ready to start small, that's perfect too. Begin with the Foundational Three. Clean up your diet. Protect your sleep. Move intentionally every day. Start building those rhythms that allow compounding results to take hold.

If you're ready to go further—to create a real, personalized strategy—Dr. West and the entire team are here to support you. You can request a consultation with Dr. West at www.AmericasHealer.com where you can explore customized care options, testing programs, and virtual or in-office treatment strategies.

We believe that health is not an accident. It's an investment. An investment that will pay you back every day of your life. Some people will finish this book and set it aside, hoping that knowledge alone will save them. A few will take action. And those few will transform not just their health—but their future. The strategies exist, the science is real, the tools are ready, the decision is yours. We hope to walk this journey with you. Because true wealth is not found in what you own. It's found in what you have the energy, clarity, and strength to experience, create, and share. You are your greatest asset. The time to act is now. Let's begin.

CONCLUSION

The Ultimate Return On Investment – Investing in YOU

Health is the foundation of everything. Without it, wealth loses its value, success feels hollow, and time slips away faster than we realize. No matter how much money, influence, or recognition a person accumulates, if they lack the physical energy, mental clarity, and emotional resilience to fully experience life, then what was it all for? The pursuit of wealth, achievement, and legacy is meaningless if the body and mind are too broken down to enjoy the rewards.

At the core of every high achiever's journey is the realization that health is not something to be managed reactively. It is an asset that must be built, maintained, and optimized with the same level of discipline and precision as any business or financial strategy. The most successful individuals understand that true freedom comes not just from financial independence, but from physical independence—the ability to wake up each day with energy, vitality, and a mind sharp enough to execute on their vision.

For decades, society has conditioned people to believe that success demands sacrifice, that long hours, high stress, and relentless work ethic are the price to pay for building something great. But the tides are shifting. The most forward-thinking individuals, the true high performers, are proving that longevity and success are not at odds. In fact, they are directly connected. The leaders of tomorrow are those who recognize that investing in their health today is not a luxury—it is the ultimate return on investment.

Imagine a life where energy is abundant, where every decision is made with clarity and confidence, where the body operates with efficiency and resilience, allowing for deep engagement in work, relationships, and personal pursuits. This is not a fantasy. It is the outcome of intentional, data-driven, health-first living. The difference between those who thrive into their later years and those who decline prematurely is not luck or genetics—it is strategy.

The first step toward mastering health and longevity is testing, tracking, and optimizing. Just as a business owner would never make critical financial decisions without reviewing the numbers, no individual should attempt to manage their health without knowing their biological data. Annual testing provides the roadmap to understanding metabolic efficiency, nutrient deficiencies, inflammation levels, and hormonal balance. It is the single most powerful tool for proactive health management. Waiting for symptoms to appear before taking action is like waiting until a company is bankrupt to review financial statements. The best outcomes happen when imbalances are detected early, when small adjustments prevent major breakdowns, when health is actively built rather than passively maintained.

Daily habits create the compounding effect that determines whether health is an asset that appreciates in value or one that declines over time. Longevity is not built in one grand gesture, but in the consistent execution of simple, high-impact routines. Prioritizing high-quality sleep to enhance recovery and cognitive function, eating nutrient-dense foods to fuel energy and cellular repair, engaging in movement to maintain strength and cardiovascular resilience, and integrating recovery strategies to reduce stress and inflammation—all of these form the foundation of a body that is built to last.

The individuals who sustain peak performance for decades do not just react to problems; they engineer their health with the same precision they apply to their business, investments, and personal growth. They do not rely on generic advice. They build a blueprint that is personalized, strategic, and adaptable. This blueprint is what separates those who merely survive from those who thrive.

A high-performance health-wealth lifestyle is not just about extending life—it is about extending the quality of life. It is about ensuring that each year is filled with strength, clarity, and capability. It is about rejecting the outdated belief that aging must be synonymous with decline. It is about embracing the fact that the human body is designed to function at a high level for much longer than we have been led to believe.

The ultimate measure of success is not just how much wealth is accumulated, but how well that wealth is lived. The greatest return on investment is not found in the stock market, real estate, or business ventures—it is found in optimizing the only vehicle that carries you through every experience in life: your body and mind.

This book is not just about knowledge. It is about action. The concepts presented here are not meant to be read, understood, and then forgotten. They are meant to be implemented. The difference between those who read and those who change their lives is execution. The information is here. The roadmap is clear. The only question is whether it will be used.

The time to take control is now. The body you have five years from now will be a direct reflection of the choices you make today. The mental clarity you experience in a decade will be determined by how well you prioritize brain health starting now. The longevity you create will not happen by accident—it will be the direct result of a commitment to a health-first lifestyle.

There is no better investment than in yourself. This is not about discipline for the sake of discipline, nor is it about perfection. It is about understanding that every decision compounds, that every choice is either bringing you closer to high performance and longevity or pushing you toward decline and limitation. The individuals who lead, create, and innovate for years to come will not be the ones who burn out young. They will be the ones who master their biology, optimize their energy, and build a future where success is sustainable.

The only real failure is in waiting. Waiting for the "right time" to start prioritizing health. Waiting for a wake-up call in the form of illness or injury. Waiting until wealth has been built before focusing on well-being. There is no better time to begin than now. The cost of delay is high, and the rewards of action are immeasurable.

This is your moment to make a decision that will impact not just your future, but the legacy you leave behind. This is your opportunity to build a life where energy, longevity, and fulfillment are not afterthoughts, but priorities. This is your chance to step into the reality where you are the greatest asset you will ever own, and your investment in yourself is the key to unlocking everything you desire.

Commit to this path. Build the habits. Track the data. Optimize the details. And most importantly, never forget that money is nothing without your health. The future of high performance belongs to those who understand this truth, and the most powerful step you can take is deciding that starting today, always remember your most valuable investment is you.

About the Authors

Dr. Jason West: Is not just a doctor—he is a force of nature in the world of healing. With a relentless drive to push the boundaries of medicine and a deep passion for patient care, he has transformed countless lives through his pioneering approach to chronic disease, integrative therapies, and functional medicine. His work isn't just about treating symptoms; it's about uncovering the root causes of illness and helping people reclaim their health, vitality, and quality of life. As the fourth-generation doctor leading The West Clinic in Pocatello, Idaho, Dr. West carries a legacy of over 100 years of medical excellence. The clinic, originally founded in 1916, has become a world-renowned destination for patients from every state in the U.S. and across six continents. With a practice built on cutting-edge science, holistic healing, and a commitment to unparalleled patient care, The West Clinic is unlike any other medical facility in the world. Dr. West's background is as diverse as his approach to medicine. A graduate of Southern California University of Health Sciences, he was recognized for his academic and leadership excellence, receiving both the Outstanding Senior Award and the Presidential Leadership Award. He has been twice honored as the Idaho Chiropractor of the Year (2012, 2016) and continues to expand his expertise, earning a fellowship in Oriental Medicine, a Diplomate in Clinical Nutrition, and a Doctorate in Naturopathic Medicine. His vast training allows him to bridge traditional and alternative medicine, collaborating with MDs, NPs, DCs, NDs, and LAc practitioners to create customized, patient-centered treatment plans that get results. Dr. West's clinic is known for successfully treating patients with complex, chronic illnesses that conventional medicine has often failed to address. Whether it's autoimmune disorders, Lyme disease, chronic fatigue, or unexplained pain syndromes, if it's not an emergency like a heart attack, childbirth, or surgery, chances are The West Clinic is treating it. His dedication to results is evident in the patient outcomes he shares through his digital blog, as well as in his numerous books, including Hidden Secrets to Curing Your Chronic Disease, a #1 Amazon Best Seller, and Hidden Secrets to Healthy Living, a health and nutrition guidebook for patients seeking optimal wellness. Beyond the clinic, Dr. West has made an impact as a global lecturer and educator. He has spoken at international conferences, taught seminars to doctors on clinical nutrition, blood chemistry, and chronic disease management, and provided high-level consulting to healthcare professionals striving to improve patient outcomes. His ability to simplify complex medical topics and inspire both professionals and patients alike has cemented his reputation as one of the most sought-after speakers and mentors in functional medicine. But Dr. West is more than just a brilliant doctor—he is also a devoted husband, father, and adventurer. Married to his sweetheart, Maxine, and the proud father of five sons, he cherishes his time with family, whether they're snowmobiling, motorcycle riding, or simply enjoying the great outdoors together. He also finds relaxation in playing the piano and continues his lifelong passion for reading, always seeking new knowledge to enhance his practice and his ability to help others. This book is a reflection of Dr. Jason West's mission: to educate, empower, and change the way people think about their health. It is more than just a collection of medical insights—it is a roadmap to a healthier, more vibrant life. Whether you are struggling with a chronic condition, seeking to optimize your well-being, or simply wanting to learn from one of the most innovative minds in medicine, you are in the right place. Get ready to be challenged, inspired, and transformed. The journey to true health starts here.

Jordan Dorsey: Is a certified AI expert and a media strategist specializing in Facebook Ads, podcast management, and online brand growth. He has played a key role in helping Dr. Jason West and the West Clinic expand their impact through innovative digital strategies, compelling content creation, and high-performing marketing systems. His ability to harness AI and automation for streamlined operations and outreach has made him an essential part of the clinic's mission to reach and serve more patients.

As a trusted partner of Dr. West, Jordan focuses on optimizing content production, podcast development, and audience engagement. His strategic use of AI tools has enhanced the clinic's ability to educate, inspire, and connect with individuals seeking advanced care. More than a technician, Jordan brings a deep commitment to delivering meaningful, patient-centered messaging that drives both growth and transformation.

Whether he's producing a new podcast episode, refining patient education materials, or strengthening digital connections, Jordan approaches every project with clarity, precision, and care. He operates from a foundational belief that when you serve others with authenticity and intention, meaningful success naturally follows. That philosophy guides every decision, every strategy, and every piece of content he helps create.

His work is also driven by a deeper purpose—to uplift others. Through thoughtful communication, intelligent systems, and strategic storytelling, he aims to create experiences that not only generate results but also leave people feeling valued, supported, and inspired.

Outside of his work, Jordan enjoys fishing, hiking, riding motorcycles, and exploring personal development and emerging technologies. He is passionate about the intersection of AI and communication and is always seeking new ways to blend innovation with real human impact. Jordan's mission is clear: to support Dr. West and the West Clinic in reaching more people with life-changing care, using the best of digital tools to amplify healing, connection, and service.

www.ingramcontent.com/pod-product-compliance
Lightning Source LLC
Chambersburg PA
CBHW031504270326
41930CB00006B/243